Growth Through Loss & Change
Volume I

How to Be With the:

Dying

Without Fear

Clarice A. Schultz

Lectures by Clarice A. Schultz
RN, BSN, Psychology BS

A Resource Book
Put on Your Shelf for a Time of Need

Order this book online at www.trafford.com
or email orders@trafford.com

Most Trafford titles are also available at major online book retailers.

© Copyright 2010 Clarice A. Schultz.
Anyone who has purchased this book has my permission to make as many copies of needed portions as necessary for use solely for their own students for education purposes only, with the condition that they give full credit for authorship and copyrights in writing on each page of the handout, header or footer. They may charge sufficient money to cover copying cost but may not make a profit on any copy. Educators may make copies from which to teach.

Except for the above permission with the above restrictions, all rights reserved. No part of this publication may be reproduced, stored in a retrieval system, or transmitted, in any form or by any means, electronic, mechanical, photocopying, recording, or otherwise, without the written prior permission of the author.

Printed in Victoria, BC, Canada.

ISBN: 978-1-4269-2707-2

Library of Congress Control Number: 2010903748

Our mission is to efficiently provide the world's finest, most comprehensive book publishing service, enabling every author to experience success. To find out how to publish your book, your way, and have it available worldwide, visit us online at www.trafford.com

Trafford rev. 4/19/2010

 www.trafford.com

North America & international
toll-free: 1 888 232 4444 (USA & Canada)
phone: 250 383 6864 ♦ fax: 812 355 4082

Dedication

To all the persons brave enough
to be First Responders

To all those who have the
courage to stay the course

*Through long periods of stress, illness, pain,
dying, death, and bereavement.*

Acknowledgments

To my students who taught me the majority of these interventions. They used them, adapted them, shaped them, and authenticated them. My part was to see what principles were being addressed and check them out with qualified personnel in the field for professional correctness.

With deep gratitude to the many professionals who so honestly shared their stories, feelings, and concerns.

Special thanks go to:

>William Scheer
>Bruce Conley
>Donna Kruger
>Rev. John Atherton
>Rev. Steve Defur
>Rev. Chuck Richardson
>Rev. Gary McCann

And with deep gratitude to the many nurses who generously gave input to my interviews who declined my invitation to present this information saying:

>"I am the clinician.
>You are the mouthpiece.
>
>If you do not present this information
>It will stay on my unit with me.
>
>You are the teacher
>It is your responsibility to give it out
>Unto those who can receive.

Appreciation

I appreciate the in-depth editorial and professional reviews of:

Bill Scheer, M. Div., MSW, Braidwood, IL
Bruce Conley, Funeral Director, Elburn, IL
Carter Crane, Editor, The Voice, Aurora, IL
William H. Schultz, BS, Plainfield, IL
John Atherton, M. Div., Hot Springs, AR
Jan Russell, RN, MSN, Pensacola, FL, Deceased 2009
Anita Scheer, MA, Educator, Coal City, IL
Ralph Kieffer, BA, My Brother, Oregon, WI
Marge Orchard, RN, MSN, Elgin, IL
Chuck Edwards, RN, PM, Batavia, IL Deceased 2001

I especially value the fact that the above professionals never ceased to pressure me to publish this manuscript.

Forward

William H. Scheer M. Div., MSW

Clarice has a profound effect on all who take her classes because she has touched us with kindness, knowledge and all the permissions necessary to embrace our loss, to accept it as our own, to grieve it while knowing that our ability to love is not diminished by our loss. She invites us to open our hearts to love once again as we slowly reorganize ourselves for our continued journey. Life is worth living and it continues to demand our participation. She prepares us to face the world again after bereavement and jump back into life.

I remember the comment of a group participant in one of our grief workshops. The woman lost her husband of many years and two grandsons. She had been stuck in grief for four years. She hadn't baked Christmas cookies or given presents since her husband died. She just couldn't bring herself to do it. Life offered her no joy and crying was her sorrowful lifestyle. After taking Clarice's class she was able to celebrate the holidays, decorate, and hang remembrances on the Christmas tree that honored those whom she loved and lost. She was able to step back into life while respecting the memory of her departed loved ones. It was okay for her to feel joy again!

This is what Clarice has done all her adult life. She has set people who were lost in grief free; free to experience the joy of living and loving once again. Her two volume set is full of information about the many dimensions of grief with insights that have been tested and refined over the years. These two volumes are an invaluable source of information for anyone working in the caring professions including nursing, ministry, teaching, psychology and social work. May you have good reading, and welcome to Clarice's world!

Twenty-seven years ago I was suffering the effects of a recent divorce. I spent many lonely weekends in my apartment hoping to find someone to fill my life with joy. I was standing in my living room one Saturday with nothing to look forward to. I said to myself, "You're not going to meet anyone sitting here in this apartment!" I decided that I needed to get involved in a community activity. I had seen several advertisements for volunteers for Fox Valley Hospice. I volunteered as a public relations speaker traveling to churches and fraternities educating the public about the importance and value of this new service in our community. By early fall I decided to volunteer as a direct worker visiting and supporting the dying patient and their family. I was informed by the director that I would have to take a ten week course.

This was my first meeting with the instructor, Clarice Schultz. Little did I know then that she would change my life in some very dramatic ways. There were twelve of us in the class. We were all profoundly affected by Clarice and her teaching style. Once you have taken one of her "Grief and Loss" classes she is indelibly etched on your heart, never to be forgotten.

Clarice introduced me to my wife in the form of a blind date. She gave me Anita's phone number as she reminded me, "Remember she comes in a package of four." I met my wife to be and her three children on March 19, 1983. We were married in April of 1984. Her children embraced me and we legalized the adoptions at the courthouse. We now have a fourth child. I invested in life and love again. That is healing grief.

Preface

How it Began

The door burst open to the Recovery room where I was nursing two critical patients. This was a quiet room with the lights dimmed and movement quick; but subdued, so as not to agitate the recovering patients coming out of anesthesia. The energy coming in from the nurse at the door was electric. She was saying, "I will take your patients, Clarice, I can do it. You go to the emergency department where a man is writhing on the floor, completely overcome with grief at the death of his wife. You are good at that! You can do it! He needs you!" I was scared. Death is always scary. I protested; but, she was already taking care of my patients.

At the emergency department I saw bewildered, kind folks, encouraging a young man on the floor. He was inconsolable and could not hear them. They had only been married a year. Swiftly I walked to him and went down onto the floor beside him. I locked in on his energy stream and reflected, reflected, coo-ed, reflected, comforted, and reflected.

That is how this all began. From then on I was often called to any part of the hospital.

I had just graduated from nursing school a couple of months before, so when the administration offered me an opportunity to attend Dr. Kubler-Ross's seminars in Chicago, I was amazed and honored. The only requirement was that I turn in a summary of her presentations and develop nursing recommendations upon my return to the hospital. I did; and I was done.

A week later I met the Nursing Administrator in the hallway. She asked me to make an appointment with her to arrange teaching times for all the head nurses in the hospital. I said, "Thanks, but no thanks. I don't teach." She answered "Yes, you can teach." I replied that it was a conscious decision of mine to choose nursing over teaching; therefore, someone else would have to teach the material because I would not be doing it. I was going to nurse patients." As I walked down the hall I heard her voice say, "Yes, nurses do teach."

About two weeks later I met her in the hall again. Her mood was different. Sounding authoritative, she said, "I asked you to make an appointment to come in to talk about teaching." I responded, "And I told you, no. I would not teach. I cannot teach. I don't know how, and I choose not to teach." Squinting her eyes, she asked in a steel voice, "Ms. Schultz, do you like working here at this hospital? If you do, you will make that appointment with my secretary." And that is how my teaching career began.

I taught two series of eight sessions at the hospital, at the local college the next semester, the following semester I spoke nine hours in the superdome in New Orleans to an international convention of emergency physicians and nurses. Decades later, it is still going on. I am still teaching.

Donna Kruger RN

It was a few years later when I heard that a nurse from a nearby hospital was at a Catholic school in Aurora, Illinois, presenting a session on meeting the needs of the dying and their families. I attended and introduced myself. The custodian locked the school but Donna Kruger and I were still in the school parking lot at 3am. It was so exciting! She had been approached by Illinois Senator Grotberg to begin a new emerging model of care for the dying and their families, called Hospice. Donna Kruger, Bruce Conley, and I founded the Fox Valley Hospice.

We divided the duties, she took the development of the administration and I developed the hospice educational component. There was no end to the growth of that knowledge. I spent days at Rush Medical College Library doing research. I loved it! I taught the hospice training course for eleven years, at which time I left Illinois and moved to Houston, Texas. I continued to teach and develop this course continuously in Texas and now again in Illinois.

Certified

The entirety of this material has received full continuation education credit for all the helping professions in numerous states on the Regional and National lecture circuits. I have taught it for graduate as well as undergraduate credit. All of it has been clinically tested in the classroom and professional institutions of hospitals, nursing homes, hospices, schools, home health and palliative care facilities.

Most years I lectured or taught on the average about four times a week during the semester. The course was designed as a 2 ½ hour session by the original college for whom I taught. It consisted of 1 hour lecture and the other hour as facilitated sharing time. The college observers quickly saw that the one hour format did not do the students justice. Grief is so intense that when the student opened up they needed time to debrief. I still keep that format for classroom situations.

Contents: Volume I

Chapter 1: *Emotional Preparation of the Helping Person* 1
    Knowledge Does Not Take Away Pain. 3
    Personal Death Awareness 8
    Tears 29

Chapter 2: *Americans: The Lonely Grievers* 61
    Role of Community in Grief Support 66
    Known Rituals 78
    Essential Tribal Family. 87

Chapter 3: *The Dying Person* 103
    Does the Patient Know? 109
    Personal Experience is Not a Flag of Credentials 118
    How to Make a Therapeutic Visit 122

Chapter 4: *Family of the Dying* 137
    A New Era Begins 142
    Dying Fully Healed. 144
    Stages of Dying. 145

Chapter 5: *Sudden Death Crisis* 165
    Typical Reactions 167
    Mutilated Body. 181
    Criteria for not Showing Body 183

Chapter 6: *Dying Event* 197
    The Caring Objective Outsider 200
    Prepare the Family............................. 201
    Do at the Time of Death 211

Chapter 7: *Pregnancy Loss* 225
    Parenting a Child Who is Dead................... 229
    Parenting a Dying Baby......................... 233
    Memorabilia Parents Want Collected.............. 236

Chapter 8: *Sexual Needs of the Dying and Grieving*...... 239
    Marriage Problems Are Really Grief Reactions....... 239
    Factors that Complicate Adjustment 268
    Concerns of the Well Partner..................... 283

Chapter 9: *Care of the Grief Support Person* 303
    Clarice's Definition of Burnout 305
    Give Only From the Overflow.................... 312
    Healing Measures 316

Contents Volume II

Chapter 10: *The Scope of Grief* 1
    Culturally Worthy & Unworthy Grief 2
    Example of Losses 4
    Grief for Someone You Don't Like 20

Chapter 11: *Normal Dynamics Grief* 53
    Definition of Healing Grief 57
    Time Line 85
    Physiology of Grief 103

Chapter 12: *Grieving Children Need Adult Help* 135
    How Is Death Introduced To Children 157
    Working With the Child 171
    School 200

Chapter 13: *Just For Teens* 213
    Grief Overtakes You 214
    What can Bring up these Feelings? 220
    Facets of Life Changed 227

Chapter 14: *Gender Differences in Grief Response* 237
    Healthy Masculine Grief Expression 241
    Physiology of the Brain 255
    Characteristics of Males 258

Chapter 15: *The Pastoral Visitor in the Hospital From A Nurse's Perspective* 293
    The Continuity Care Person 298
    Different Views of "The Minister" Role 301
    The Minister Nurse Team 307

Chapter 16: *Spiritual Handling of the Holidays* 329
    Gift from Your Grief Experience 329
    Holiday--A Time of Pain 342
    Expect that Grief Will Surprise You 344

Introduction

My intention is to publish these unedited versions of my lectures so that others may use parts of them to augment their own presentations. It is my desire that readers find the material helpful in their personal as well as professional lives. It is a body of work that has proved useful throughout many years.

If something were to happen to me these lecture manuscripts will die in my file cabinets. It is to avoid this fate that I put them on the internet for the use of anyone. That is what they were developed for, that is what I devoted my life to, and may the ministry to the suffering continue.

The manuscripts were developed by request of the sponsoring agency for presentations at professional regional and national conventions. Therefore they are meant to stand alone. To achieve this, I often cut and pasted from existing manuscripts to provide the proper introduction and background for the material. Therefore you will find some repeats of material.

They went together nicely for the college courses that I taught. You may use them as you wish to best serve your audience.

Course Name:

Many versions depending on the institution sponsoring the program or course.

Sensitivity to Loss
Death & Dying
Grief & Grieving

It is an assumption of this course that all who are bereaved,
Are also placed in the role of helper

This role occurs both in a present loss situation as well as in future losses, so that any healthy coping patterns learned in this loss event will be available with adaptation for future losses.

Course Description:

This course focuses on the principles, theories and intervention methods that underlie the care and support of the dying and bereaved. Emphasis is on identifying the dynamics of loss and discovering practical means of support in the personal and institutional setting.

Content Includes:

Dynamics of grief for the adult and child, tasks of the dying person, the grief impact on family and institutions, and the role of the community in support of mourners.

Intervention methods are taught which are related to the cultural and emotional aspects of, dying, grieving, sudden death, grieving children, and caregiving.

Target Population:

All persons in the helping professional and paraprofessional fields, e.g. nurses, physicians, teachers, counselors, ministers, funeral directors, EMT's, respiratory therapist, police, fire, hospice volunteers, grief support facilitators, church visitors, and all lay persons who are sensitized to death and grief. Continuation education credit for this material has been granted to each of the above groups.

History of Course:

Content of this course has been DEVELOPED and taught by CLARICE SCHULTZ for 30 years in a variety of settings, colleges, hospitals, hospices, churches, workshops, seminars, and inservice programs around the USA. Ms. Schultz published some of the content in professional journals.

Goal:

To enable the students to: develop a therapeutic presence that they can offer to themselves and others coping with a loss, in family, community, and institution.

Chapter 1

Emotional Preparation Of the Helping Person

Experiential Journey

Welcome to this book that will take you on a journey. As you go through each chapter you will find that your life will change. It will be more of an experience for you than an academic learning of facts. There will be academic material but the information affects you experientially. As you travel through the pages of this book life will be different for you. Through these pages you will find a safe place to search your own life's history of loss and come to terms with your own personal death awareness.

This will give you an opportunity to define your personal value system. Through this you will be able to define your individual skills of self knowledge, self healing, and self growth. In this way you will be able to reach out to heal others through the experience of your wounds, not in spite of your own wounds.

Your decision to read this book indicates that you want to help others as they struggle through their life's passages. I also believe you are interested in learning how to process your personal losses in a healthy way so you can continue to grow and love into a rich old age.

This book is designed to help you look at your own life. The information contained here will assist you in gathering the gifts of grief from your life and from there to reach out to support others in their losses. The principles and dynamics of loss are presented here in a way that can be applied to oneself as well as to other people.

This material is presented from a holistic health model. We are holistic by nature. We are a composition of several facets; social, physical, intellectual, emotional, and spiritual. When working with a dying or a grieving person we need to be aware of each of these dimensions in their life, and at the same time, it is important to be aware of these dimensions within ourselves.

Writer's Contract

I have been privileged to be on this journey with many classes of students. I, too, have grown as the students shared what they read, discussed, and put into action. The students have been my teachers. It is from them that I have learned much of what I share with you. Just as I have grown immensely from the sharing of others in my classes, you also will benefit. I am glad to share this material with you.

Congratulations

I want to acknowledge the difficulty that people have when they decide to study bereavement. It is hard to make the decision to help others in grief. So, along with my welcome to you, I want to congratulate you.

I really do mean congratulations on reading this book. If you evaluate how you felt about studying the subject of bereavement and you were straightforward, you would likely admit that it was a difficult decision. It may have been an effort to put one foot in front of the other or you might have felt like walking backwards. You probably thought of a million things you had to do before you got involved, or needed to get involved with this thought process. You may have felt that you wanted to postpone the study of death and dying, grief and grieving, until next season. Reticence is the name of this game. Be candid: you would have found it easier to sign up for a course on precious gems, CPR, or aerobics.

Why is it so hard to take a course on death and dying? Because deep down you know you run the risk of bringing up some of your past unresolved grief. It is daunting to think of it coming to the surface. You wonder, "Can I handle that?"

Not Denying Grief

By your opening this book you are different. There is a screening process that takes place when people choose to acknowledge loss. Some people choose to avoid all reminders of loss. Your presence tells us that you are not denying the reality of grief in your life. You are saying by your behavior, "Since grief is real and does exist; since sorrow is a part of all of our lives, I would like to know more about what is normal in the bereavement process and how I can assist someone who is grieving."

You recognize the actuality that in time you will have a grieving friend, a fellow worker, or someone in your church family who is going through a tragedy. Many of you are presently relating to a bereaved person, a grieving Mother-in-law, sister, brother, or friend. You want to support their healthy behaviors.

A Screening Process

There is a self screening process that takes place when the opportunity to study attachment and loss arises. Many choose to avoid the subject and therefore the opportunity to learn more about this taboo subject. You are special. You are different. What kind of people study death, dying, and the principles and dynamics of loss? I don't think that there is a common denominator other than that there is a genuine depth of caring in these people. They are all beautiful souls; they all want to use their lives and skills in a therapeutic manner to make life a little easier and healthier for themselves and others who suffer.

Knowledge Does Not Take Away Pain

For yourself, the knowledge of principles and dynamics of dying and bereavement will not take away your pain; because, if you have loved, you will grieve. Grief is a love story and you would not grieve so, if you had not loved so. Grief follows attachment as surely as night follows day. The pain of separation will be there for you.

One of my students, a young innocent looking 19 year old burst out in class saying. "But that is why I came to this class. I don't want to grieve. I want to learn how not to be sorrowful." She went on to say, "I was a late in life baby. My parents are old and because of health conditions, I know they will die in the next ten years. I do not want to grieve. I do not want to feel bad!"

Her intensity shocked the other classmates. It sounded as though she had an attachment difficulty. It sounded as though she was without feelings. Stunned, a young minister in the class asked, "Do you love them?" she broke down sobbing, "Yes, I love them so much." The minister responded, "That was your first mistake. Now you are destined to grieve." She wept. Then she spoke of her parents saying, "They are the nicest people I have ever known. They mean the world to me. I cannot imagine living without them. I don't think I can survive their deaths. I am so afraid. I hoped the class would tell me how not to grieve." The other students were sensitive and supportive to her and during the semester she gained confidence that she could indeed survive the grief. She grew determined to gather all the gifts of having loved and in time lose those two wonderful parents.

There is something different about suffering pain when you know that what you are going through is normal. It doesn't seem so frightening to go through the process.

Birthing a New Self Image

An analogy that helps is childbirth. When a woman enters labor without any knowledge of the process, she becomes frightened. Once the pains get beyond the intensity of menstrual cramps, and once her body takes over and spontaneously responds to each new stage, the new mother tends to panic because she has lost control.

Wood's People

At 16 years of age I worked in a busy obstetric department in northern Wisconsin. In those days there were people referred to as, "Wood's people," since they lived in the forests. As a little girl I went with my mother as she drove down the forest fire lanes to find them. She seemed to know when they were sick or without food. I recall her saying they were people who couldn't live in a community; some for personal reasons, some for psych reasons, others were alcoholics, but all of them wanted to isolate themselves. My uncle George was one of them. He was very spiritual, a hermit, and he loved the forest. He was a good man; I loved him dearly.

These people had babies and the girls grew to puberty at which age many were impregnated. In the 1930's and 1940's most or these children did not go to school. Later the school buses stopped at the mouth of the lane and the children walked back into the forest. These children had no amenities. Their babies were born in shacks and the birth not wisely attended to, if at all. But by the 1950's there were an increasing number of pregnant girls found on the roadways waving down cars for help. They were in the middle of complicated labor. Their lives were in danger. Sometimes they were alone and sometimes a person would be with them. But that person seldom got in the car. When they came into the hospital the nurses loved these young mothers. There was empathy and gladness at the opportunity to save their life and perhaps their baby's life.

At sixteen years of age I was so impressed with their fear. They had never seen electric lights, masked people, or stainless steel. Injections and IV's were torture instruments in their eyes. They were terrified! They were totally unprepared, much less prepared than the third world people of today. Of course there was no TV and they had never heard of a telephone or seen running water in pipes or toilets, or a building over one story high. I don't remember one girl whose support person came into the hospital with her. They were alone. We kept someone at her side to ease her fear.

Not the Time to Patient Teach

The most a support person can do at that time is to stand beside and encourage. In the time of deep fright, deep pain, or deep grief, it is not the time to patient teach. During crisis the recipient cannot deal with more than one thought at a time since the ability to make rational judgment is impaired. The nurses could only assure her that we would not leave her alone and when we had to go home another person would sit with her. We could gently stroke her and make calm parental sounds. That is all.

Can the woman in the height of labor learn all about child birthing while she is in labor? No. And so it is in grief. When we are talking to someone in the state of crisis, we cannot share with them all the wonderful helpful knowledge we learned about the grieving process. We can stand by, be supportive and offer our warmth. We can say, "Lean on me, you are not alone. We recognize what you are going through, we've seen it before. I assure you that it looks normal to me."

However, those mothers who have been through the child birthing education process understand the birthing phases. Even so, they too, have to experience labor. But when the contractions take over, the body submits to labor and the pregnant mom loses control, she asks, "What's happening?" The nurse answers, "You are in phase II or Phase III." The mother responds with, "Oh yes," as she identifies what she is experiencing to be a normal process, and panic ceases. It is the unnecessary pain of grief that we want to prevent, not the necessary pain of birthing a new self image.

Necessary Contraction Pain

I ask you, was that mother who attended the child birthing classes spared pain? Is she spared one contraction that is necessary to bring that child into the world? No! So it is in grief. After losing precious people in your life, the knowledge of the normal dynamics of grief will not save you one necessary contractual pain as you birth a new self image. But it surely makes a significant difference to know the pain you feel is normal, instead of fearing that you are going insane. You can then make plans on how to work with the grief to facilitate its processing.

Emotional Preparation

Permissions

It is important to prepare yourself for the emotional component of this work by giving yourself permission to experience the full range of emotions. The time you spend reading this book may be a sad time for you. Many students of mine have said, "I am very sad the day after class." They wonder, "Perhaps the course is not good for me if it makes me so sad." Some wonder if they are not good candidates for grief support work because they feel so sad after working with this material.

Let the Sad Flow Free

I think it is good to permit the sad to flow freely. I don't think the sad is in the course, the sad is in you. If you have lived this long; you have lost. Losses are part of life. You could not have gotten to the age you are now without experiencing loss. Many of the losses you are dealing with are unidentified. Identified or not, you still expend energy to repress your feelings as you keep them below the surface.

This book will give you permission to let the sad flow freely. I'd like to suggest to you that you use this period of time to practice getting comfortable with all of your emotions. When you feel them, simply identify the feeling and allow it to emerge. You will be a much freer person when you no longer have to expend energy controlling those feelings.

Night Dreams

Also be prepared for the night dreams. Perhaps your story or someone else's will keep circulating in your head and in your dreams. That is okay. Allow the dreams to occur. Dreams are part of processing exceptional material; however not everyone remembers their dreams.

Feeling of Love and Joy

As you experience deeper feelings of sad you will go deeper and deeper into your feelings of love and joy. It is a process. That is just the way it is; there is a balance to life. The more your sadness is liberated, the freer you are to feel feelings of delight and love, because the same energy that restrains sad holds out love and joy. When you are no longer using that energy to put a cap on sad, love and joy quietly emerge. You won't have to will it to happen. It just does.

You become sensitized to all of life during the time of grief study. Take time to notice the colors in the sunrise and sunsets. They will excite you more, music will touch you deeper; poems and thoughtful meditations will be more meaningful. You will enjoy seeing other people loving one another and supporting each other in a special way.

Use of the Therapeutic Self

You will be aware that you have become more observant of how people reach out and touch one another. You will be conscious of how people stand supportively beside one another, and how they demonstrate caring for each other.

Take this opportunity of renewed sensitivity to soak in the love and joy you are experiencing. This is a good time for you to become acutely observant of others using their therapeutic-self. You will see it in the grocery store, on the ball court, street, and in the work place. You will recognize it by the tone of voice, open body language, eye contact, soft eyes, parental tones, and gentle touch. The period of grief study is a time when we are acutely aware of the therapeutic use of self.

One day you may be in line at the bank and notice the teller reaching out to cover the hand of an elderly person and understand he is changing the name on the bank account from two persons to one. That is hard. I was at a tennis tournament when a young woman lost the championship game. Her coach husband ran unto the court. I could see that he was talking continuously to her. I assumed he was coaching her. He had his forehead against her forehead and his arms around her neck. Then I saw her crying and he tenderly wiped her tears. He was not coaching. He was encouraging her. They were alone in a public arena.

Personal Death Awareness

Mirror Effect

Looking at those who have lost is like looking in a mirror. We see ourselves and those we love in their eyes, their stories, their yearnings, and their love. It is scary, intense, exciting, enriching, touching, and sad, all at the same time. Here we touch the essence of being alive. This is where the rubber hits the road. This is where attachment lies and where love is born. This is where the heart is torn asunder. This is the wonder of life and living.

That Could be Me

A phenomenon called the mirror effect happens when we look at a grieving person and for a moment we see ourselves. Suddenly we realize "That could be me! That could be mine!" Instead of seeing that other person we see ourselves, our mates, our child in that car crash, our Dad on that death bed. With that happening, innocence is lost. We will never be quite as naïve again.

The reaction to the mirror effect is one of terror. A part of us thinks as the Psalmist, "Thousands will fall to my right and thousands to my left, but I will be standing." Usually we live with thoughts like, "It happens to the other guy. I am gifted and from my bounty I want to help others who suffer. My role is the helper, not the helpee."

Role Confusion, Victim or Rescuer

My husband and I lived in our wonderful home for twenty nine years. I planted every known flower and many trees on our lot. We brought our babies home to that fine house and they left it to live their independent lives. It housed my dreams. From there I attended colleges, taught, and nursed in trauma and disaster programs. Then one day in thirteen seconds a tornado wiped out a lifetime. It took the mementoes of our history and spread them over twenty miles and filled our yard five feet high with other people's torn memorabilia.

I was in shock. For days I walked the devastated neighborhood that I used to know so well, but now could not even tell whose lot was whose or where the occupants had gone. Twenty nine people were dead and countless injured. All went to live somewhere else. Disaster teams of every ilk were everywhere. I walked and walked with one refrain, "Lord, I am supposed to be out there with one of those disaster teams, not in here as a victim." I couldn't get over the role confusion of being victim or rescuer.

We think, "I take care of my children, teach them, provide a good example, disaster won't happen to them." We think, "I drive carefully, I made good choices, I save my money, I have good insurance. I plan. That ensures it won't happen to me." But, suddenly the time comes when we are face to face with a suffering person and realize, "It could happen to me! It could be someone I love!"

Grieve Your Vulnerability

The mirror effect happens to most people. Most likely it will happen to you. What to do? Live through it. Process it. Grieve your vulnerability. It takes months for a helping person whether neighbor, church member, volunteer or staff, to go through the adjustment of working closely with the dying and bereaved. During the time of adjustment it is sad, frightening, and humbling. Let it be. Accept your place in the human condition and it will pass.

You will never go back to that period of naïveté, that period of innocence again. But the terror and the pain will pass. Out of your compassion will come true empathy and a maturity of spirit. You are no longer above it all, no longer superior. You have a sense of oneness with all people, awareness that we are all connected, and a sincere, "Today is not my time. Today is your journey. I am here with you."

Unless we are willing to face our vulnerability through those who suffer, we cannot work effectively with them; therefore it is necessary to be open and vulnerable to do this work.

Be Gentle With Your Self

This means that during this period of grief study you will become extra sensitive and this affects other parts of your life. Certain movies and stories won't be for you right now, just as particular jokes and bawdiness may not be for you now. Do not bombard yourself with them. As you open yourself to deeper levels some experiences will remain with you for a time. You may need to turn off the TV. You will think, "This program is not for me now." You will know that you are too emotionally fragile to deal with harshness. Students think they will be sensitive forever, but after this material has been processed, some of that sensitivity moderates.

So be gentle with yourself during this time of grief study. Do nice things for yourself. Since you will be more emotionally vulnerable and open spiritually, give yourself more time to walk, to muse, and time to just sit and be.

Use a Debriefer

When working in the field of grief and dying one of the most important aspects of self care is the effective use of a debriefer. You will need a person to whom you can spill out all of your reactions; the angry ones, jealous ones, feelings of being scared, lonely, sad, joyful, and happy. You need to process the guilt of could I have done it differently, and could I have done more? And yes, you need someone to share the ecstatic feelings that are so much a part of this work. There is a euphoria that occurs when working in the field of loss. Dr. Garfield from Berkley said the elation is the major reason people stay in this work.

You will find that very dear friends and relatives cannot be a debriefer for you. You will need an objective outsider who knows how to listen to what is happening to you and be supportive in all the facets of your feelings as you process grief experiences. Students tend to choose their dearest friend who they have always been able to say anything to. But we found that very few people can listen to what a bereavement support person has to say. This is different than what you have shared in the past. Friends are not prepared for what grief support persons have to talk about. Very few people are prepared to hear what it felt like to look at what you looked at, and to hear what you heard.

It is important that you make a contract with an outsider, preferably someone trained as a people helper such as a therapist, counselor, teacher, nurse, social worker, or minister. This special person needs to agree to be available to you at all reasonable times when you need to emote and debrief. This person needs to care about you. It is not necessary that your debriefer be particularly interested in grief dynamics. You need someone who is interested in your physical, spiritual, emotional, social, and intellectual needs; someone who is interested in all facets of your holistic self and how each aspect is affected by your grief work. In the debriefing session it is wise to go over each aspect; social, emotional, intellectual, physical, and spiritual separately and express how that part of you has been affected by your grief work. Put tabs in your journal and make a separate section for each one. Believe me, each of your facets are affected when you are immersed in grief. To keep from burning out each of them must be kept filled.

Awareness of Your Losses

A Life's Review

You have already grieved. I know that. Whether identified or not, most helping persons have already tasted the bitter sting of loss. It is through the gifts, the insights of their grief-experience that they became sensitized to the needs of others.

Visiting with the dying and grieving causes the support person to review his or her personal losses. It also provides a revelation of losses that are to come in the future. This review is ongoing. It is the ability to live and work with life's review that is a crucial attribute in a helping person. Those who achieve this ability cannot keep themselves from grieving. This leads to healing and growing. It is to this purpose of personal death awareness, along with the knowledge of the principles and dynamics of loss, that an education course for those working with the dying and grieving must be focused.

These permissions must be considered when facilitating grief support groups because, even though the members of the group are considered lay people, lay people are the major caregivers for family, friends, and sometimes neighbors and church members. Burnout healing and caregiving skills are always appropriate as part of an educational package for the bereaved. There is no way to separate people who are dying and grieving into another category of people. It is an assumption of this book that all who are bereaved are also placed in the role of helper. This occurs both in a present loss situation as well as in the losses that will come in the future.

I have yet to talk to someone in grief who is not concerned about the grief of another. If a woman tells me her husband was killed, she is likely to follow with statements of intense concern for the grief of their children. It is likely she is also anxious about helping his elderly parents in their time of extreme grief. She wants to be a knowledgeable caregiver even though she is a primary griever herself. It is the lot of those who grieve to be concerned about others who also grieve for the loved one.

Central Task of Life

Processing losses, integrating the meaning of past loves, hopes and dreams into the image of self, and then letting go in order to move on is a central task of life. This is a continuous process as we go through life's passages. It does not become less painful even though healthy coping patterns are developed. Losing is not negative. It is a part of life. However, losing, integrating, healing, and growing, is not an easy process. Its success and amount of work depends on growth and development strengths and the number of new coping patterns that are necessary to develop. It depends on perceived support from those around, and the ability to develop a sophisticated philosophy to include the possibility of loss. These are tall orders.

Many people do not succeed. Others succeed through a succession of losses but at a later bereavement seem to give up. People get stuck at a stage or passage and some people give up and never again risk loving. Some are broken because there is such a thing as too much, while others choose to wallow in their losses as a life style because they like the power of victim position.

It is important to be in touch with your personal death awareness. Check yourself. Are you stuck in a stage of loss? This book will help guide you through the various stages of grief.

Lose Control

Don't worry about losing control. You will not lose any more control than you want to. It is a choice to utilize this opportunity to free up some material and grow. Our purpose is to urge the reader to judiciously use a carefully chosen debriefer and to change debriefers when new needs appear. Many students choose to go into counseling during this time to gain help with clarifying their thoughts and short cut the process. It is sensible to provide a safe and confidential atmosphere for yourself.

This process of healing and growth depends on how support from others is gained. It is an example of how human beings are interdependent.

As helping people, it is important that we identify our own need, ask for the support we need, and develop the ability to integrate that support into our self image growth.

Grief Comes Onto You

Therefore it is necessary to be willing to be open and vulnerable to do this work. There is no way to separate the dying and grieving into another category of people. In supporting them we expose our vulnerability because, Kubler Ross says, "There is no way to work with the bereaved without their grief overcoming us." We feel not only their pain, but our own past pain, present pain, and future losses as well. This is a strange work, for the helping person cannot deny he is destined to become the helpee.

Need for Death Education

Need for Academic Discussion

It is important that grief classes and seminars take place in secluded rooms in order to discuss this subject openly. People are interested and want to learn. In a classroom setting the concepts can be explored in safety. It is constructive to do this away from the scene of intense grief. It is helpful to do this before one encounters one's next personal grief.

In a group or debriefer experience it is valuable to practice speaking and reacting sensitively. You need a place to rehearse before going to families and clients in the midst of grief. It is sad that people's first discussion of loss happens to them when they are in intense sorrow. During crisis it is very difficult to weigh alternatives of action and to choose options with a clear head. The American culture denies grief and squelches discussion of bereavement; yet expects its people to manage mourning well and quickly.

Taboo Subject

Talking about dying and grieving is taboo in our society. Even with all the books and classes available, it is still forbidden to mention one's feelings about this topic. This forbidden subject is quickly enforced by our cultural mores. When someone shows emotion while talking about their loved one who is dying or dead, we are quick to say, don't cry. Yet, crying is often the most appropriate action in that context. We say, don't cry, because when the other keeps a composed demeanor we do not have to deal with their feelings. The use of don't cry, is for the benefit of the listener not for the benefit of the griever. Often crying is the best expression for them at that moment.

People follow sheep-like in the culture mores of their society. Groups tend to go along with the expectations set up by the social order. If someone does not respond in the expected manner they are punished with a cultural mores which is seldom recognized as such. It is seldom acknowledged even when it is recognized. Yet punishment is quickly metered out. It is socially unacceptable to mention the sting of chastisement and many people will not even permit the feeling to come into awareness. This is difficult to change. It is easier to change a behavior that is scripted by parents or religion than it is to change a behavior that is ascribed by culture.

Telling the Children

Another cultural expression which shows the culture mores at work is, "We didn't tell the children because they are too young to understand." The assumption is that it is possible to be too young to grieve; that is not true. There is no such thing as too young to grieve a primary person. Even children adopted at birth need to process that loss. Processing loss includes not only missing the absent person but also the loss of roots, history, biological background, integrity of the family unit, and freedom to project an unlimited future.

Prayers at Church

You will hear this cultural denial of grief in churches as people pray for those who are ill. Often you will hear an announcement similar to this, "Judy is home from the hospital after having major surgery. We thank God she is home now and doing fine." The loss from major surgery is not well identified. Do you really believe she is doing fine? Major surgery represents an assault to our bodies and an insult to our sense of integrity. There is always a loss to process. Even if it is only the presence of a scar, the person must deal with the loss of skin integrity.

We are setting up an expectation of behavior when we make such comments. We need to discover what her perceived loss is. Is it body image change, body function loss, loss of reproductive ability, changes in sexual adjustment, or immobility? Then there is always the difficulty of processing the, betrayal of the body; to come to terms with the knowledge that my body can kill me. Many times the patient expresses a willingness to live with a loss such as an amputation of a limb or reproductive ability, yet, they still have to process the meaning of that tremendous change in their physical, emotional, and fantasy lives.

Whatever it is, the adaptation process will take place a long time after the person is home from the hospital. People often need more support after returning home than they do while in the hospital. The hospital represents a protected environment with help readily available because there are people and activities all around. After hospitalization the days and months at home can be lonely, frightening, and full of adaptation to the loss. Yet, we continue to give the impression that when someone has come home from the hospital the worst is over. There is a reason for this. We are setting up the expectation of, don't bother us with your adjustment problems.

People should be encouraged to visit the recuperating person at home more often than at the hospital because it is lonelier at home. It is more convenient to arrange for company at home and more conducive to confidential conversation. Perhaps the physical crisis is past, but the time required for realigning spiritual values, emotional reactions, social changes, and the need for intellectual understanding are all just beginning. Our culture mores cut off discussion of these adjustments.

As a culture we have forced our grieving people into emotional isolation so that they must process their grief without help. So if you can bear to listen or just stand by with persistent presence through the months and years of integration of loss and change you are giving a very precious and rarely given gift. Many people go through their mourning without this kind of support.

Response of Mourners

A commonly heard answer to the question, "How is John doing since his son was killed?" is, "He is doing just fine. It has been two weeks now since the funeral and the whole family handled it well. They are all back at work and school." If you go to John and ask, "How are you doing?" He will answer according to the culture expectation by saying, "I'm fine, thank you." The truth is that he is not fine. One is not fine two weeks after a son is killed. We know he has a minimum of two years, likely many more, of hard grief work to integrate the meaning of the loss, fantasy, and life style changes by this death. Mourners comb their hair; put on the cultural mask and respond with, "I'm okay, thank you; I'm doing as well as can be expected." They must process their grief in isolation.

Next Party

If you do not believe that it is taboo to talk about death and grief try bringing up what you have read in this book at the next party that you attend. Then watch how the people react to you. How quickly do they try to change the subject? Failing that, how quickly do they walk away to join another group? How did people react to you when you told them you were going to read this book or take a class on grief and loss? Did they wonder what your problem was? How did members of your family react? Looking at the reactions you received helps you to understand grieving families better. It helps to understand how much they are shunned when they bring up their losses and adjustment problems.

When I began work with the dying I found there were very close friends of mine who simply told me, "That is alright for you but I don't want to dwell on it, let's change the subject." Some clearly avoided me during the semesters when I was teaching. They came around only in the summers and interim when my mind was not as involved with grieving people. In the years since, these are the very people who call and want a lot of my time, effort, and comfort, when they suffer their losses. Some even express anger when I am not 100% available, saying, "You like this subject." Suddenly they will not share any of their joys with me, wanting to get the most of their time with me for grief discussion. I am effectively excluded from their happy conversations which they save to have with other friends. Yes, I am willing to be vulnerable and used by my students, clients, and patients but not in my personal life. As I mentioned before, this is a strange vocation.

Lack of Language

A cultural taboo against discussion of a subject tells you that the people of that culture have no language by which to express feelings on that subject. We never talk about it so we don't know how to express it. Therefore, be patient as you struggle for words during this time. You may practice an idea over and over until it, feels right to you. Much of the task in preparation to give grief support is to develop verbal and nonverbal language by which to communicate feelings of grief, love, and support.

Because people do not have a language, an important art of grief support is learning to read non-verbal expressions of heartache. These are often expressed as physical aches and pains, eating disorders, relationship difficulties, and lack of joy. The people you are supporting do not have word tools readily available to describe their inner struggles.

Death Pornography

An interesting phenomenon happens when a culture decrees that something basic to the human being is taboo. The need to express this basic component of nature comes out in pornography.

Death pornography is increasing. Examples of death pornography are horror movies, certain cartoons and other aggressive films and video games. These provide the people with an outlet to express concerns about dying and grief. This increase in death pornography is partly due to the fact that our population is further away from the old cultures that provided outlets for death anxiety through story telling, nursery rhymes, religious and civil rituals. The older people grew up at a time when their culture or religion provided rituals through which they could express grief. Young people have no rituals given to them for this manifestation of fear. The basic concern about death must be expressed somehow.

Academic about Taboos

It is not acceptable to express personal feelings about sex or death. However, it is okay to be vulgar and tell sex or death jokes. It is alright to be academic about a taboo. For instance, we can draw diagrams of sex organs and explain their biological function but we may not discuss emotional concerns about our own sexual functioning. Worries like, how the drugs we have to take or how aging will affect our sexual performance, whether we can live a celibate life now that our mate has been killed, how to entice someone of the opposite sex to become our sexual partner from the perspective of the age we are now. So too, we can, study a cadaver and isolate the nerves and blood vessels. We could discuss the biological cause of death, but it is not acceptable to discuss concern about our dying or our loved one's dying.

Lonely Grievers

We thought we did away with grief when we did away with the rituals surrounding it. We discarded the armbands and the widow's veil; we changed organ music to guitar music. We thought we discarded grief along with them. All we did was isolate the griever.

There are people who would dispute this concept saying that there are myriads of books about death, and that everywhere you look there are seminars and workshops about death. Yes, if you want to read about grief you can. If you are a professional you can attend educational programs. That is wonderful and such an advance over the state of the subject as it was in the past.

Illusion the Bereaved are Better Supported

However, do not let that lead you to believe that the bereaved are any better supported. It is an illusion that the bereaved are better supported. I ask you, when you are concerned about a friend who is overwhelmed by grief, to whom can you go for help? Do you know? Some people have a sensitive doctor, social worker, teacher, or minister, but for those who do not, and that is the majority of people, to whom can they turn for support?

Now let us say the person you care about lives seven hundred miles away from you and is lonely since the death of a loved one. You would like to support your friend or relative but you live far away. How can you mobilize support for your friend? It is true the professionals do have more opportunity to learn about grief dynamics than they did thirty years ago. But the grass roots griever is in a lonely unsupported process. If you can be that support person for someone you are doing a beautiful deed.

Grievers Respond to the Expectation of Society

Grievers respond to the expectation of society by dressing well, combing their hair and putting on a calm demeanor. They respond to inquires in the culturally expected manner of, "I'm okay, thank you," or "I'm doing as well as can be expected." Yet, under many a coiffure hairdo and well dressed person is a broken heart. There are lonely mourners everywhere. If you can be that one person who can listen, you will have done a rare service.

An Honor Plaque

I had a marker event near the 5 year anniversary of my son's death. He was honored in a public occasion. I sent out an e-mail to several of my friends mentioning the event. I was greatly surprised at the number who responded with concern, "I see you are still grieving," and "I am surprised your son's death has such a strong effect five years later." Clearly my friends were worried about my mental health.

My friend, Lynn, came to visit me and said, "Let's grab a cup of coffee and talk about Craig." I asked if she wanted to hear the story of what happened. It took about an hour to relate. It was a fascinating story! It involved a trip to a distant city and an honor plaque installed for him. It was a week of great pride for me. Yet, no one in my daily life would let me relay the details of it. I asked her, "Now do you see why the repercussions of his death are not 5 years ago. It is today." These events are in my life today but I have to deal with them in silence.

Confidentiality

The purpose of a sharing group is to provide a safe place to be vulnerable to each other. It is a safe environment to share thoughts, experiences and insights as well as feelings. Helping persons are professionals and paraprofessionals who are expected to keep professional confidences.

When You Use Skill

When ever you use your skill to encourage someone to emote, tell, or share information that is difficult for them, you have an implicit understanding that you will respect the information as confidential. In this field your skill is the look in your eye. The manner in which you handle your body by leaning forward and the tone of your voice. These are your tools. Your body is your tool. It is the instrument you use to express your thoughts, feelings, and understanding. It is through your body that you show and express empathy. You console others by your words, gestures, and touch. By doing this the other person is encouraged to share information that they would not have shared if you had not verbally or non-verbally led them to believe it was safe.

It was your skill that invited them to emote. Therefore, it carries with it a professional and paraprofessional responsibility of confidentiality. This includes both verbal and nonverbal sharing such as crying. It is so tempting to tell friends that, "John is feeling badly, he cried last evening when he talked about his daughter." If you used skill to get someone to express you may not tell anyone that they cried in your presence. They may tell anyone anything they wish. It is their story. However it is not your place to repeat what was said to you in trust. You may tell no one without their permission, except in a professional debriefing or guidance session. In that case, the recipient of your information, your debriefer, is also burdened to keep your client's confidentiality.

Their Stories Are Their Property

You do not tell stories that belong to a friend, classmate, client, or family. What is shared in confidence must stay confidential. If you need to talk about it call your debriefer, minister, therapist, or someone trained to keep professional confidences.

Confidentiality is a difficult concept to teach but it is absolutely necessary if you are to honor the mourner and their story. The important concept to grasp is that confidentiality is not about the information, it is about the person. People tell me they have a secret; they verbalize how difficult it is to say it out loud, they warn me that I will be shocked. Often they will come back several sessions before they have the courage to say their secret out loud. They struggle so hard with shame and worry to tell me something; only for me to realize it is a subject I hear all the time. The information is no big deal.

It is not about whether it is shocking to me; but rather, it is about whether it is shocking to them. It is not mine to tell. We may tell no one! They may tell anyone, everyone, or no one. It is their prerogative to keep it a secret for ever.

How to Share a Case Study

There are ways to share a story without breaking a confidence. Learn how to do this. Practice with a professional to check your method. When you want to use the story as a case study, pick out the point or points you need to share. Then change the details such as sex, marital status, number of children, and locations. However, some cases are so well known that you cannot even safely do that, so you must skip the story and share only with your debriefer. There are many wonderful case studies I use in my lectures, but must eliminate them when I am teaching in the territory of their origin.

Consequences to Keeping Confidences

There are some consequences in keeping confidences. In order to keep the confidence you will sometimes need to act dumb about a situation. This puts you out of general conversation. You may be misunderstood. To be effective in grief work, you must be willing to be vulnerable which means you must be willing to be used at times, misunderstood at times, and criticized unfairly at times for the sake of another. I find that lay people have a difficult time understanding confidentiality. They either say nothing at all about the event thereby building a separate life leading to burnout, or they tell freely in the manner they spoke before participating as a paraprofessional.

Techniques in Loving

When I studied at Berkley, my instructor, Dr. Garfield, author of *Hospice* and *High Performers*, encouraged us to observe people who were using the therapeutic self. He wanted us to break down what we observed and write it as a skill. He advised us to find out what makes it work and teach it to others. There is an attitude that if we watch the activities of empathetic behavior and then break it down into a skill, we somehow desecrate the act and it is no longer as beautiful. That is not true.

Who is the Ideal Grief Support Person?

Who helps those who grieve? Who should help those who grieve? Do we need another specialty? Who is the ideal grief worker? Who is it who should be supporting the grieving persons? We wonder if it should be the minister, social worker, or would it be better if the grief worker were a psychologist, psychiatrist, minister, nurse, or do we need to develop another specialty?

Grief work is not a profession. No one has dibbs on grief. It belongs to our humanity. If you have a profession it will add to your effectiveness as a grief support person. The grief worker is the person who is next to the griever at the time of need. Your interest shows that you would like to be helpful to others in the time of their grief.

Think back to your own life at a time of distress, sorrow or disappointment. Think of a time when the news was really bad and you felt really sad. Who was beside you? Who touched you? Who give you an idea about their caring by the look on their face? Do you remember someone who reached out and patted you on the shoulder as you walked out of a crowded room? Did someone reach out to give you a hug or squeeze your hand? Who cared and showed their caring? How did they do this?

Perhaps it was the way they looked at you across the table or across a crowded room. Maybe they had a tear in their eye, perhaps it was the gentleness of their voice. Was that person a professional grief worker? Chances are, no. Do you wish they had been a professional? Chances are you prefer that it was the exact person who was there for you at the time.

In the time of my grief, I want my friend, my lover, and my relatives near me. Yet, I am a professional grief worker. Grief work comes out of your love for others; out of your humanness.

Era of Specialization

Dr. Granger Westberg said it so well when he remarked, "How sad that we live in an era of specialization where we have relinquished our human caring in favor of recommending a specialist." In our good will for others, we want them to have the very best support they can get and often say, "Oh, you are feeling so bad, you should see a minister, doctor, therapist, or the school social worker."

He adds that we mean well by that, but, what we witness when we observe sorrow in another's face is often only a desire for a little human caring. All that most grievers want is a little love, a little caring, and touch from you. They do not want to be recommended to a faraway stranger who is a grief professional. It is your fate in life to be the desired support person for those that love you and seek you out in their hour of grief.

This means that you will often feel that you are over your head. You may sense that there are deeper needs present than you are prepared to meet. By all means recommend a specialist at this time. However, my experience is that when I recommend a specialist only a small percentage of persons follow through and get the counseling they need. Grievers often immobilize. If they perceive you as safe they do not go to others for help.

Where does this leave you? Many times you will have to make an appointment with the minister, doctor, school teacher, or therapist in order to upgrade your knowledge so that you can help your friend. A large number of the calls coming to me for grief counseling come from friends who are standing beside and supporting the bereaved. There are many times when you have to be humble enough to accept that, while you are second best; you are all they've got.

Feel Inadequate

The difference between a grief worker and one who holds back is that the one who does the grief work is willing to feel inadequate. Death and grief represent failure. They represent our inability to call upon the parent figures of society like great medical specialist, healers, and religious rituals to save this person. It may be that the family and friends have tried everything. They prayed so hard, yet were unable to move God with their plea. Money was impotent to buy a cure. They went to so many specialists, tried so many medicines, tests, and treatments, yet failed. The loss still occurred, the person still died or the relationship still failed.

Inadequacy is the nature of death and grief; therefore, do not expect to feel adequate. Cold hands, shaking voices, and tears are part of being a grief support person; therefore you must be willing to accept them. You need to give yourself permission to feel deeply the grief and overwhelming sorrow as you work with the dying and the grieving. You need to accept your tears and to work with your tears, not hold them back.

Look at what happens when a person is being strong for another or expending effort to keep a professional front. Where is the energy going? It is directed inward toward the self to maintain external body control. But if you say, oh well, here I am, with my entire humanity showing, and let the tears flow, then your energy is free to flow out to the dying and the grieving persons.

For example, we can prepare ourselves as helping persons intellectually. We may learn as much as we can about helping those who grieve. Yet, when we are in that sick room with the dying person our stomachs may churn and our eyes shed tears. We become acutely aware of the betrayal of our body. We may want desperately to have a friend near us and our hearts may scream out to God, why, why?

It is this willingness, and openness about you that is the genuine human quality others respond to. The bereaved sense your willingness to communicate your deepest feelings. Grief affects everyone who is near it. You need to be willing to let your feelings be noticed.

Personalize This Subject

I would like to invite you to personalize this subject as you read. If you have a role you play when working with mourners, I invite you to take it off and lay it on the back of your chair. It will be there for you when you need it. But while you are learning and thinking, do so from your personhood; for you come to each dying situation, each grieving situation with the sum total of the person you are up to that moment. If you were to prepare yourself in terms of technical expertise you would be looking for a technique to use at a time when intelligent loving is what is required.

Intelligent Loving

These two words put together may seem incongruous, intelligent and loving. Yet in the field of grief they are both necessary.

We all know of loving that is not intelligent, as in the case of abuse where the abusing parent or mate loves the abused victim. We would not call that intelligent loving. So, it can also be the reverse. Many persons with whom I worked got the intelligent portion together very well. I have had the privilege of working with students completing their master's thesis or doctoral dissertation in the field of loss. Yet, some were not well received by those in mourning. I know the student's heart was in the right place. They were very well intentioned and caring. However, the grieving persons were unaware of this. Mourners will not be vulnerable but remain safeguarded if they don't trust. In order to help a griever you must be perceived as loving. All the good intentions in the world and all the enviable information will not be of any use if the dying person or bereaved is defended.

The first time I was assigned a 5 year old abused child my heart just hurt. I had small children at home and abuse was unimaginable. This child's father beat him so badly that one leg and an arm were broken along with multiple bruises and contusions. I went to him feeling so glad that he had been brought to the hospital where we could love and care for him. He did not want me. He fought me. He cried for his Daddy. His grief of separation from Daddy was so great that I could not get him to cooperate with his care. This shocked my naïve soul.

Have a Big Head

Then my supervisor said I was assigned to teach his father parenting skills. I said, "What!" That is not how I wanted to confront the father! I had to work on my attitude. At the appointed time the Dad came in. He was so concerned for the boy, genuine about wanting to go to him and kept repeating, "He will be scared alone." Dad wanted so bad that the boy grow up properly and not have a, "big head." That was the only reason he had disciplined the child. It was "because I love him so much." It was then I learned about love that was not intelligent. I had seen abused children before but never when love was present.

Recently I heard on the news that a surveillance camera in a parking lot had photographed a young Mother opening the trunk of her car and proceeding to feed an infant and toddler who were locked inside. She diapered, kissed them, closed the trunk lid and went back into the store. A couple of hours later the surveillance camera caught her doing the same thing. When the tape was viewed it was discovered the young Mother worked in the store. She came out on her breaks to feed and care for her children. She had no money and no one to care for her children. She needed the job to buy them food. Did she love them? Was it intelligent love? Doesn't your heart just break for her?

Hone Skills to be Perceived as Loving

To be effective one must be perceived by the recipients to be caring. Otherwise they cannot receive the benefit the helper offers. Therefore, it is important to enhance one's skills in loving. Professional or paraprofessional lovers must develop skills to be understood as kind persons. One must learn how to use one's bodies, one's voice, to know when to reach out and touch, and when to stay silent. One needs to develop listening skills, therapeutic touch skills, and verbal skills which convey caring and support. Without these, all your knowledge will stay only with you and will not be effective in the lives of others. All that love in your heart will make you a better person, but it will not be much help to those you reach out to.

One of the best ways to develop the therapeutic self is to get in touch with your personal death awareness by learning, reading, listening, and growing from your personhood. You will discover that all the richness of your person will be there for you at crisis moments and that your professional knowledge and skills will augment your personhood. It will happen, so take in this information with your whole person, for you come to each dying and grieving situation the sum total of the person that you are in that moment.

Got It All Together

I don't know about you but some days I've got it all together. I feel good about the world; I am glad to be alive and present. If someone has a tragedy or sorrow I am sorry they have to go through that experience, but I know my running away will not remove their trial. So I say to myself, "If they have to go through this, I am glad to be here for them. I am glad to be supportive and to help them." Do you ever feel this way? It is a wonderful feeling!

Those Days!

Out of Step; Out of Rhythm

Then there are other days when I feel just a half a beat out of step with the rhythm of the drummer. Do you have those days also? On those days my elbows knock things over and my hips bang into things. I say things I do not mean. Do you have those days? Have you noticed that people need you on those days also? And have you noticed that you are functional and beneficial to them even on those days as well?

Own Well is Empty

Then there are the days when my own well is empty. It is hard to get out of bed in the morning and I have to talk to my feet. Have you experienced those days? Yes, people need you on those days as well. You may have wanted to avoid people because you knew you wouldn't be therapeutic for anyone. If there was a hole to crawl into you would. Do you have those days? And have you noticed that people need you on those days too? Your own heart may be absolutely broken as you sit listening to someone else's feelings.

Have you had the experience of someone saying to you on one of those days of deadness of spirit. "Thank you so much. You helped me more than you will ever know." And have you gone away throwing your hands into the air saying, "From where did they receive when my own well is so empty?"

This is the humbling part of grief work. Often people draw support from you just because you care, not because you are so brilliant. It appears that in this work you have to do your part by reading, discussion, and mediating. You have to take the time to integrate the meaning of this material into your own life experiences, put your priorities in order, clarify your values, and then you need to let go and be free to respond from the heart of your beautiful humanity.

There is a real difference between being unprepared and adlibbing. As someone once said, an excellent off the cuff speech is a presentation that has been well rehearsed many times in the mind. Grief work demands the best of preparation and also the best response to the needs of the moment. One cannot spontaneously respond intelligently to the needs of the moment if one is not grounded in an excellent base of information. It seems like a computer to me. You have to program the material into your brain. Then you have to spend time getting your heart and information in order. In addition you have to spend hours reading, discussing, meditating, and evaluating attitudes and priorities. Then, you have to let it go and be free. You will be on automatic pilot and it will work for the person who is in need. All that has to happen is a mourner's story to push your buttons and you respond automatically.

Have you had the experience of comforting someone and at the same time listening to what you are saying as the mourner hears it? And have you wondered, where did this come from? I never thought about that before. I never put those words together like that. That is the computer working. Some people refer to this as the workings of the Holy Spirit; others refer to this phenomenon as E.S.P. You may have other symbols or frameworks to make sense out of these phenomena. The point is that you are professionally responsible to have an excellent data base.

Tears

Show your tears. Practice by letting your tears flow freely. Use this time to learn that you can think, hear, and function well with tears in your eyes. Tears do not interrupt the learning process. It is an American myth that tears mean you are out of control. Look at films of other cultures and you will see men crying freely as they work. No one thinks they have lost their intelligence.

In America athletes and firemen are about the only groups who recognize this. Often you see a film or picture of a fireman carrying the burned body of a child out of a building with tears streaming down his cheeks. We don't think that fireman is incompetent because he shows his tears, or that the athlete cannot return to the game.

It is impossible to have your arms around a sobbing mother as she stands by her dead child's body without the tears streaming down your eyes, so don't try. If you are using energy to hold in your tears so you can put forth a strong front, your energy is directed inward to yourself. Often there is little left to comfort the mourner. However, if you accept yourself exactly as you are, with tears, your energy is free to go to those who grieve.

Medicine Room

Much of being an effective grief support person is being willing to show tears. Many people care but run away because they are unwilling to show feelings. Tears do not take away from your dignity.

When I worked in obstetrics I often heard patients talk about a particular Doctor or nurse saying, "She is so cold that ice water would not run in her veins." I would think, "I have coffee with him or her and they do not seem cold hearted to me." As I entered the medicine room I'd find the nurse or doctor crying. Yes, physicians do cry at times. I looked at the medicine cups and thought of that poor Mom or Dad weeping in the other room and thought, "Why did you cheat her of your tears? Go; let her see that you are affected by her sorrow. Your tears do the medicine cups no good. How much good your tears would do for that Mom or Dad whose baby just died. Stand with them; walk with that father in the hall. You are not going to get any work done in the next five minutes anyway. Do not stay in here, go to the grieving person."

I mused to myself, "How tender-hearted and caring that person really is. It is so sad the patient feels rebuffed and endures a sense of rejection added to the pain of the death of their baby." When helping persons struggled to keep emotional control until they left the patient's room, the result was interpreted as cold hearted. Many people are perceived as being cold who are not cold at all. This is because they don't allow themselves to be witnessed as vulnerable.

What is Helpful to a Crying Person?

Gently Touch

How can you best support a person who is crying? Put your hand on their arm, knee, or shoulder. Often people want to hug a crying person. This stops the tears and the story. Just touch them to pass your warmth and energy. You may hold your hand close to their body, not quite touching, about and inch away, but near enough to transfer energy to them. If it seems all right, hold your hand gently against their body's neutral zones, such as shoulder, back, and arms. Show acceptance by your body language. If there are others near, have them put as many hands gently on the crying person as possible to pass energy. If the crying person is capable of taking in that energy, that can be comforting.

Ways of Interrupting

Stroking

There is a tendency to stroke a crying person. This eases the nerves of the helping person, but is distracting to the crying person who is working. Think about what the person who is trying to process grief has to do. They have to stop thinking of their story and must deal with the stroking. It is a way of interrupting the grieving person's thoughts and emoting.

Mention Crying

When someone starts crying a support person is often heard nervously repeating, "It is all right to cry. It is all right to cry." Well, the griever believes this or they would not be doing it. When people get in touch with their sorrow they frequently need to cry. If they are putting effort into stuffing feelings they cannot emote. Tears are part of the work of grieving. Do not talk about their crying. They are in the process of telling their story and talking about their crying is to interrupt their story. You are changing the subject. By doing this, you now make them deal with their crying and not with their issue. If they mention their crying it is usually a plea for permission. A gentle repeated response of, it is okay, is usually all that is wanted.

Get Tissue

If you truly believe it is acceptable for them to show their tears do not hand the mourner a tissue. This discounts their tears as if to say, "Something is wrong with your tears dripping. Please get rid of them in a tissue." Handing them a tissue likely interrupts their working. In my experience, one of the first signs a crying person's work is completing is that they will get their own tissue. They had it with them all the while. It just wasn't wanted until now. If they don't have one, they usually look around or ask for one, just as we all do in time of need.

Stops Talking, Wait

If someone has been talking and leaves a long silence or cries broken heartedly-- wait. They usually start speaking again in exactly that part of the sentence where they choked up. Just wait expectantly and you may gently give the permission such as, "It is alright to cry here. It is okay to have feelings here." Do this quietly as an echo, in parental tones.

This silence can last two minutes which seems like an eternity to the listener. The griever who is wordless is usually unaware or uncaring about the passage of time. The stimuli they are dealing with is just too much and they are taking a little reprieve.

Give Hug

Many times when someone cries we say, "You need a hug." That isn't where they are at right then. They are trying to tell us something and we smother them. There is a place for holding, hugging and stroking. This appropriate time is after the struggle to put their story in words is finished. There are times, however, when someone needs to be held before they talk. Some people need to be filled with enough love and energy before they can release. As a grief support person you will sense the various needs of the griever.

Toward the end of an outpouring of words and emotions you will often see a great release of energy. Sometimes this will be in the form of free crying, a great sigh; or you see a full release of muscle tension. It is kind to refill them with your loving touch. Many people benefit from a gentle, cuddling, touching, or holding for five to twenty minutes. As they regain energy you will feel it in their muscle structure and their skin. You will physically feel them replenishing energy and putting on the muscle armor to face the world again.

You will know then, that a sacred moment has passed. For a short time you were permitted into the sanctuary of their soul. Because they were able to reach deeply into the self to release pent up emotions, they will be freer persons because you were there and you cared. It is strange, but it is the nature of humans to need another person as a catalyst to their healing.

When is the Mourner Finished?

Incremental Grief Healing

You have heard of incremental learning. Well, I speak of incremental healing. Grief is not something that is over quickly. It takes several years, so it is a long process. It builds up to a point where the mourner has to let out steam. After the pressure release the person is relieved but it builds up again as concerns about the lost love and need for new coping patterns rise. Then they have to let off steam again. Out comes more release from grief which is smoldering, creating more sorrow. What you see is an incremental release of pressure. It is very much like watching a pressure cooker on the stove. They valve pops up, steam is released, and the valve closes again, only to repeat itself until the fire stops stimulating steam to expand. So it is with the person in grief.

Your caring and presence often stimulates a mourner to release some grief pressure, and with that some of the physical side effects such as headache, sleeplessness, and anger are diminished. At that point they stop talking. Many times you are still caught up in the story. For the moment they have no need to continue looking at the sadness. But you are caught up in the story and want to know the resolution. You are not ready for them to close. It is common to be caught off guard and disappointed. It is frustrating because often you do not get the details.

Not There as a Journalist

You want them to continue because you are keenly aware that this outpouring was healthy for them. That is the time to remember your purpose; your purpose is to help them progress in the processing of their grief. You do not need to know the rest of the story. You are not there as a journalist. You are interested in the health of their processing.

There are signs that provide clues that the mourner is closing. Often they express free broken-hearted crying. That is a wonderful release. You may notice muscle armoring. While they are emoting you may feel that the skin and muscles are very relaxed under your touch. When they are progressing to closure you can feel the turger first at the bone, then the muscles, and finely you can feel the skin tighten. That is a sign to you that even though they are still talking they will close soon.

Muscle armoring is what we all do in order to go out and face the world. We cannot go out being too vulnerable. If you are unaware of this try it out the next time you go in a crowded elevator. Let your body be very limp as people press against you. If you are in America, you will get some disapproving looks. At the end of class I always ask my students to receive touch from at least three people in a way that is acceptable to them. Since students open up much deeper than they are aware during class, this is a way to accomplish muscle armoring and more objectivity before they leave grief class to go play with the traffic.

Value of Seeing Helping Person's Tears

Professionalism Not Diminished by Tears

Your professionalism is not diminished by tears. Tears do not take away one iota from your ability to splint a leg, direct traffic, put in an IV, bandage a head, move an injured person, make telephone calls or comfort grievers. The difference between empathy and sympathy is easily recognized by co-workers. You can be empathetic including flowing tears, without becoming the victim, and without breaking down. You can be the comforter with tears streaming from your eyes without needing to be the comforted.

Many a grieving person has said the greatest comfort they received was seeing the tears in the eyes of the helping person. After the first concerned glances of your co-workers, they will accept your competency when they see by your demeanor that you are continuing well with your work.

Seeing tears in the eyes of the helping person validates the intense grief the griever is feeling. Your tears, shaking voice, trembling cold hands say better than any words, "Your grief is real. Your feelings are legitimate to this situation. I share them with you; I do not run. I am here professionally and humanly."

You do not have to know the dying person nor his family to feel his pain. That is your humanity. John Donne said, "Ask not for whom the bell tolls, it tolls for thee." Man is not a social isolate. His soul is in tune with all humanity. You do not have to have experienced a son being killed to understand a father's grief. Therefore, accept your sorrow, rage, anger, and guilt as being appropriate and legitimate. When a fellow man sorrows, a part of you is affected and a bit of his misfortune becomes your grief; for we are all a part of a bigger whole, our humanity. You need to accept this philosophy when working in a field of high loss. Otherwise burnout comes too soon.

Emotions Close to the Surface

Tragedy Part of the Days Work

This does not mean that each time you are around tragedy you will grieve. Sometimes tragedy is just a part of the days work. Perhaps this is a day you've got it all together and can be an effective comforter while remaining separate. You are a person who can look with loving compassion on another without getting caught up emotionally in their experience. That is alright and good. I always say, "I borrow no sorrow."

Identification

There are times in your work when your emotions will be much closer to the surface than at other times. One of those times can be when you personally identify with someone or something in the story. When the man you are working on looks like your father, you will react. When the boy whose wasted body you pick up is the same age as your son. That will get to you.

You will be affected when the happening confirms your worst fear. My son was a police officer. When a local police officer was killed-- do you think that bothered me? If you are a jogger and a jogger is hit by a car, that will affect you.

Life Crisis

We all experience life's crisis. You may be supporting another when you are having family difficulties, or when there are losses in your own life. We act as though helping persons should not have life crisis and personal grief. However, if you are a helping person for ten to thirty years, the reality is that you will be comforting others during the time of your marital difficulties, child rearing problems, and other losses. You will be holding a grieving daughter while you are also grieving the recent death of your own parent. Tears will be there then.

The person you are helping does not need to know. If they inquire, a simple one sentence explanation, "I have a recent grief," is usually enough. Then return the focus to their issue saying, "This is your time now." When they apologize for causing your tears, simply say, "I don't mind my tears." There are times when your personal feelings are too close to the surface for you to be therapeutic. This is the time to call a peer as a replacement. Take care of yourself.

My Mother Died

I had taught this concept several times when one day my Mother died. I returned to Illinois several hours early to keep an engagement as a speaker at a local church. It was on the "Normal Dynamics of Grief." If that was not ironic enough, the phone was ringing as I walked into the house. Words tumbled from the caller, "My Mother died two weeks ago. I don't think I can make it. This grief is overwhelming--." It was a case of where she needed someone to listen to her outpouring for 45 minutes. I did. Then I went off to the church. I did not tell the audience of Mom's death until after the presentation as I was afraid I might not keep my composure.

I am always amazed at hiring practices that require an applicant to be a year post-primary-death, such as a Mom, Dad, brother, sister, spouse, or child, before the candidate can be considered for a grief support job. However, for those already on the job like police, fire, nurses, physicians, social workers, hospice employees, ministers, paramedics, and EMT's, they get the regulated four days off for the funeral.

In Love

Emotions will be close to the surface when you are in love. Times of high love for a lover, children, hobby, or work, are times when emotions flow freely. Emotions of love and grief are part of the same continuum, for grief is a love story; you would not grieve so, if you had not loved so. Tears flow easily and appropriately at both weddings and funerals.

Those Days

Then again, there are just those days. I sometimes say, "Name a subject and I will cry about it." People need you on those days too, and with all your emotions you can still function at a high level of professionalism. So sit back, relax and be a person, let your feelings show. Accept your sense of inadequacy and let your love flow freely.

Appendix A

Handout, required for students in some classes that I teach.

Role of a Debriefer

Ideally a debriefer is someone certified or degreed in people skills. Needs to be someone trained in listening skills

It is caregiving that we do as fellow students in a *Coping with Loss* Class. The student therefore needs to talk with an objective outsider on a regular basis. The student needs someone who is concerned about their holistic self as it is affected by the information and stories of others.

The student will benefit by being encouraged by a debriefer to talk about each component of their self, to identify how they are affected physically, spiritually, emotionally, socially, and intellectually, by this involvement in grief study.

A debriefer who listens with love to the story of the student/caregiver is essential for burnout prevention and burnout healing. The primary concern of the debriefer is the student/caregiver, and the effect that grief caring has on his or her family relationships.

A Debriefer:

- Agrees to be available for a debriefing session at all reasonable times.
- Is a support person who will share your feelings in a safe and confidential place.

- Gives you permissions to feel, cry, be angry, laugh, be grateful, and have joy.

- Helps you evaluate your skills and growth as a person.

- Helps you define what motivates you.

- Helps you keep your values and priorities in order.

- Help you assess what additional communication may be necessary and with whom that communication should be directed.

- Helps you assess your caregiving as it impacts on you and also how it impacts on your family.

- A debriefer's concern is not to the client first, but you are first to them. Their concern for the client is how that client affects you. [During the class the client refers to your fellow students.]

- Is someone to relate to in your time of joy and in stress.

- Is someone who has love for you.

The duration of a contract with a debriefer is open ended: Agree upon the length of your contract. Typical contracts might run 4-6 months.

Agree on the terms of the contract, for example:

- Each individual is responsible for his/here own feelings

- Confidentiality

- How often the meetings will take place, where, and under what circumstances

- Who will call for the appointments

- Add any other terms important to the two of you

Contract:

The undersigned, acting in the roles of debriefer and student agree to interact with each other for a period of _____ months. This agreement becomes immediately effective upon the signing and dating by both parties.

_____

DEBRIEFER DATE

_____

STUDENT/CAREGIVER DATE

Appendix B

I often adapt material for specialized groups. In those cases I cut and paste as you will notice in some of the class exercises following. It looks like a repeat but is not for a specific group that does not receive the entire document. You may do the same with your sessions. Feel free to use parts of my material for your work. Just give authorship rights when appropriate.

Non verbal communication is the essence of communication with the dying and bereaved. In order to be effective at grief support one must hone and become efficient at this skill.

Non Verbal Communication Exercise

What is Helpful to a Crying Person?

Gently Touch

How can you best support a person who is crying? Put your hand on their arm, knee, or shoulder. Often people want to hug a crier to stop the tears and the story. Just touch them to pass your warmth and energy. There is a tendency to stroke a crying person. This helps the nervous helping person, but is distracting to the crying person who is "working." Hold your hand close to their body not quite touching but near enough to pass energy to them. If it seems alright, hold your hand gently against their body and show acceptance by your body language.

Mention Crying

Do not talk about their crying, they are in the process of telling their story. To talk about their crying is to interrupt their story. If they mention their crying it is usually a plea for permission. A gentle, "It is okay" is usually all that is wanted.

Offer Tissue

Do not hand them a tissue if you truly believe it is alright for them to show their tears. Do not discount their flowing tears with the behavior that says, something is wrong with your tears dripping; please get rid of them in a tissue. My experience is that one of the first signs that the crying person's work is completing is they will get their own tissue which they had all the while. It just wasn't wanted until now. If they don't have one they usually look around or ask for one.

Stops Talking

If someone has been talking and stops to cry, wait, they usually start again in exactly that part of the sentence where they choked up. Just wait expectantly, you may gently give the permissions such as, it is alright to cry here, it is OK to have feelings and alright to have them here.

Give Hug

There is a place for holding hugging and stroking; that is, after the struggle to put their story in words is over. Sometimes they need o be held before they talk. Some people need to be filled with enough love and energy to be able to release. Toward the end of an outpouring of words and emotions you will often see a great release of energy. Sometimes this will be in the form of free crying; sometimes a great sigh, and sometimes you see a complete release of muscle tension. It is kind to refill them with your loving touch. A gentle cuddling, touching or holding for five to twenty minutes is great. As they regain energy you will feel it in their muscle structure and their skin. You will physically feel them replenishing energy and putting on the muscle armor to face the world again.

You will know then that a sacred moment has passed. For a short time you were permitted into the holy of holies, the sanctuary of their soul. And now that they were able to go deeply into the self to release pent up emotions they will be freer persons because you were there and you cared. It is strange but it is the nature of humans to need another person as a catalyst to their healing.

Non Verbal Communication Exercise

The following exercises are important in life. They come easy and natural in any conversation, they do not take forethought; nor do they take any of your own energy. The only requirement is intention. My objective is that you get in touch with a personal power that is just there and that you make it available on a conscious basis through your choice.

Soft Parental Sounds

People use this personal power instinctively. They give off non-verbal communication while they talk, such as when loving someone, much of the communication is non-verbal and the verbal words uttered tend to be nonsense words said in nurturing tones.

We also nonverbally let people know how to treat us, such as when defensive, we give a look that conveys, "Give me good reason--," or when we need to isolate we give that look of , "Don't bug me; I am not with the program right now." We give off vibes, measurable energy, to affect these behaviors.

Harness Personal Power

Let's look at harnessing a personal power that has always been with us. You may choose to use this personal power for the good of others. Like any good skill it will serve you well all of your life, including your personal life.

We are talking about a power that is just there in you. It cost you nothing. When you give it away, you have no less of it. When you leave the scene, you still have as much of it as when you came. That is truly remarkable.

People say, thank you so much for what you gave. You marvel, saying to yourself, "If I gave, how is it that I have no less when I leave this situation? In fact, at times I have more than what I came in with." This is truly a phenomenon of your power!

Information on burnout discusses the problem of caregivers who say they get fatigued, they tire from giving. The key is: to open to the flow from outside of yourself. What is this flow? Different peoples from different parts of the world have different names for it. Use the name that works for you. Christians often use the term, grace. "Lord, make me an instrument--," and "Let your wind blow through my vessel."

You Communicate by:

Approach, in a calm, quiet manner
Providing simple explanations
Verbal cues, tone of voice
Non-verbal cues, body language
Providing verbal and non-verbal encouragement
Visual cues

These are often non-verbal behaviors

Non Verbal Guidelines:

Always ask permission to touch, can be a non-verbal request and a non-verbal acceptance
Gentle touch, lots of skin contact to neutral zones, feet, shoulder, arms, outer thighs, and back

Need for touch continues as the person ages
Touch people when arriving and when leaving
Have eye contact when you touch

Permission assumed in:
Deep grief
Deep pain
Deep fright

Always Sit

Even if you only have a couple minutes

Feeding literature says it is a feeling of tyranny that a person feels when someone stands over them and pushes food at them. However, you decide according to the situation. I stood because of the angle, when I fed my brother who lay flat on his back.

Studies of Doctors who stood over patients for 2 minutes vs. those that sat for 2 minutes. Patients estimated those who stood were present about 30 seconds; those sat were there from 5 minutes to 15 minutes.

Demo and Return Demo

At this time, Partner up
Be prepared to move at each exercise so you experience different partners = different energy
Be prepared to discuss each exercise

Sitting Visit

This position allows for hugging or backing off when appropriate

Chairs facing each other
Thigh to thigh

#1 show a closed body language
#1 show an open body language

#2 repeat

Discuss: How did that feel? Which do you prefer?

Energy Field

#1 person - close your eyes
#2 person - slowly move your hand to the others cheek
#1 person - let your partner know when you feel their hand in your space

Notice the feeling

#2 repeat

Discuss

Hand Shake

Personal space for Americans is hand shake distance apart. Within 15 feet we drop eyes; it gives privacy to the other. If we inadvertently make eye contact within 15 feet, social manners dictate we need to apologize by means of recognizing them such as, saying good morning or sorry.

#1 shake hands
Use a double touch – sandwich their hand with one of your hands on top of their hand and the other under their hand
Keep hands open, do not squeeze. This will not hurt arthritic hands
Have eye contact

#2 repeat

Next:

#1 first, offer one limp hand
#1 second, tighten your muscles in your hand and arm, keep hands open, do not squeeze, offer double hand shake

Notice the feeling difference

#2 repeat

Discuss

Hug

Neutral zones
Back
Arms
Thighs–outer
Feet, for bedridden persons

#1 do a double touch of inclusion, with one hand on the upper arm, other hand on thigh or knee, careful – certain areas may be painful
Now feet

#2 repeat

Discuss
When might you use the feet?

Stand For The Following

Body Hug

Never impose a hug upon someone! That is a violation of personal space. One sees bumpers stickers, "Did you get your 20 hugs today?" The thought is, "You are going to get one now!" Many vertebra, especially in persons with osteoporosis, are broken from an enthusiastic hug. One often hears, "You need a hug," and then it is imposed. No, no!

Invite them into a hug by your body language. Always cause them to step or move into your space, unless they are handicapped; they move, you do not. This allows them time to open up emotionally to receive the good that comes from being enfolded in a caring embrace.

Leader Demo

Tight muscles but a light touch

Students demo & Return demo

Discuss

Embarrassing Hug – How to Get Out

Leader Demo

\# 1 hug
\# 2 resist by tensing your entire body
\# 1 slowly without changing the stride or tone of your voice, withdraw one hand, back away from one side to a distance of hand shake away, turn your body to be along side rather than facing
Leave the other hand on your partner
Slide it down to shoulder or forearm
Continue talking as though nothing happened

Usually this is discreet and neither person needs to deal with the event. You may choose to release your hand and gently step away.

Repeat Demo

Discuss

"No Touch" Person

There are many people who do not want, nor can they receive caring touch from another.

Leader Demo

\# 1 open arms and body with verbal and facial expression of intent
\# 1 extends that greeting and hug from across the entire room which is filled with many people. Your distance is safe and not embarrassing to them. Do not step forward at this time.

\# 1 say goodbye
\# 1 extend a hug form – squeeze and tickle
Blow a kiss
Be gone, turn around and leave so that they feel safe. This allows them to receive and take in your loving intention.

There was no touch to scare the other person
How did that feel?

#2 return demo

Discuss

Standing Over

#2 sit
#1 relate from a standing position. Include some cues

Reverse demo

Both sit for this demo
Reverse demo

How did the difference feel?

Hearing Impaired

How to speak for the hard of hearing, actions truly speak louder than words. Nearly all persons past the age of 60 do some lip-reading, though they are not aware of it.

Make sure the:

- Light is on your face
- Light facing you
- Maintain eye contact; however, the other may be watching your lips closely
- Use body language, smile, and look sincerely interested in them
- Speak in a low pitched voice
- Space between each word
- Spit consonants
- Spit the beginning of each word

Often when working with a hard of hearing person you do not have to speak out loud. The tendency is to shout. No.

Assignment:

#1 lip sync a message of 3 to 5 words

#2 did you get the message?

Repeat demo

Discuss

Feel Energy Flow

Forehand and Neck

#1 without touching your partner's skin
Move one hand near their forehead
Place the other hand behind their neck
Be aware of what you feel

#2 be aware of what you feel and prepare to give feedback

Return demo:

Discuss

Cheek Cuddle

#1 without touching their cheek, cup one of your hands near their jaw and cheek
slowing move your other hand to the other side of their cheek
feel the energy – let it flow from hand to hand
be conscious of what you are feeling

#2 be aware of what you feel and prepare to give feedback

Discuss

Hands Draw Away

#1 place your hand near your partner's cheek; very slowly draw your hands apart.
be acutely conscious as to when you no longer feel the energy

#2 close your eyes, be aware of what you feel and give feedback when you cease to feel #1's hand

Return demo:

Discuss

Your Hands Are Powerful
Your Hands Perform Miracles

Appendix C

On Hands
History Now

Let's start by taking a few moments to center ourselves
To get in touch with our "Self," "The self within," "The inner self"

Go to that special place in your heart where you
Converse with your God
Come to the Garden of your heart
Where you:
    Walk with Him
    Talk with Him
    Listen to Him

Get in touch with the feeling of the why you are here
Be in touch with the motivation of the why you volunteered

There are many reasons you volunteered; all legitimate, the core reason comes from your values

Let Reflect on some Thoughts:

Many were called, few were chosen, why you?

Feed my lambs, feed my lambs, feed my sheep who feed my lambs
What you have done for these the least of my brethren; you have done for Me

Quiet yourself
Come here to this room to be with these people

Think of the busy day today:
Look at it, let it go, it is history now
Getting up, look at it, let it go, it is history now
Dressed for work, look at it, let it go, it is history now
Drive here, look at it, let it go, it is history now
So quickly life becomes, "History now."

This morning, meetings, work, people, phone calls,
Look at it, let it go, it is history now
This afternoon, the rush of it
Look at it, let it go, it is history now

All the things you have to do later
Look at them, let it go, for now
Later will come soon enough
Let it go for now, it too will become history
So fast, your life becomes history

Be here, in this room, with these people

Hands & Energy

I invite you to let pictures come to your mind for each phrase
Some images will be of you and some will be of another
Let this be a slide show in your mind

Look at your hands
Gaze upon your hands
See them
Really see them

Magic hands
Powerful hands
Hands that hold
Hands that touch
Hands that work
Hands that include
Hands that shut out

Hands that are lovers
Hands that are tender touches
Hands that carry
Hands that caress
Hands that strike
Hands that guide

Oh, marvelous hands--what miracles you perform!

Stretch out those hands of yours
Stretch; reach them--way out beyond the fingertips
Stretch them into long fingers, long thumbs, long palms

Light

Open up your mind to the light
Let the light come into the place of your body where you let the light come in

See the light, feel the light come into your body
Filling your body all the way down to your feet and up again to your arms
Flowing out your fingertips
Feel it flow out of your finger tips at a very high rate of speed
Let it flow, let it flow, let it flow

Now lift your hands up
Palms facing out
Keep the light flowing in your body and out your palms, a rapid energy flow

Direct Energy

Now, lightly rub your hands together vigorously.
Build up the friction on your skin

Without looking at the person across from you
With your palms out held outward
Direct that energy across the table
Move it up and down the other side of the table by the position of your hands

Staying in your quiet center, putting none of your energy into this
Choose to stay open, let the light energy flow into you
Though you, and out of you through your hands
What color is the light?

Now, let an image of someone who is not here come to your mind
Direct the energy flowing out of your hands to that person
Let it flow, be consciously aware, here in this moment

Now, let an image of someone in your family come to mind
Direct the energy flowing out of your hands to that person
Let it flow, be consciously aware, here in this moment

Now, let an image of the world come to your mind
Direct the energy flowing out of your hands to all people
Let it flow, be consciously aware, here in this moment

Ball Energy

Rub your hands rapidly together again
Slowly separate your hands, being very aware of the energy flowing between them

Form that energy into a ball
Bounce the ball a very little bit
Dent the ball with your finger

Feel Energy Flow

Without touching your skin
Move one hand near your forehead
Place the other hand behind your neck
Be aware of what you feel

Without touching your body
Cup one of your hands near your jaw and cheek

Slowly move the other hand to the opposite side of your cheek
Feel the energy; let it flow from hand to hand
Be conscious of what your cheeks are feeling

Very slowly draw your hands apart
Be acutely conscious as to when you no longer feel the energy

Close your eyes
Put one of your hands about 18 inches away from the side of your face
Palm toward your cheek
Bring your hand slowly to your cheek

Be aware as to when you feel the energy first touch your cheek
Quietly look at where your hand is
How far away from your cheek is it?
Are you surprised?

This energy is real
It can be can be measured, it can be photographed
You have power in your hands

Contemplate Hands

Quiet your soul, quiet your mind, and let us spend several minutes contemplating - Your hands

Hold them out in front of you
Look at your hands–slowly–really look at them

Contemplation is different than meditation: Contemplation is:
To muse
To observe
To look at intently
To gaze at
To think about intently, to study, to consider

Hold your hands in front of you
Muse about your hands
Observe your hands
Look at your hands intently
Gaze at your hands
Think about them, study them, and consider them

Look at your hands–slowly--really look at them

How are they the same?
How are they different, one from the other?
Look at the shape of your nails
Look at the shape of your fingers
Look at the length of your fingers
Look at the width of your fingers

Look at the palm of your hands
How are they different from each other?
Look at the lines in your palms
Where do the lines of your hands go?
Are there few lines--or many lines on your hands?

Look at the back of your hands
Where are the veins
How are the knuckles
What directions do the lines of the back of your hands go?

Look at your wrist
Do they look sturdy?
Do they feel fragile?
Do they feel strong?
Stretch them
Tense them
Feel their strength

Bend your wrist down, way down, way up
Turn your hands over and bend your wrists way down and way up
Sense the feeling as you do that, up & down

Press your fingers together in a steeple, press hard
How far backwards do your fingers bend?

Interlace your fingers
Wiggle them
With palms facing up interlace your fingers, wiggle them
Look at your fingers all mixed together, keep wiggling them
Which fingers belong to which hand?

Hold your hands out in front of you
Now let your hands flop down
Let them be totally limp
Limp like dishrags

Flop them round and round--use no voluntary control
Think of them as totally separate from you
Flop them this way and that way
Have no control over them
Let them seem disconnected--to have a mind of their own

Now totally limp, let them slowly flop unto your lap
See how they fall
How do they crumble, lay there
Slowly, still disconnected drag your hands to your knee
Down your leg, to your shoes, totally limp, run them around your shoes,
    over straps, and laces
Notice the feeling

Keeping them limp, bring your hands back to your lap
Do they flop in a different position on your lap this time?

Limp and dangling, move them up to the table top
Across your papers, pen, and book

Move your limp hands across your imaginary computer keyboard, i-pod,
    and your imaginary telephone

Move your limp hands across your imaginary plate
Dragging them across your food
Now across your silverware, around your glass of juice
Gently flop your limp fingers across the handle of your coffee cup

Let your hands flop back to your lap again.
Feel the disconnectedness of your hands
Let us hold that feeling--stay with that feeling
In silence--for awhile

Take the Strength

Take the strength of your hands back
Own your strength! Rejoice in your strength!
Shake your hands with purpose!

Look at them!
Thank your hands for the creativity they do for you
Thank your hands for the love they express for you
Stretch them--long hands--long fingers
Make a fist--tight--tight

This is your journey now--hands that work
Hands that yield product now
Hands that express loving and caring--now

Thank you God for hands
Look at your hands
Really appreciate your hands
Thank your hands for what they do for you

Thank you God for the present moment - the present time
I am here Lord; I am here--for me--for You

Chapter 2

Americans: The Lonely Grievers

Whenever we talk about supporting persons emotionally, we need to look at the culture to see how that culture supports its people during emotional crisis. If the culture supports its people well helping persons simply assess the need, identify problems, and check to see that the need is being met. If it is being met by the culture we say, "Fine, the problem is identified and being met well." If, however, the culture is not supporting the persons in the time of emotional stress, the helping person needs to provide intervention. Helping persons need to suggest a plan. If the recipient agrees to accept that support, the helping person needs to arrange for provision to have the support actualized. Often all they need to do is to connect the giver with the receiver.

Ideally the support of mourners and their families are best met by those who are primary to them, family, work, neighborhood, church, and community. This is healthy both for the recipient and it is also important for the extended family of the community. A helping person ought to be careful never to interfere or hinder the flow of caring that comes from the primary circle of the grievers; but rather, needs to facilitate the enhancement of that indigenous support.

When there is no support within the mourner's community helping persons need to design a system of support and facilitate its happening.

Purpose Statement

In this chapter we will examine the nature of a person's relationship to their community. We will identify some of the functions of community in support of the grieving. We will look at the culture of America and identify some of the tasks to be achieved on our way to developing a supportive community for our grievers.

Not Social Isolates

Persons are not meant to function, much less heal alone. There is nothing that lets you know more quickly that persons are not social isolates than to have tasted grief. You know that you belong to a system when you are caught up in grief and bowed down, then you know you need other people. You cannot manage yourself or your family without support of the system. How warm the hand feels that touches your arm when one of your family members dies! How comforted your heart is when someone else reaches out to touch your grieving child. It is at times like this that you know keenly that you belong to a system. You are aware that other people affect you, and you begin to realize that others are involved in your life.

Grief is Not a Private Affair

Grief is not a private affair. You recognize at the death of a loved one that others are involved as grievers themselves because they also mourn the person who is dead. Others are involved and hurt because they care about you, and your grief brings them pain. Still others are involved as nurturers to your family. You are deeply affected by how your community supports or does not support you. Individuals are not isolates; they belong to a group that is part of a system. The pain of one member affects the entire group and the individual or family incapacitated by grief needs the support of a group to heal.

Grief Injures

In grief the emotional aspect of self has been severely injured. The death of a primary person, husband, wife, parent or child, is a severe blow to the emotional aspect of self. The whole person reacts to this injury. Grief for a primary person is such a severe blow to the emotions that if that person had been dealt an equally severe blow to their physical body they would be in an intensive care unit.

We need to know how to treat the grief injured. Let us look at how we treat the physically injured. How do we treat the patient in the intensive care unit? We do not go to them and say, "What do you want your children fed for breakfast?" Rather, we go to the intensive care unit and say to the parent, "You have gone through a lot. Your work right now is to heal your body by working with the machines, drugs, therapists, and people here in the hospital. We will take care of your children. We will clothe your children and feed them. When they cry for you, we will love your children until you are able to come back to be with them again."

That is how we need to recognize injuries that occur to the other facets of the person, not only to the physical facet. Grief is a severe injury. It is an injury to the primary griever, the family, and to the community. When someone is dying in a family; we now have an injured family. That family is a unit. It is a system. They need someone from the outside saying the equivalent of, "We will give you the medicines and treatments that helped other people with similar injury." We can say to those who are emotionally injured, "Others who have gone through experiences similar to yours have found this helpful or that useful." We can ask them if they would like us to facilitate that happening. People need outside support to heal from severe emotional injury just as they need outside support from their community to heal from severe physical injury.

Representational Model of Self

The injury that occurs in grief is to the representational model of self, that is, the way they always thought of themselves has changed. The picture of self that they envisioned is wounded. If a woman thinks of herself as a Mother of living children and the children are now dead, the grief task is to rebuild the representational model of self to that of being Mother of dead children. This is very difficult and takes a long time.

The future for this person has been fragmented. The vision they projected for themselves has been shattered. For them, looking to the future appears as though looking through a mirror which has been shattered. One cannot see clearly through the glass, everything looks broken. Everything they counted on is not predictable. Health is not predictable; money is impotent to help or is gone. All their best laid plans are shattered.

These people feel fragmented; they do not know where their center is. They will often tell you they trip easier, forget often, and fall without reason. They feel disjointed as though their arms and legs are not connected to their body. They need to feel their perimeters physically. They need to feel where they end and space begins; where they end and someone else begins. One of the greatest helps for them is to experience a hug or touch. When someone else touches their arms, they feel their perimeters and can draw back from that fragmented feeling to their center again. If they can allow themselves to be held in the caring arms of another for 20 minutes they pull themselves back into their center and for a moment feel somewhat solid in a world that is no longer solid by any of the perimeters or measurements they tested before. Every perimeter that they used to measure the world by has been shifted or broken. Now the long task of rebuilding their philosophical world and their representational model of self lies ahead. In the meantime they are vulnerable; they need to be supported by their community.

Institutional Grief

Fragmentation happens to an individual who is grieving. It also happens to a family in grief and to any system that is strongly affected by grief. If a primary person or persons of any system are killed, the shock and need for reconstructing the image of the institution needs to be done. That is why we can refer to institutional grief. Sometime the entire system is affected.

One of my students told of being part of the flying medics over the Gulf of Mexico. There were several teams who went out into the Gulf on rescue and transport of critical patients. There was a tremendous bond between them because of the teamwork necessitated by their rescue work. One day one of their helicopters crashed, killing the entire team aboard. The student told of the sorrow.

She told of how heavy their bodies felt as they worked. Gone was the joy of running to the call. She told of how difficult it was to accept the newly hired members. The former team was not ready to accept replacements for their dead partners. The grief process had not occurred yet. Many spoke of quitting, of entering another line of work. This was a grieving institution and its very existence was being threatened by grief.

They needed outside help to come to terms with the deadness of their members, and the fragmentation of the image of the institution for which they worked. They needed help to process that grief. Then, only then, would they be ready to rebuild an image of the new institution with new and old members as part of it.

Many institutions become grieving institutions and must process that grief as a unit. Those individuals who cannot fit themselves into the new institutional model become misfits or leave.

Some examples of a grieving institution are: three of my son's high school classmates were killed one day in a car accident. The administrator made an announcement over the P.A. system saying that they were killed. He asked for a moment of silence. After that-- nothing, he turned off the speaker. He said no more. Classes were expected to go on. One teacher told of the effect, "The students were looking at me stunned. They looked at the empty desk of one of the dead students. A boy sniffled. I looked at him and realized he was a friend of the boy who was just announced dead. I saw the wide eyes of a girl who flirted with him the day before. God! I couldn't teach after that! And they could not concentrate." She asked, "What were we to do? We were all in a state of shock."

I remember seeing a nurse waiting for me one morning as I came to work at a small 75 bed hospital. She wanted to tell me of the suicidal death of one of our most vibrant peers before I went inside. You could feel the shock in that little hospital. All the phases of grief had to be processed by that institution. You could hear it in the hushed tones from the huddled groups in the hallways. Outsiders knew something had happened the minute they walked into the building.

When President Kennedy was killed we had a grieving nation. A sufficient percentage of the population was deeply affected so that the nation had to take the time to mourn. We have also seen this mass grieving process affect the whole world in the death of Princess Diane. Grief support is necessary for individuals and systems as well. That system can be a family, congregation, institution, workplace, community, or on a much larger scale such as a country or world.

Role of Community in Grief Support

Who is Community?

Who is community to the griever? The answer seems to be, "Those who belong." How does one belong to a community? The answer is, "By being there."

Individualistic Americans tend to think of personally supporting those they choose to support and those who choose them. We want to decide who it is that we will support. That is not the definition of community. Community is all the people who belong. All need our support when they are down and out.

Think of your blood relatives. Let your mind think of each one of your extended blood relatives. Do you like each and every one of them? Are you proud of each and every one of them? If they were not related to you, would you go out of your way to seek the relationship of each and every one of them? Probably not. Yet, you claim them all. When they are happy you are affected and when they are depressed they affect the entire family system. If those you are not proud of were to be mutilated, injured, or terribly sad, you would care. You would care that they hurt even though you may not like them as individuals and even when the only response to news of their death is relief, you still care that they suffered.

Yes, often we love people only because they belong. That is reason enough for the community to gather round to support them when their road gets too tough. Thinking in terms of tribe makes it easier to understand who is community and therefore deserving of our support. Think of the tribes. You expect them to care if a member sorrows. So it is with your tribe of neighborhood, church, and work. You need to reach out to support each and every member when they are incapacitated. Community does not support only those whom they like. Community supports all those who belong.

A good example is that a call to 911 brings about an instant response to any person. The operator at 911 does not ask if the victim is our type of friend, whether he has money or not, what church he goes to, or what name he calls his God. The community provides an immediate response from police, fire, EMT's, paramedics, and trauma personnel to anyone in their community who is in need, just because they are there. Never mind if the victim's home is in another state or country. We still provide money for salaries of trained personnel and sophisticated equipment to support him in his time of need.

The Function of Community

When the family is shocked by grief, when a significant member is dying or dead, this family is no longer sure of its boundaries. It is fragmented; the sense of unity is broken. The representational model of self, that is, the way in which they pictured themselves as family has been shattered. The old methods of communicating no longer work and new coping patterns to support one another are not yet developed. This is a family in crisis. It is an injured system. The function of community is to gather around this family that is fragmented and push against it hard, as a pressure bandage is pressed against a wound so the shattered pieces can mend together. This family needs to heal, but the wound is in need of pressure-love and the time of healing is long. So the community needs to press hard against this family to facilitate healing just as a cast needs to be firm to facilitate the aligned healing of a shattered bone.

The wounded family needs to feel a community hug. Just as a wounded person feels safer in the arms of a caring individual, so the wounded family is safer when it feels the support of community. The rituals of the old cultures were designed to achieve this.

Value of Rituals

If you look at the rituals of other cultures to see how they supported their mourners amongst them, you will see rituals that look very different from one culture to another. The grief rituals of the Chinese look very different than the grief rituals of England. These rituals may look silly and without meaning to the casual onlooker. However, even though they look very different, all cultural rituals are found to support the same basic human need in the time of fragmentation from grief. The ritual achieves the function of pressing round the grieving family to prevent undo fragmentation. The ritual allows time for healing.

The Jewish people have many healthy rituals around the support of the mourners. One ritual is that during the week of the death and several days after, they go to the house of the mourner each day. We who are not Jewish wonder if this is an imposition on the family's privacy. We hesitate to go to the house of grief. We need to look at the effect of this ritual. What the Jewish community is saying nonverbal by coming each day is, "Yes, you are hurt. Yes, your sense of future is gone and you may not know why you should live. You may feel like weeping forever and not facing anyone, you can mope, and you can cry, and you can curl up in a ball. You can pull into a fetal position in your bed; you can pull the drapes and go into your realm of isolation all day long because you really do hurt that badly. However, once a day you are going to have to face us, you are going to have to look at us. You are going to have to look us in the eye and admit to the fact that we exist and care about you. Once a day you are going to have to face the fact that you are part of community. You have a community around you in your pain even if you do not know why we exist." Once a day the recipients of that ritual must deal with the fact that they belong to a system that cares about them.

America's Isolationist Culture

Contrast that assertive, slightly aggressive, ritual and its effect upon the mourner with an American mourner who is the recipient of our mixed cultural, transient society's method of dealing with people who mourn. Many people have moved into a new area without extended family. They have no one, neither relative nor social family. If a wife is killed leaving a fragmented nuclear family, what happens to them? In our cities they are likely to be living in a small apartment of a great big apartment complex. No one notices whether they come out or not. No one realizes that the green car was not in the parking lot during the days the young husband and child took the Mom's body back home for burial. Their absence goes unnoticed. For the majority of our grievers struck with the terrible blow of a primary loss there is no one who faces them to say, "We care that you exist." All it takes is one telephone call to work saying, "I cannot come in today. I do not feel well." There are no caring questions asked. They are likely to be told, "Take all the time you need." In fact, people in the work place are relieved that they do not have to deal with a co-worker in acute grief. From then on we let them curl up and isolate, alone in their grief. That is not natural to human beings. They get disorientated, day runs into night, weeks run into months, confusion and problems begin to occur. Humans need the feeling of a group around them in order to heal. This isolation of mourners is a product of our transient, mixed culture that does not have a common ritual to greet, talk to, and support victims of tragedy.

The task of our times is to develop a ritual that works in our society. The framework of the ritual may look artificial. However, it is effective if it serves the function of assisting the mourner to process his grief. It may be as artificial appearing as arranging a call to the mourner each evening at 8 pm, or it may be to bring a meal into the house every third day. Whatever serves the need of supporting the mourner is acceptable even if it seems unspontaneous. Community is very important in the support of mourners. Remember community to Americans can take many different forms; the workplace may be the only group of people for a particular mourner. An institution or work place must devise a way to be community during the time of grief fragmentation of one of its members.

Many Subcultures

When we check our needs assessment list for a mourner, we need to look at those items taken care of by the culture and say, "Fine." Then we need to stand by and continue to assess the effectiveness of this care over the weeks, months, and years following the inception of need. Sometimes needs are met well during crisis but help disappears over the long haul. For those needs that are not being met we need to design and implement a system of support.

To make this assessment is difficult in America because we are not one culture. We are a conglomerate of many different cultures. Therefore, it is difficult for the helping person to recognize behaviors which are helpful to a particular mourner. It takes work, effort, and preferably a group of caregivers to assess and make sense of what is happening to this particular family.

America has many subcultures. Some things are common to all Americans. Some behaviors differ from state to state. The way mourners are supported in Oklahoma is very different from the way mourners are supported in New York City. Some rituals and methods differ from one nationality group to another. The inclination is to ask, "Wow, with all these differences how can we support a grieving person in America?" What ritual can we design that will be helpful to all the people we serve?

The American challenge is to develop a framework. To do this we need to identify the normal dynamics of loss and the type of support mourners must have in order to process the tasks to achieve healing. I envision this framework to look like a French door with many little panes of glass within it. If the frame is defined and firm, that is, if the knowledge of the normal dynamics of grief are defined, and the tasks which the mourner must process are clearly known, the mourner can choose their own glass for the windows. By this I mean that the mourner can choose their own way of processing their loss and their individual coping patterns for their changed lifestyles incurred by the loss. As long as it helps the mourner to accomplish the tasks of grief; the manner in which they cope can be as individualistic as is the mourner.

Some mourners may choose all clear glass. Others will fill their French door with blue glass. Still others will create detailed stained glass panes, and others will use finely cut crystal etched glass. The point is the view through the door of grief may be as individual as is the mourner. Yet, if the frame and hinges are strong and well designed, meaning they meet the growth and development process of bereavement, the door of grief will function well. That door is the entrance into the future that will exist without the loved person, place, or ideal, which was lost.

Differing Reaction to Loss

All people do not react to grief in the same way. We recognize there are many different ways to react to loss. It is possible that any reaction can be normal for that particular person. No reaction can be used as a measure of the love the mourner had for a lost object. We cannot look at the grief reaction to measure the love they had for a person who is dying or dead. Sometimes we may look at a mourner and see no reaction to bad news. We may think, "Perhaps they did not love the dead one very much." The reaction does not answer that question. It only tells us something about the coping pattern being used, and something about where the mourner is emotionally at the time we are assessing them.

How do we know what is normal and what is abnormal when relating to grieving people? If all Americans were of one cultural group who processed with the same rituals we would be able to know if they were healthy quite easily and quickly. When we are dealing with Americans we simply don't know. We always have to be mindful that there are many different ways to react to loss. Even so, we must assess our mourner's growth and development in the grieving state to know when to intervene in order to assist and support them through this time of vulnerability.

Nurses often express this confusion by saying, "We just called a family to the unit to inform them that their Dad was dead. They didn't react!" Nurses wonder, "Maybe there was no love between them?" There seems to be no real way to measure the initial reaction as intensity of attachment. People can react in many different ways and none are a measure of the love the mourner had for the dead person.

Reaction Culturally Appropriate?

What we need to ask is, "Is this person's reaction culturally appropriate? Is it appropriate to his past behavior?" If you come upon a person in crisis you will seldom have information about their culture, past behavior or personal support system. In that case you need to stand by, tune in, look, and ask the question, does the behavior seem alright for them at this time? We need to be aware that what will seem very okay in one culture may be very unusual behavior in another culture.

We need to find out if this behavior is appropriate to the mourners past behavior and also to his culture. If it is, you want to support him in that behavior. If the mourners behavior is very different from their past behavior and culture, you take notice, watch, stand by, and be ready to intervene.

You want to be watchful even though the behavior would be appropriate to you. Sometimes we look at someone and say, "I understand what they are doing, I would do that too, or, "That is the way my Mom would react. What they are doing is familiar to me and looks alright to me." However, even if your Mom does react effectively in that manner and it works well for her, but if it is not in accordance with this person's usual pattern of behavior, you want to be alert and ready to intervene.

Normal Reaction to News of Death

There are some behaviors that differ from state to state. One characteristic of Americans is that they try to fit into the culture where they are living at the time someone in their family dies. They adopt the funeral and grief support ritual of the areas to which they moved. This means the wake, memorial, funeral planning, time of funeral, visitation, and the after-care they receive is likely to be very different than anything they have experienced before.

What this means is that many mourners do not have the coping patterns by which to use these rituals. They are puzzled by the proceedings and confused by the actions of those who come to support them. Sometimes mourners are insulted by the seemingly uncaring behavior of either more aggressive or less intrusive actions of their new friends than was common in the area they grew up. Mourners in America do not have a known way to bury their dead child or mate.

Mixing Oil and Water

Dr. Warden gave an example of observing differing grief behaviors. He said, "I come from a hospital in Boston. If you want to have an experience, go there to watch my people. The hospital serves basically two cultures. Approximately 50% of its clientele are Italian and the other 50% are English." He said, "They don't mix. In fact, it is a little like mixing oil and water." He continued, "If you really want an experience, come and work with the two cultures all day long. It is a little like eating ice-cream and drinking hot coffee at the same time-- makes your teeth crack. That is how you feel when working with two such different cultures all day long. You have to shift gears very fast." It leaves you with an emotional whip lash.

"The Italians come in," Dr. Warden said, "Notice I used the plural, there is no Italian singular. They are always in a group, and they are always talking, and they are all talking at the same time. Not only are their mouths always moving, but all of them is moving, their arms and whole body are always moving. Italians, he said, have the ability to fill up all available space. So you take them into the treatment room. They quickly spread out and fill up the entire treatment area. While you would like them to be there, they get into your sterile field and tangle in the equipment. Now you have to ask them to please step into the hall. Then they immediately fill up the entire hallway."

He goes on to say, "If you want to see something funny watch an English couple come down that same hallway and try to get passed this moving mass of humanity. The English persons pull in their skin, get very close to the wall and walk by very carefully, hoping that whatever the Italians are doing-- it isn't contagious."

There really is a significant difference between cultures. When you call an Italian family into the Emergency Department to say, "I'm sorry; your son was brought here. We were not able to save him, he is dead." You get a lot of reaction! It may be crying, flailing, hugging, and falling on each other. That does not worry you a bit. Because you know it is culturally appropriate for them to express feelings with overt behavior.

Now when an English family is called to the hospital, they come in twos or threes. They come quietly and sedately. They respond to news of a death with a simple response of, "Oh, my, how did it happen?" They are very methodical. These reactions of the Italian and English families are very different. Yet, neither reaction is a measure of the love for the dead person.

Accordance with Past Behavior

When you are working with a family whose background you do not know, you can quickly assess whether you should worry or not. For instance, if the Italian family were to respond simply and sedately to news of the death of a primary person, would you worry? Yes, you would become very alert. Why? Because it is not in accordance with his past behavior. You would want to be alert, stand by, and watch. Perhaps the Italian gentleman is in shock. When it wears off he may react strongly in an unsafe environment. Perhaps he is about to faint. Maybe he is on medications which are inhibiting his understanding. Perhaps this is just how he chooses to react right now and he is really all right. All you want to do is be around and aware that he may need intervention. Many persons with delayed reactions leave the place after receiving bad news to find that they are a driving hazard to themselves and others. They tell of unbelievable driving events. Some are not able to walk without help, some tend to stumble and fall easily. Others have breathing difficulties and cardiac events.

The same approach must be used with the English father. If he reacts overtly with arms flailing, you would be ready to act. Anything might be happening to him. You are concerned even though this behavior would not concern you if it were displayed by the Italian father. You are concerned about one father's behavior and not about the other father who displays a similar reaction. You simply want to be alert as to whether the action is culturally appropriate and in accordance with their, not your, past behaviors. This is the principle you want to keep in mind when working with people.

Tasks of the Decade

There are many questions we need to be asking as a society. The first task is to identify the questions. After the questions are identified, the answers come very slowly.

Each decade has its task. A society needs to come to terms with the deficit before a new ritual or method can be developed. To come to terms with this means the society needs to identify what is lacking. They need to design a system to meet that need in a way which is healthy for the society. In the 1950's there was a need for research. We researched everything. In the 1960's we needed to come to terms with overpopulation and the birth control issue came to the fore. In the 1970's the task was to come to terms with death. Those who were saved by medical advances in the decades earlier were coming to the end of their viability. The increasing life span for the majority of citizens was maturing with many elderly in our population. The country was dealing with the termination of natural death and the creation of prolonged unnatural dying made possible by technical achievements in medicine and machines. A sufficiently large percentage of the population had buried a parent after prolonged unnatural dying. So much so, that a cry arose in our nation saying, "I do not want to die the way I watched my Father die." The time was ripe to face the issue of death and dying.

Now we have many questions to ask. We need to be astute as to how and where the answers will come. We need to discuss questions such as, "Why do we need special classes on dying and bereavement?" "Are we so much weaker than our grandparents who took their losses in stride?" "Is not support of the dying and grieving something we should do naturally and spontaneously from our hearts?" We need to ask, "Why do we need the Hospice program that sends strangers into the homes of grieving families while someone is dying?" "Is not that an invasion of their privacy?" "Why do we need self help groups for every different kind of struggle?"

Problems Peculiar to Our Generation

We need to ask ourselves why we need to concern ourselves with death, dying, and grieving; so much so, that we even have special classes on the subject. Is it because we are a weak generation? Are we a weak people, as some foreign cultures view us? Are we pampered and unwilling to make the adjustment that loss requires? Are we so much weaker than our grandparents? They took their losses in stride. Isn't this something we should be able to just do naturally? Shouldn't grief support be something we do spontaneously as the need arises? What is the matter with us that we struggle so much in our losses? Could it be that we are so selfish and self-centered as a people that we will not help each other in their time of need? Are we too busy in our work to lend a hand? Are we really so much weaker than our grandparents? Are we big bad Americans? Have you heard these questions?

Dying and Grieving are Different Today

The fact is that dying and grieving are different today. Our great-grandparents did not have to go through what we must go through. They did not have to die as we have to watch our loved ones die. They did not have to grieve in the manner that we must grieve today. We are dying and grieving in a way that never happened before in history. We need to get together in an academic setting at a time when we are not emotionally caught up in personal grief. We need to discuss many things such as, how are we dying today? We need to look at those answers objectively. We need to look at how our culture supports its families who have dying persons amongst them. We need to ask, how do we want to die in the future when it is our turn to die?

Home Dying

We need to ask, where should our people die? Should they die in acute care hospitals with the very best in technology being done to the very last? Or is it better to die in a Hospice setting, a special wing or building used for the care of the dying? We need to ask about dying at home with hospice support. If we like that concept we need to address some hard questions. We need to look at home dying in the context of:

Amount of Care

Those of you who have been close to a dying person or taken care of a long term dying person know how much work that can be. We need to look at home dying in terms of the amount of care needed, in the context of:

Working Women

The reality is that a high percentage of people who will become the caregivers of those dying are working women. Those houses in suburbia are empty monuments to the economic levels of their owners. They are not homes during the day hours. Many working people including women travel overnight for their job. Isn't it ironic that just as the nation has abandoned its houses it begins to talk about supporting the dying at home? There may be no one in that house to care for the dying person or for the community to support. Think about this question: In your family, if someone was to begin a long term dying process, would there be a caretaker free and available? What kind of changes would have to take place to free a member of your family for caregiving?

I work mostly evenings so I exercise during the day. I often ride my bike through the subdivisions near my home. I would like to suggest that sometime during a regular workday you go to a subdivision and observe. Choose a subdivision that has been built within the last 20 years and therefore unlikely to have retired persons. I find perfect peace there. There are no children running around the streets to disturb me. They are in day care, pre-schools, day schools, and after school programs. There are no sounds of radios and televisions coming from the houses to disturb my creative thinking. There are no smells of bakery wafting down the streets.

There are no groups of laughing, talking persons with coffee cups sharing their insights and pleasures of the day. The people are all busy somewhere else. They are going about their day's business. These suburbs are perfect peace. They are as peaceful as any cemetery. Suburbia is as nice as a park. It is nicely landscaped and has pretty flowers with trees. It offers the bonus in that it is usually safer for a woman to be alone in suburbia than a forest preserve or park. I like to meditate in suburbia while riding or walking.

Could it be that as our women have gone to the work world and our houses are empty, we are talking about the value of home dying? Could it be that home dying will not fill the needs of our families when the homemakers of yesteryear are no longer amongst us?

Family Burnout

We need to address the question of, "How many deaths can one nuclear family support?" After going through the dying process with two parents, each taking several years in their dying, there are still two more parents to die. In addition most families have a relative or child for whom they will be the primary support person during their time to die. Can one family do this for years that stretch into twenty or more? At some time can we wear a family out? Is there a limit to their giving ability? I did not say willingness, I said ability. Can families' burnout? We need to look at the energy level of families who take care of a dying person when the dying takes a number of years. Are they ready to start all over again with the next person?

I remember a staffing meeting at our hospice after the death of one of our clients. As was our custom, the hospice nurse asked the caregiver, the sister of the dead man, how we could best support her. The sister responded by pleading with us to intercede for her with her relatives. She wanted us to explain to them that she could not travel several states away to take care of an aunt who was dying. As the story unfolded we began to see that she was the only family member without a paid position. Therefore she was considered free to take care of the ill in the family. Over the past 10 years she had no respite, going from one illness to another. Her brother was the third significant other she had helped in their dying process. She was single, emotionally drained, and burned out. How she wanted to take care of the old aunt, but her body was refusing to get up in the morning. This is not an unusual tale.

Support of Families

As a society we do not support the dying and the grieving amongst us. We are hesitant to reach out for their friendship, to include them in our social circles, and to draw from them the richness they have to offer. We tend to ostracize them. The help we give is given to victims, not to equals. It is not acceptable for the dying and the grieving to talk about their struggles at public functions or social gatherings. We respond quickly with our cultural mores to shush them. We say, "Don't cry. Don't talk about it." We have many platitudes to shut them up, such as, "It will be all right," or, "Everything happens for the best." If those remarks do not quiet the fragmenting mourner, we use, "God never gives you more than you can handle." Imagine a suffering person trying to continue after those put-downs. So grieving people suffer in hiding, dress well, wash their hair, and respond to inquires, with, "I'm doing as well as can be expected." To greetings they respond, "I'm fine, thank you."

Known Rituals

Are We Really So Selfish and Cold?

Why has this happened in America? Are we really so selfish and cold? Do we really not care about another's sorrow? Americans do care very much! We need to look upon ourselves with sympathy. We do not know how to help each other. We do not know what gives each other comfort. Many of our well intentioned efforts at comforting are rejected and misinterpreted. Think of the person who sits across the room from you at your place of social interaction. Do you know what gives that person comfort? Much of the time we can look at the people in the groups to which we belong and say, "We are all approximately in the same broad age range, economic level, educational level, and often the same racial or ethnic group? One would assume with so many similarities that we would know how to comfort one another. Yet, you do not know what the person on your right needs in their time of loneliness. There is no known ritual that is acceptable to both of you that you could perform to symbolize your caring.

When you are sad and lonely, when your day is out of sorts, what gives you comfort? One person answers by saying they putter in the garden, another plays the piano, some curl up in a chair to think, some to read a book, and some sleep. The comfort measures are as broad a variety of activities as there are people. Our tendency when attempting to comfort another is to provide for them the same opportunities that give us comfort. So we have these weird patient care plans. The piano player urges the sleeper to play piano saying, "For your own good." The "Curl up in a ball," person tucks the jogger up tightly in an afghan on a comfortable couch saying, "This will make you feel better." The "Putter in the garden," drags the bookworm outside, saying, "Fresh air will do you good." Is it any wonder that we are not receiving great accolades for our efforts?

To find out what gives a person comfort we must ask them. This presumes that the person being asked is self knowledgeable enough to know the answer. The tendency of the mourner is to immobilize, to curl up in a ball, to be rendered into the child self. The grief injured person is emotionally injured as severely as a physically injured person with a wound which would cause hospitalization. This helps you to understand why it is so important not to wait until they ask for help. You must go to them with a plan. You must go to them without insisting they have it together enough to know what it is they need. They are not able to ask for their needs to be met. You must offer them symbols of your caring without them asking, such as calling at 8 pm each night or bringing them a loaf of bread. Perhaps the content of the phone conversation seems meaningless; however, it is the symbol of a caring community that makes the call or loaf of bread so important. It is not about the bread.

Because people are so individualistic, cultures have provided known rituals surrounding the important events of life. These rituals are not to replace the individual needs but are meant to provide a symbol to both the giver and the receiver. The symbol is to show the extent of the caring of a society to its sufferers. Our society does not have rituals that are known and acceptable to its entire people. It is this absence of known rituals that isolates the sufferers and makes our American grievers so lonely.

America a Dispersed Society

We need to look at where we are as a society in terms of grief support. We are a dispersed society, a society in transition, we are in interface. The coping patterns of grief support from yesteryear no longer work and the new coping patterns of tomorrow are not yet developed. There are many contributing factors to this period of transition.

Pluralistic Society

Americans come from a wide variety of backgrounds, countries, nationalities, life styles, religious beliefs, and economic levels. We have been open and welcomed all peoples. Our parents and grandparents brought their rituals with them to the new territory but wanted to be tolerant of others. Therefore they did not impose their rituals on other people. We have paid a high price for our tolerance. We now have no common rituals to support families in stress and crisis. Other cultures where sameness of rituals exists, know they can reach out in a certain way to give support and receive support.

In our efforts to be accepting of other people's routines, we did not even give our children rituals. We have raised entire generations to adulthood in America who has no known rituals by which to express their grief in community. Nor do they know how to extend their condolences to another. We have raised entire generations to adulthood who have no experience and therefore no adeptness at receiving the comfort from rituals. Those of you who are older are more fortunate. You can remember the rituals of your childhood. Even though you have not partaken in them for years, you can bring them up in time of need.

We see this often among mourners. They establish for themselves a ritual of comfort that stems from their youth. This is healthy. But we must be aware that many of our mourners were given no examples of healthy grief processing. Therefore, they need even greater support from their communities in time of grief.

The present task of our society is to develop a known ritual of support for healthy grief processing where both the giver and the recipient of the ritual can look beyond the act, to understand the symbolism of caring and support that is expressed by this ritual. By itself the ritual does not mean much. However, it is an identifiable, abbreviated public behavior that extends all the love and caring of an entire society.

Who Are We?

Your great-grandparents knew who they were. They said, "We are Greek, we are Italian, we are Irish, Jew, Chinese, Indian, or German." They knew who they were. In the time of grief they would say, "We Turks do it this way, We Japanese do it this way." They knew how they would design the wakes and funerals of those they loved. They knew the meaning behind the symbols they would receive as mourners. They had a known ritual. The mourner knew this ritual. The mourner of the old societies knew how to derive the comfort from the meaning behind the ritual.

But you-- funny people-- you did not even marry your own kind, did you? Jews have married Polish, and the Irish married Italians, Danes married French, and Spanish married Russians. If your great-grandparents knew you did that they would turn over in their grave.

It is my guess that those of you who did not marry your own kind, did not sit down during your engagement period and say to each other, "If our child should die-- what would give you comfort?" Did you discuss this with your new mate? Likely, you did not. So what we have happening in America is that, at the time of grief we have one member of the family wanting to do this activity for comfort, while another member of the same family wants to do something very different. It is common to see families pulling apart in grief instead of pulling together in comfort. What is comforting to one makes the other member of the family think that he is going crazy. It is not uncommon to find a mourner thinking their mate has lost their mind in grief, when, in actuality the mate's scary activity is historically and culturally appropriate to him.

Comfort Rituals of Childhood

When we are injured severely we are rendered back to our child self. We are placed in a dependent position by our injury. We tend to revert back into behavior and activities that were ours when we were young. In times of great grief, pain, or fright, we let others take control, put needles in us, tell us to go to bed when it is not bed time, and give us medications for which we do not know the names. We would not put up with that external control of others when functioning from an adult state. In grief, we go back in time to wanting the comforting measures which we received as a child. This is appropriate because it is our child self that wants to be comforted. Therefore it is common that our grieving people want to hear the sayings, songs, and prayers of their youth. They want to do the activities and rituals of their childhood. They yearn to hear the language of their youth and music from the old days.

Very often what gives comfort to one person is very disturbing to another person, even within the same family. For example, often you will find one of the mates wants to go to the cemetery every day. The other mate is commonly heard to worry out loud, "I think my wife is going crazy. She goes to the cemetery every day; she can't seem to realize her child is not there. She talks to her and cries at her grave. I really think she needs a psychiatrist."

If you ask, "What did her parents do? Did they visit the cemeteries of their dead?" It is likely you will hear a response of, "Oh, those crazy people, they were out there all the time." Then you ask, "What about your parents? The person will likely say, "Well, the cemetery means nothing to us. You know the spirit of our dead are not there. The cemetery is nothing." So you can see how we have mixed cultural rituals even within marriages. This lack of common ritual around a taboo subject not only confuses our communities but also the very core of family interactions. Just a simple understanding of the reasons behind these behaviors can bring release from tremendous tension and worry within the family.

Not only is this wife's heart broken with grief for her dead child, she now feels she has a husband who does not love her enough to stand beside her when she weeps. She perceives she has a double loss. He on the other hand, is afraid to go with her to the cemetery because he does not want to support behavior that appears crazy. With outside help he would quickly understand her ritualistic need and gladly go with her out of love, even though not out of his personal need. Can you see how grief behaviors are often misinterpreted to be marriage problems? This woman thinks her husband doesn't love her. He does.

Value of Ritual

One of the values of rituals is to provide a complete message with a short symbolic activity. An example of the value of ritual can be seen in movies that depict two women from an old world culture. They are dressed in black with babushkas covering their heads. You recognize the scene. One woman can be seen expressing her sorrow as the friend pats her on the arm saying, "Ah, Sophia, life is hard for you now. I know you feel so bad. I will go to the church and light a candle." The church bells toll the evening Angeles, both women know it is time to prepare dinner for their families; life goes on even when you know not why. Sophia heads to her home. Her heart is comforted seeing her friend pad across the courtyard to the church. Later when Sophia is making dinner her heart is feeling great pain. Then she remembers the pat on her arm and still feels the warmth of its touch. She thinks of her friend. She thinks of the candle flickering in the lonely church. Sophia is comforted all over again.

Contrary to popular opinion, Sophia probably does not believe the candle is magic, nor does her friend. Each of them knows the tremendous caring that is symbolized by that lit candle. The friend is pleased to help Sophia by expressing such depth of caring. Sophia's heart is warmed knowing the number of hours the candle will burn, a symbol that she and her pain belong to a greater community. The beauty is that all of this was conveyed in the shortest of time. It took one sentence of promise spoken to Sophia, the trip across the village square, the time to drop a coin in the cup and light a taper. That is the function of ritual, to convey a lifetime of meaning in a symbol. This is particularly appropriate in time of loss because mourners can only deal with one small thought at a time. Volumes said in caring words often only make the mourner nervous.

Would you like to try this symbolic gesture with the grieving lady at work? You may discover that she thinks lighting candles is voodoo. We do not have a known way to reach out to others, to simply let them know of all the caring that we have for them who are in community with us.

Rituals No Longer Work

Another example of rituals having meaning is the custom of bringing food to the house of a family in crisis. I was to speak at a discussion group in a church. This group had become very close and supportive to each other through several years of association. The leader asked for time to make an announcement before I began my presentation. He said to the group, "As you know, Bill Jones was suddenly taken gravely ill last week. Please do not bring any more food over to his house." Bill was 46 years old, a pillar of the community and church. He and his wife had four teenage sons.

Now let us look at our culture. What do we do with healthy 46 year old productive family men who have sudden severe unexplained illness? We transfer them to a specialty hospital in a city far away. That is what the physicians did with Mr. Jones. However the neighbors brought over dishes of food to the house. Now, let's look at our culture again. Where does the family go when someone is acutely ill? They go to be near him in the city of the hospital that is far away. So there was no one in that house to eat the food in the dishes that were so lovingly prepared by a caring community.

Five days later Mr. Jones died. Let us look at our culture again. Are most 46 year old men living in the town where they grew up? Many are not. They have moved to pursue their work. When they die unexpectedly, where do the families tend to have them buried? They are likely to be buried in the home town cemetery of their ancestors. That is what happened to Mr. Jones. His body was transferred to a distant state for funeral and burial. Where is the family at this time? They tend to follow the body and attend the services. The Jones family went directly to Kentucky. There they decided to stay with relatives for two weeks to mourn, rest, and receive comfort from each other.

In the meantime word of his illness and death spread from his neighborhood, to the communities of his work and church. People continued to bring dishes of food to the house. Kindly neighbors kept the house intact for them. But there were no eaters to eat the food in the dishes so lovingly prepared. The man making the announcement said, "The food has filled the refrigerator, overflowed unto the counter, and now fills the kitchen table. There is some green stuff beginning to grow on the edges. Would those of you who brought the food, please go to the house, find your dish, take the dish home and throw out the food? It is no longer safe to eat."

How does that make you feel? The people took their dishes home, washed, and cleaned the kitchen so that two weeks later when the Jones family came home there was not a tangible sign of the massive display of love and caring that had been present in their community for them during their time of sorrow. Are people likely two weeks later to go back to the family in the same way that they do at the time of death? No, they are not. This family had no visible, touchable, symbol of the outreach that was truly present for them.

We often hear that we have become a cold and uncaring society. I wish you could have been in the room that day. There was so much caring and frustration, the people wanted to help. But, they had no known way to convey that love and caring to the family in need. We often hear it said that, "People know the caring is there for them without the outward signs." I'm not sure that is true. We are holistic persons. We need to give something tangible. We need to receive something tangible. We need something to be looked at, fingered, and gone back to for reassurance in the moments of doubt when the night is just too long.

Have any of you received a precious letter? Did you keep the letter out on the desk or table weeks and months after you received it? Why? You knew the message. We are holistic persons. We want something tangible. Have you ever received flowers, and did you sometimes walk to that room just to look at them or to smell them again? Why? You knew the flowers were there. Oh, yes, we are physical as well as spiritual, emotional, social, and intellectual. That is why donating money to a medical fund or charity just does not satisfy comforters in the same way as taking a dish of food, running errands, or sending flowers.

Gave Our Children No Rituals

Some of us are lucky. Even though we do not partake in rituals in a regular way, we do have memories of them from our youth. In time of need we can set some of them up from which to derive comfort. But our children have no rituals. In fact, our children do not even know who they are. How many of you had the experience of a teenager coming home saying, "Mom, I've got to do a geneogram, what are we?" Are we Irish, Arab, Swedish, Columbian? They usually follow this up with, "I forgot, Mom." Chances are they are a hybrid, a mixture of ethnic groups. I have even forgotten the exact mixture of our adopted children. When they came to us over 30 years ago I thought I would always remember something so important. That generation is middle-aged now. They do not even have the memory of a cultural ritual.

About middle-age, life's losses come quickly and furiously: As career height is reached, downsizing and career marketability become real, the glass ceiling becomes visible, age prejudiced becomes palpable, children develop fantasies foreign to parents, ones own parents age and become terminal, dear friends move away, a percentage of peers choose the depressive approach to life, and some peers begin chronic illnesses. So the need to design a cross-cultural support ritual for a mobile, fragmented, nuclear family, blended familied society is an immediate need right now.

A Known Ritual

When I was young we lived on a farm. We had no telephones. There were two churches in our little village. Both had beautiful bells but very distinctive sounds. When someone died we all stopped our work in the fields and barn to count the tolls. I remember my folks silently standing and counting. As soon as the bells stopped they went into action. The women went in the house to cook and bake, the men went to the sheds to get the machinery of the season. We knew by the tone which church the dead person belonged to and by the count of the tolls how old the person was. We also knew who was ailing in the town and if it matched we knew exactly who died. If it didn't match it was likely a tragedy. In that case, a car would soon drive in the farmyard, shouting out the name of the dead person. Everyone knew what do. Everyone knew what was needed. People didn't ask. The mourners knew what to expect. Farmers arrived and went directly to the barn to milk the cows. They drove into the hay fields and commenced to bring in the bales. Women prepared a huge feast for the funeral day which was always the 3'd day after death. Women knew the leaders in the church to coordinate the food. No one bothered the bereaved. It just happened.

How to be the Receiver

The most important aspect of a known ritual is that the receiver knows what to expect and knows exactly their role. I was driving with my little children up to Wisconsin to see my Mom and Dad when nearing their farm I saw a field with about eight tractors and balers. I knew that meant tragedy. A few miles further I pulled into my brother's farm intending to greet him on my way to the folks. No Barn! Just a smoldering pile of ash still burning. Several fire units were still working on it. It was easy to find my brother. He knew his role as victim very well and knew exactly what to do. He was standing in the middle of his yard, directing traffic, "Take those wagon loads to the Weber farm," and to the next driver, "Take 6 wagon loads to the Nickels farm," then to someone in a car, "Send those sandwiches to the back forty and the next batch of food goes to feed the crew at the Weber farm." You see, he had been at many barn fires in his life. Now it was his turn to receive. He knew exactly how to take in and to be the receiver.

The fire was discovered about 11pm. It was quickly designated as a five alarm fire activating fire departments from several towns. When the sirens wailed farmers counted the number of wails, and went directly to that area of the township where all they had to do was follow the stream of cars and trucks heading to the lighted sky. They herded the cattle and other farm animals, checked for injuries, fenced, watered and fed them. They worked the entire night. The women did not drive toward the fire. They drove to the little village nearest the fire and knew that when they arrived the grocery store would be opened with lights on. They went directly to the shelves and gathered what they needed. No Check out. No pay now. Someone would take care of that in the days to come. "People working fires need a lot of food and drink." They went to the local designated place, prepared, and delivered food all night and the following days. A known ritual. They knew exactly what to do to support their hurting community members.

Essential Tribal Family

Nomadic Society

Another characteristic that defines us as a dispersed society in the period of interface is that we are a nomadic society. It is said that one out of three Americans moves more than three hundred miles every three years. This is still true even though companies are transferring personnel less often than they used to. It appears Americans move just because they like to move. That makes us the most nomadic society in the history of the world. Most of us thought the nomads were more nomadic than we Americans.

The nomads only moved from winter hunting grounds to summer hunting grounds. They moved 30 miles up the mountain for summer grounds and 30 miles down the mountain for winter grounds. We move further and more often than other groups ever moved. However, being Americans we do it differently. We are the only group of people who ever tried to migrate without taking our cultural rituals with us. We try to fit into the culture of the area in which we move. As helping persons we have seen many families move into our area with a terminally ill person amongst them. They have no idea how to derive comfort from the culture of their new environment.

Americans also are the only group of migratory persons who do not take the extended family with them. The nomads took the grandparents and the entire extended family, including the tribe. They also took the same rituals for celebrating holidays and occasions of joy and loss.

Who is Your Social Family?

It appears that people are not meant to function in nuclear families, much less heal from grief without an extended family around them. The human being is a group animal. That extended family is not always defined by blood. Sometimes it is defined by tribe or community. We are group persons. We need to be in a group of about thirty people to function well. The small tribes were about thirty people each. When the group became larger it divided itself into several tribes that formed a clan. In other parts of the world, people had an extended family that lived together in one complex or under one roof. They built onto the house when one of the young persons married. If the group got beyond thirty the young newlyweds would move to the house of the in-laws. Throughout the cultures we can see the natural need to be in an extended family system of about thirty people.

I would like you to count the people who are important to you. Be sure to count the children whose presence makes your eyes light up. Be sure to include the old people in your life. We tend to eliminate these two groups from our consciousness if they are not blood related. Chances are, if you are healthy in your interactions and have been in a location for awhile, your number will be about thirty. That is healthy.

When counting be sure to ask yourself, who is the child you miss when he hasn't been in the street for a few days? Who is the teen you always touch? The one you just cannot seem to walk by without running your fingers across his shoulders. Who is the old man whose absence you notice when he is not at church?

Now look at how this is manifested in your places of work. See how the members divide into groups of about thirty. Again look at your churches, if a church has ninety members, chances are you can see three subgroups of approximately thirty. I bet you call these factions. This is a natural division. But not knowing this can be disturbing.

Social Family vs. Blood Family

If you are healthy you have a social family. It is good to identify who these people are. We need to recognize that man is not meant to be a social isolate nor are we meant to exist as unconnected nuclear families. The fact that we have moved away from our blood families does not change the fact that we need an extended family. Healthy people do have an extended family. It is not blood defined, it is socially defined. We need to recognize that when we are working with the dying and the grieving we are working with the social family system.

It is important to identify the primary members of this social family. I would like you to answer to yourself, who is it that brothers you when you need a brother? I hope you have brothers whether you are a man or women. I hope you have many friends of the opposite sex. We are the only society who ever expected to go through life experiencing the hugs or the cultural equivalent of a hug from only one member of the opposite sex. We exclude over 50% of the population as potential friends based on sex alone.

In times gone by the extended families were large. Large families meant there were many brothers and many sisters to hug or give and receive the cultural equivalent of a hug. There were many uncles and aunts from both sides of the family as well as parents and grandparents.

In our society we have small families producing a small number of blood relatives whom we do not even live nearby. Many urban people do not even know their first cousins or know why they should want to. They make zero effort at contact; much less effort to obtain the depth of relationship that supports one in times of loss.

It is common to hear someone say, "I am so different than my blood relatives; my friends are much more like me. My friends are interested in similar things as I am and we share values. I choose my friends; I did not choose my relatives. I have nothing in common with my farmer or small town relatives" This sounds reasonable. However, when these urban reared people get old, they are likely not to find the friends they gave allegiance to. The friends made during their children's youth are not likely to sit at their bedside in the nursing home or to stand beside them in the time of mourning. The blood relatives of the rural areas far away are still able to be traced after many years. These relatives likely have a cultural ritual of support that quickly takes in concern and consideration of relatives that were separated. However, each decade there are fewer of these people to make the connection.

Social Families are Important Bonds

When you need sistering to whom do you go? That is a special kind of relationship. When you need an uncle to whom do you go? We all know there is a special place for, "uncling and aunting" in our lives.

When parents must discipline, a child needs to go to someone else for comforting. In the old extended family there was a kind lap of grandma or auntie to go to for comfort, not to negate the rights of the parent, but to soothe and provide a philosophical explanation by which the child could emotionally cope with the disciplining parent. When we are adults, aunts and uncles are caring people to bounce ideas off including concerns about our parents. They are a bit more objective than parents, yet they care. They are a special relationship.

Yes, we never grow too old to need a parent. When you need fathering and mothering to whom do you go? It is well to identify these persons. They may be younger than you are chronologically, or all of them may be older than you. The chronological age is not what defines their relationship. It is the nurturing and caring that exist between you that defines social family.

Then too, you have parenting to give. What child is it that causes your eyes to light up? Which child do you miss if you have not seen him lately? These are your social children, your social nieces and nephews. They are all important people to you. If they were killed or moved, or angry at you, you would be destined to grieve.

Part of the task of aging is to develop this social network of extended family. Life is such that there is a continuous loss of members from the extended family. To age successfully one must be willing to continuously work at developing and communicating with an extended family while grieving for members who must leave.

After you have identified your social family by name and identified the relationship each one has with you, such as uncle, sister etc., take the time to identify as many members of your children's social family as you can. Since these relationships often function well but are rarely identified, we seldom know the persons who are primary to our children. Another reason we do not identify our children's primary social family is that we do not mix in their social worlds. We may never witness the significant relationship between our child and their social aunt.

Children Bond to a Social Family

Librarian Was Auntie

My daughter was hyperactive. To sit in a classroom all day was more than she could manage. When she was in the fourth grade, her school recognized her need for movement and variety. To keep her from disturbing the class the teacher came up with an innovative idea. She told Lisa that she could leave the classroom whenever she needed to move. They put a stop sign at the door. While Lisa was at her desk the stop sign read, "Stop." When she needed to move she was instructed to get up quietly without disturbing her neighbors, tiptoe over to the sign turn it around so it read, "Go." Lisa loved this power. The teacher said she could see her heading down the hall very fast, long hair flowing out behind her. Shortly after she would return, turned the sign to "Stop," and tiptoed back to her desk. The teacher began to wonder where she went but knew all the teachers in the building were alerted to watch for Lisa. The teacher found that each time Lisa headed to the library. The librarian learned to expect her visitor and always knew what she would show Lisa that day. One day it was fish in an aquarium, another time it was a flower outside the window, many times it was a pretty picture in a book. This secret love affair went on for an entire year. What I did not realize is the importance of that relationship in terms of growth and development. The librarian was aunt. I am sure the loss of her aunt at the end of the school year was extreme. I did not recognize her behavior as reacting to a significant loss.

There are many children who are grieving the absence of a primary person. Yet, neither they nor we identify the moroseness and the behavior changes as being grief behavior. We just do not realize the importance of social family. We do not identify the members of our personal social family or those of our dear ones.

Little Old Man with the Wheelbarrow

When my son, Craig, was four years old he was permitted to go to the end of the block on our side of the street. Yet, he persisted in going to the house behind the one at the end of the block. He insisted that he was not being disobedient because he did not cross a street. Finely I checked to see the source of the attraction. There, in that house, lived a little old man who enjoyed yard work. Every day my son would follow this little old man and his wheelbarrow around the yard. Looking back, I now realize the importance of the little boy to the old man who had been a family man, but lived alone since his wife died.

It never occurred to me that the grandfathering my son was receiving was from the little old man with the wheelbarrow. If anyone asked my son who his grandfather was, he would answer, Grandpa Kieffer who lives in Wisconsin. Grandpa Schultz was dead. My son heard me tell this story during a lecture when he was a junior in high school. He said to me, "I didn't know you knew Mr. Schroeder. I still go to see him. He always gives me soda pop." Now, I had no idea that my son continued to see him all those years. When my son is a grandfather, whose coping patterns do you think he will use with his grandchildren? Will they be the patterns of behavior that my father used? My father who lives 300 miles away, who Craig saw for two days at a time, two times a year? Or will he use the grandfathering coping patterns of the little old man with the wheelbarrow at the end of the street that he followed daily. Yes, he will probably give his teenage grandchildren soda pop.

Little Kids Grieve in Isolation

We need to look at this dynamic. It is important to children. When my son was young, what would his response have been if the little old man had been suddenly removed to a nursing home? Do you think I would have even known of the old man's condition? I don't think so. Would my son have grieved? Would I have identified his behavioral difficulties as a grief reaction? I doubt it. How would he have made sense out of the absence of that precious old man in his life? How would he have done his closures? Yes, little kids grieve in isolation.

Always There, Across the Lot Line

Knowledge of the existence of an extended social family is essential in order to identity the mourning individual. Often the loss is never validated and the mourning process is puzzling to the individual as well as to the family. In one of my classes a Nurse told of an old man who lived alone next door to her. He remained kind and pleasant but did not mix with anyone. Her son was born and grew up with the old man who was, "Always there." How the little boy loved that old man! As soon as he could crawl on hands and knees he would go as fast as his little limbs would move him across the lot line into the arms of the welcoming old man. When the boy was twelve he came home from school. His mother was working in the hospital and he followed his usual custom of going to the home of the old man before going to his own home. This afternoon there was no answer to his knock on the door so the boy just went into the house. He saw the old man in bed. The bed was on fire. The boy carried the old man to the shower, wet him down, called the ambulance and fire departments, and accompanied the old man into the ambulance to comfort him in his pain. The boy was refused permission to ride in the ambulance. Worried and distraught, he called the hospital for information. He was asked his relationship to the old man and the boy answered, "Neighbor." The hospital personnel answered him, "Sorry, we cannot give information to anyone except relatives." The boy tried repeatedly for the next four hours until his mother came home. He was beside himself with grief and worry. The mother was so sorry that he had to be alone through all his grief. She and the boy tried to visit the neighbor, but were refused admission because the next of kin from a distant state had requested no visitors be allowed. This boy who acted maturely enough to do everything right in an emergency was considered an unfit visitor as well as unworthy of receiving any information.

Two days later the boy saw a stranger go into the old man's house and begin to throw the old man's belongings into a dumpster. To the boy's objections the stranger said, "It's alright. It all belongs to me now. The old man died last night, I'm his only relative." The boy was beside himself in grief. He asked which funeral home the visitation for the old man would be. He told the stranger, "I want-- I must go to his funeral." The relative replied, "Oh, there will be no funeral. He was an odd person, lived like a hermit, and knew no one. We sent his body directly to the crematoria. It is all done with." The boy then asked for the old man's watch. From the time he could crawl on hands and knees, the old man would put the watch to the boy's ear to hear the ticking. The old man always said, "This will be yours when I am gone." The boy wanted and needed something tangible to hold as he grieved. The relative said, "No, I don't have time to sort through his junk. I've wasted enough time already and want this whole house cleaned out in a couple of hours so I can go home this afternoon. I have to return to my job."

Who was the primary person to this old man? Can outsiders always know who needs to mourn? Can a private funeral fill the mourning needs of the social family?

Months later the boy was morbid and distraught. His mother knew he had not said good-bye to the old man who was her son's primary grandfather figure. With the help of a caring clergyperson, they designed a memorial service to say their good-byes. The boy needed a place for the old man. It is common for mourners to need a physical place for the dead. He chose a tree in the cemetery. With his Mom and the clergyperson he buried a letter of thank you and goodbye to the old man along with a picture of the two of them and some other mementos. The mother noted a physical relief in the boy's demeanor. The sadness was there at times but he began to invest in boyish life again. Often we do not even know our children are grieving. We think their distraught behavior is simply abnormal.

Health Care Teaching

When working with the dying and grieving we need to help them identify: From whom do they need to hear forgiveness? Who is it they need to tell that they love them? To whom do they need to express the meaning of their relationship? Who is it they need to sit close beside for awhile? That person may not be blood related. The question is not only, "Who does the dying person need?" but, also, "Who needs to do closure with the dying person?" Those who will continue to live have needs in this dying time also. It affects their quality of life.

I want you to think, if you were to wake up tomorrow between two clean white sheets, because of an accident or illness and they tell you the prognosis looks very serious. Not counting your mate, who is it that you would need to sit quietly beside you? Which someone would you want to be there, to just hold your hand? I ask you, is that person blood related? Chances are they are not.

Look at the way in which we give health care. We tend to give our health care teaching, sympathy, and comfort, to the long distance relative who flies in from a distant state and will be present only during the dying days. How do we treat the neighbor women as they show up at the time of crisis? We say, "Go home now. There is nothing you can do." Who will be supporting that mate and children in the months of grief to follow? It is the friends, work associates, neighbors, and church people. Yet all our precious health teaching flew out of state on the day after the funeral.

We need to identify the primary social family, primary caretaker, and primary mourners. This is not easy to do. It is least well done among our teenagers. So often we forget to identify, who is brother to this dying boy? Who needs to be with him at the bedside? Who needs to grieve? Who needs to be part of the funeral? It may be a girlfriend or a boyfriend.

It is common to see several carloads of teenagers in the hallway of the emergency department after an accident involving a teen. Quite often the teens are referred to as gawkers, voyeurs. They are sent home. We must carefully assess the motives of these young people for being present in a very difficult situation. These may be primary social relatives. Their relationship may be the equivalent of a brother or cousins. If behavior has meaning their presence speaks very loud.

Born on the same Block

My son, Craig, and the neighbor boy were born on the same block, played together, went to kindergarten together, the same grade school and high school. They walked home together each day. When they were sophomores the other boy was hit by a car with sufficient force to knock his boots off and pop his eye. My son was refused permission to stay with him in the hospital. He spent hours calling the Emergency Department and later the intensive care units. I heard him make the calls and so nicely plead for information, yet they would not inform him as to whether his friend was alive or dead. The injured boy's family did not return home until the wee hours of the morning, so it was not until the next day that my son could know if his friend, his social brother, was alive or dead. The cruelty we inadvertently inflict upon our young people.

How should we Treat the Social Family?

How should we treat the friends of the injured or ill person? While the injured person is waiting on the cart for treatment the friend should be given the opportunity to sit with him. The friend needs to be prepared as to what they will see in physical injury and also the state of consciousness. The friend benefits from being given a meaningful task such as wiping a brow, stroking an arm, holding a hand. Friends should be coached how to give information to the injured, such as, "I am with you, you are in a hospital, you were in an accident, we have called your Mom and she knows you are here." This involvement is important to both the concerned friend and to the injured or sick person.

Opposite Sex Friendship

The validation of the extended social family can ease our lives in many ways. It can help us reach out to nurture others from our position as a social uncle or nurturing mother. Instead of confusing all man-woman relationships as being sexual in nature we can pursue these necessary friendships in healthy non-sexual ways. This does not mean we do not recognize the sexuality of the other. Yes, as a brother or a cousin we recognize and enjoy the sexuality of each other. In this way mature adults can enjoy the wide range of close intimate relationships and maintain sexual boundaries that are appropriate to that relationship. Not only is the individual blessed by this freedom, but the mate is also freed of unnecessary concern which could lead to unnecessary pain of jealousy.

Sorry to see a nice Person go

A man came to me a week after hearing me speak on this subject saying, "A tremendous burden was lifted from my shoulders." He had felt weighted by confusion and guilt. He could not understand his emotional behavior. He related that he was an executive of a large corporation. For eight years he had the same secretary, taking her for granted. Her husband was transferred to another state. She gave her resignation. They said their good-byes and wished each other the best of luck. He remembered identifying no particular feelings other than the usual, "Sorry to see a nice person go," feelings.

It was only in the last week since my presentation that he looked at the time table of his emotional reaction and connected it to her leaving. About a month after she left he began to feel a real heaviness while in the office. Then in a couple of weeks he had difficulty breathing in the office. About another month later he realized he was purposely going to the plant in the mornings before going into his office. In about the sixth month after her leaving he identified the office as a place of great sorrow, a place filled with the emptiness of her presence. Then he knew how much he missed her and he cried.

The feeling of emptiness stayed and his crying jags persisted for several months. In the years following there were moments of deep unexplainable sorrow. He examined his conscience, not liking what he thought he saw. He said, he was an elder in an evangelical church and was very sincere about his ethics and morals. He loved his wife and children. Now it appeared to him that his secretary must have meant more to him than he had admitted. He felt it must have been sinful if he grieved her so. Yet, try as he would, he could not remember ever being, "Lustful in his heart," for her. He never felt that he might be emotionally unfaithful to his wife. He was thoroughly confused.

Now, after hearing the concept of social family he immediately saw what relationship she filled for him. It was aunt. He recalled his loneliness as a child for a significant mother figure. His Mom died when he was four years old. Much of the grief he suffered when the secretary left was unfinished grief work from his childhood loss.

His secretary had been very healing for him. Her qualities as he described them were, "The office was light and warm when I arrived. She always greeted me with a sincere good morning, and how are you today? She cared if my child was sick. She was happy when my wife and I had a pleasant weekend." He said, "It all seemed part of a days work. It wasn't until she was gone that I knew the office was cold and gray and that there was not always a source of caring in it."

The sad part of this is that the relationship, healing, healthy, and wholesome as it was, was not socially validated. Now that the lady moved the relationship was terminated. This is less likely to happen in blood relationships. It is easier to reestablish closeness in blood relationships when one has moved. A reason for this is the significant social people in an individual's life are not integrated into the family or even known to them. So when the external reason for their being together such as a work project is terminated, there is no longer a socially acceptable excuse to be together. Any attempts to continue the relationship appear clandestine. Too bad. This is sad. We all need extended relationships with members of both sexes who encourage and support us as we grow through life.

Task of Every Society

Mandelbaum says the task of every society after its members have been dispersed and reassembled into new groups, is to define how each group is to be supported when they are dependent. One of the very first tasks is to decide how to die, how to support the dying, and how to dispose of the body. This newly assembled group has to decide how to support the mourners amongst them during the long bereavement period, a time in which they are vulnerable to illness, attack, and accident.

The major difference in societies of old and now, is that the old societies felt they could not afford to lose any members, so each member's safety and well-being was protected by society. We do not mind losing people in our society today. We are overpopulated and while we respond to a death on a nearby highway by remarking, "That is too bad," we go right on with the day's activity unaffected by a death that occurred in close proximity to us. Death only affects those of the immediate family and communities of work, social, and church, to which the dead person belonged. Even for most of those communities the emotional effect is short lived. The effort is on replacement of the dead, not on support of the mourners. The care we wish to give our dying and mourning members of our society has to come from our spiritual and intellectual caring. It does not result from our personal need. If we are not involved, we don't need anyone. We go on living our individualized isolated lives.

Our society has been defining this process for several years. What system can support the dying and grieving in a mobile, multi-cultural, multi-ethnic, and multi-religious, blended families, fragmented nuclear family society? Some encouraging signs have appeared in the form of hospice to support families with dying persons and with support groups for those who feel the disintegration of coping patterns after severe loss. There is evidence of a new compassion demonstrating itself on our landscape where friends band together to support those among them who are dying alone. However, these meet only a small percentage of people with a need.

The Hospice Structure

In the former days of migration the method of support was to take the extended family and cultural rituals with the people when they migrated. The present system of support seems to be to have a known structure present in each community so the individual can move into and through the system. While they are in the system the structure provides an extended family. The structure provides support and a known ritual. For example, the mother of school children may be diagnosed with a terminal illness in Denver, Colorado. Her husband may receive a transfer to Chicago during the last months of her life. This is usually an unsupported situation. Members of the new community do not reach out to make friends with a couple when one of them is dying. At school the children do not verbalize the entirety of their situation. Their home is not a fertile place to nurture new friendships with either school pals or neighborhood children.

With the hospice system of care, the family can receive hospice support in Denver, find a ready supportive extended family in Chicago at hospice, and if they move again before she dies, hopefully there will be a hospice to welcome them in the lonely new location. This system appears to work well to fill the needs of the dying and their families in our society.

Our hospice had a case such as this. The lady wanted nothing more than to go to a large shopping mall for Christmas. She wanted so badly to hear the Christmas music, see the Christmas decorations, and feel the holiday hub bub. The church people cared so much but were unsure how to handle a wheel chair client and they whispered, "afraid that she might die in the mall." Hospice had several volunteers that were adept at wheel chairs and perfectly comfortable to attend to her if her time to die was at the mall.

The Compassionate Friends

A similar support is experienced by members of *The Compassionate Friends*. If parents move shortly after a child has been killed, they find themselves mourning the loss of their home and all that it stands for as well as the loss of the dead child. In the new location that loneliness is intensified by the recognition that no one knew the dead child, no one mourns his loss with them. Again people tend to avoid making intimate friendships with someone who is actively grieving, especially if it is made more awkward by not having shared history. With the support system of *The Compassionate Friends* in operation the family can receive support immediately at the time of the death of their child. When they transfer they can find a ready structure in the new town, providing them with sincere extended family support and caring immediately upon their arrival. At the compassionate friend's meetings they will find others wanting to see the pictures of the dead child, hear of his life with its hopes and dreams, and there will be people who want to be called in the middle of the night when the darkness seems too long.

Designing and making available structures that can provide a system where the grief injured family can find loving care and an instant tribe of approximately thirty support persons, knowledge about their grief work, and rituals to process this grief is the task of this generation. A very rewarding task! You are part of that generation.

Appendix A

I Spoke to the River
Then the River Spoke to Me

Grief over the Transfer of a Friend

Hope is not the projection of our wishes onto the calendar of the forthcoming year. When my dear friend was transferred to a place so far away my grief and pain were almost unbearable. I talked with my sister for and hour and then went down to the river to talk to the River and then the River talked to me. The River said, "Look back." I rarely look from where the river comes; I look to where it goes and meditate on the meaning and growth of life, but the River said, "Look back from where you and your Friend have come." And I saw it was beautiful in that direction also. The colors were taking on a fall hue of rusts, the weather comfortably warm with deep cool shadows. The sounds of summer and birds was noisy and peaceful. Then I noticed it. There was a fork in the river from where the waters came. They came from separate sources.

Separate lives to flow together under the bridge. Then I noticed there was much material, sticks, and leaves. being carried by the river, mingling the goodies of both sources. And so it has been in our lives. We mingle the material of both and are so much richer for it. Then the River spoke again. "Do you see how beautiful each of the forks was before you met? I gasped, looked from one to the other. Both incredible beautiful souls, lives, being joined together to go hand in hand down the river of life, to mix, to blend, to share, to ripple, to shimmer, to gurgle with a joyful sound, to bask in the sunshine and feel its warmth, to grow.

Then the River spoke again. It said, "Look ahead." I answered, "No!" Not today! I don't want to! But the River was insistent and again said,

"Turn around and look to where the waters go." I did and screamed, "Dam that island! Dam! Dam that island!" The River was speaking but I, with hand over mouth in pain would not hear. Slowly, I let the words come in. They were gentle. "It is only an island, only an island. Don't be so afraid. It is only an Island what is so scary about an island?" I answered, "It separates the beautiful waters." The River asked, "Does it take away their beauty?"

Through blinking eyes I reluctantly saw the beauty was not diminished one iota for its separating. But I saw the debris it had shared with each other went with each in a mixed way so that what was one before they joined was now part of both as they separated and I noticed also, that now instead of touching two shores the richness of the river touched four shores. And then I said to the River, "So what! The world is richer. It doesn't make up for the pain, the loneliness, the hurt. I am tired of making the world grow richer. I need to be fed too." The River spoke firmly, "Don't you see? It is only an island; it is not a fork in the river but an island. Waters go around islands and join again."

Amazed I looked as the water parted each so beautiful and I heard the echo, "Don't be afraid, it is only an island - be joined again - be joined again - peace as the waters flow down the river of life, don't fight the current so hard. Go quietly my soul; go peacefully with the eternal plan." Standing there on the bridge I felt the peace of the fast moving current as it carried my friend and me to the base of the island. Quietly I asked, "When will the waters rejoin? This life or the next?"

The river gurgled, rippled and swished, the noises of summer sprang up and I felt the warmth of Sunshine on my neck, I had asked one question too many, the River no longer spoke English.

Chapter 3

The Dying Person

What does the dying person think, feel and do when he becomes aware he will die soon? We wonder what persons think about after they learn their life span is limited. What do they wish to do? How do they wish to talk? How do they want to have others respond to them? What are their needs? How can we best help them meet these needs? How can we assist the family to process their own grief with the dying person? How can the family best assist the terminally ill person in the dying process?

These are questions that come to mind when we hear of someone dying. Can we know the answer? Or is it true that everyone is very different? Must we go without a plan to each dying person and family?

There are some growth and development processes which we share with our fellow human beings. By looking at others who have died and tasks they needed to achieve, we can prepare a patient care plan for those that follow.

Death is a normal process. It is normal to die when the balance of nature has been overcome by trauma, disease, or the aging process. By accepting the normalcy of dying we can have less fear in approaching those who die at any age.

If we view dying as a normal process we don't have to treat the dying as abnormal or tender, like a fragile egg. We can approach them more confidently. We can encourage the family to reach out and risk in interactions, knowing that where there is love there is room for error. Where there is love it is possible to go back to rectify misunderstandings.

The Normal Way to Die

Is there a normal way to die? What is the good death? How is the best way to die? How can we help a terminally ill person achieve this? Asking the dying person is the most often forgotten step.

Standing around in a kitchen at the home of the dying person, it is common to hear family and helping persons say, "I think what Dad needs is--, or, those huddled at a nursing station in the hospitals or nursing homes saying, "I wonder what would please Mom the most--?" Seldom does it occur to anyone to walk to that bedside, take the hand of the dying person and ask, "What is it you are wanting most right now?" "How can I help you get that?"

Remember that the terminally ill period can be a long time. Many persons have remissions after the diagnosis and go back to their daily lives and work. We need to ask these persons, "Now that the doctor has told you that your time may be limited, what is it you would like most to happen?" Let them know then that you are committed to supporting them in achieving their goals. Ask how you can best help.

This is a good time to have a check list in your mind such as:

Holistic concerns:

- Intellectual desires
- Business affairs
- Will and trusts
- Funeral plans
- Social desires
- What do you need to know about your disease
- What do you need to know about the dying process
- Whom do you need to see, forgive, hear forgiveness from

Follow through on the emotional, spiritual and physical needs. Be prepared to go over these several times at intervals as some goals are met and others surface.

To Die in One's Own Style

Each person needs to be encouraged and supported in living out his remaining days in the style that is appropriate to his past life. He ought to be supported in dying according to his own style and in the way he wants to live until he dies. If you are caring for a person who always prided himself in the upkeep of his property it is likely he will want to continue this at some level, even though it may appear hazardous to you. This can be scary to the family and confusing to the helping person. Our responsibility now is to check to see if the patient clearly understands his limitations, the risks he is taking, and if, in sound mind, he has chosen to live potently, even though it may shorten his life.

Many a person chooses to take the chance of dying sooner with his boots on, rather than live several more years in a severely restricted manner. My Dad was a retired farmer in northern Wisconsin. After a snowfall he prided himself on having the best cleared farmyard for the milk truck. He carried this pride in keeping up the property to his retirement home in town. After a heart attack the doctor told Dad to avoid exertion in the cold and to stay indoors on particularly cold days. My sisters and I were home visiting with Mom at the kitchen table, watching the large beautiful snowflakes fall when suddenly Cleo said in a shocked voice, "Do you see what our Daddy is doing?" We had come home to see this man because he had a heart attack, and there he was outside, bundled up with muffler, running the snow blower.

Do you think this is difficult on families? At this time it is the families who need you more than the patient. They need you to give them permission to allow the patient autonomy in choices. Margaret Mead said, "We think we have free will until we receive the diagnosis, "Terminal." At that time others decide what we shall and shall not do, whom we can and cannot see. Others screen our visitors, tell our friends we cannot see them now. They read our mail and keep mail from us. They decide what we shall hear or not hear. This is an infringement on our rights.

Back to my family in Wisconsin, all of us sucked in our breaths watching Dad with the snow blower. Carol asked, "Should we stop him?" We had never stopped Dad in any activity before. This just didn't seem right. Elaine wondered if it was possible to just sit and watch him continue in what might be a death activity. Cleo wondered if not stopping him meant we did not love him. Yet, none of us wanted to take away his dignity by role reversing.

I said, "I know there is a method of approaching him that would be appropriate. I teach it." Yet, when it was my own family member, I found it hard to remember. Then I said, "The family does have a responsibility. We need to assess whether Dad understands the doctor's orders, the risk he is taking, and the consequences." My sisters voted me to be the emissary. Reluctantly, I bundled up and went out into the howling snowstorm. "Daddy," I asked, "How do you feel?" He answered, "Oh, I feel okay except for tightness in my chest. I can't get enough wind. "I said, "Did you understand the doctor? He did say this was dangerous for you to work outside in the cold." Dad gave me a squinty look and answered firmly, "I do okay. I can do as much as I have always done. I just have to stop and rest more often. I take one row up and one row back. Then I sit on that little stool in the garage until my wind comes back." I was stymied! Now, what could I do? I tried one more time. "Have you thought about what would happen if you got a heart attack out here while you were doing this?" He gave me that look again and said decisively, "A guy has got to go sometime." Had my Daddy thought it over? Did he understand the risk he was taking? Had he made a clear, informed, mature decision? Did I or any member of his family, have a right to scold him? Did we have the right to talk down to him as though he were a delinquent child? Did we have the liberty, now that he had a heart attack, to take away his right to continue to be a responsible property owner?

It is said that when we hear the word terminal about someone we immediately neuter them and treat them as a child. That translates into; we take away the sex role tasks that are so much a part of a person's self-image. We talk down to the person.

I invite you to go to a nursing home. Walk the halls slowly and listen to the tone of voice used when speaking to the physically impaired. Listen to the language structure. Then determine at what age level that message is directed. Has the visitor's role reversed and have they neutered the patient?

When visiting a dying lady in her home it is common for her to greet you with, "Oh, how wonderful it is of you to come. Let me get you a cup of tea." Think of what that behavior means to her, it means feminine, mother, nurturer, hostess, and power to do something for another. Let her prepare tea for you even though she is feeble and oh, so slow. If you have the time, let her. If you do not have the time, clarify your reasons and take care of your needs.

I went on a 300 mile journey to see my mother in Wisconsin. it turned out to be the last time I was to see her alive. though in bed, she immediately offered me the cup of coffee which she knew I always appreciated. I watched this woman's pain struggling to get out of bed. I watched as she leaned on the counter to get her breath before she could put the water in the pot. I could hardly restrain myself. Her hand shook so badly while pouring the scalding water. Oh, yes, I checked often to see if she wanted help but it was clear that she desired nothing more than to do something nice for me. Her eyes sparkled with a light I had never seen when she was in bed. The triumph she exuded 25 minutes later when she finally sat with me at the kitchen table to share that coffee and toast was communion. In her powerless position of dying she had the power to nourish me physically, socially, emotionally, intellectually and spiritually. And I--, did I want to take that from her? How easily I might have done just that. How I would have cheated myself! to be fifty years old and still mothered. what a privilege!

One of my students came back to class after I told this story to say, that the exact occurrence happened to her. She told us that it took 25 minutes for her terminally ill friend to get a cup of tea on the table. She went on to say, "It took such self discipline for me not to say, I'll do it for you. Here, it will only take me a minute. Let me. I know I would have made her feel impotent. I could have had that tea and toast on the table in three minutes flat but that is not what this was about. She nurtured me. In my busy life it was important for me to be nurtured. However to be a receiver took a lot of self discipline." What a beautiful gift this student gave her friend.

The Good Death

When it comes to the time of dying we have a picture of the good death in our minds. The scenario reads something like this; the dying person is to be propped up in bed with at least two pillows. He is to fold his hands over his chest, roll his eyes back and say with resignation, "I am ready to go. I have lived a full life and I am ready to die." Pictures like this can be found described in literature and in art throughout the ages. I think of it as the good death because it leaves those of us who are behind feeling so good.

However, take this scenario; a hard driving business man comes to the office each day, pounds on the desk and yells, "Why aren't those trucks in from the west coast?" He grabs the phone and calls the west coast yelling, "I want an explanation!" When this man has his heart attack right on time according the statistical time table at age 46, is in intensive care, and the doctor comes in. The Doctor says, "I'm sorry, the results of your tests do not look good. According to the statistics, you may have a limited time to live. If there is someone you wish to see, please phone them. If you have unfinished business, you may wish to get that in order." Is this man likely to roll his eyes upwards to the heavens, fold his hands gently over his stomach and say, "It is all right." I have lived a full life and I am ready to go. No! He is more likely to yell, "What do you mean? How can you say such a thing to me?" He will pound his bedside table, call the west coast and demand a consult. He will want another opinion and will expect to know why it is a serious diagnosis.

Is this behavior difficult for his family? Are families embarrassed by patients who act out particularly in the specialty units of a hospital? Yes, very much so. The family needs you most right now. The patient is doing all right. He is finding energy to do his closures in his own style, but this can be very embarrassing for his family.

Family Needs

The family will need to know that they are accepted by you; that they have not lost status in your eyes because their relative is not behaving in a socially acceptable manner. They will need to hear permission from you not to scold, permission to let him choose behavior that may shorten his life. True, some behavior needs to be curtailed and this man will need to be quieted. With gentle permissions the family can be involved in a healthy way to the benefit of all. First they need their own fears quieted, some role modeling behavior suggested to them and permissions given. They need help in understanding that the good death is the death that is appropriate to the style of life their relative lived and the style of dying he now chooses.

Does the Patient Know?

Many persons are afraid to visit a terminally ill person because they do not know what he has been told. You need to have your goals clearly in mind. If your purpose is to listen, you do not need to have the formal information. If the patient asks you if he is going to die you reflect his remark in the same manner as you would with other information. You simply reflect what he said, such as, "You ask if you are going to die? What is on your mind when you think of dying?" Then be quiet. Listen to the response. It is often something you would not have anticipated. One man said to me, "Nurse, I want to know because I have been in and out of the hospital several times with this illness. My grandson wants to come before I die. I want to know if this is the dying time so he won't make a useless trip. If I'm not going to die now my grandson and I can talk on the phone. He can't afford more than one trip from California. I would rather he be here to comfort his Mother after I die."

Don't worry so much about telling them of their dying. Rather, prepare yourself to listen in a therapeutic manner. Reflect, "It sounds as though dying is on your mind. What do you think about when you imagine dying? Is there something you want to do? Someone you want to talk to? Is there someone you need to say forgiveness to? Someone you need to hear forgiveness from? How can I help make that happen for you?"

When terminally ill persons are looking for honest answers you need to remember that honest answers are not death sentences. Know again, what your goal is. What outcome do you want from the telling? Sometimes a simple, "Yes, I think this is the time," is all they want. Or, "It looks serious to me right now. I am concerned about your condition."

When should a person be told of his terminal diagnosis? Are there persons and times when it is best not to tell someone that their life is limited? Is it a problem when a person is not told of his diagnosis?

The answers to these questions seem to be quite simple. Almost all dying persons know they are dying even though families and medical staff may insist they have not been told. If you want to know how aware someone is that he is dying ask them, "How sick are you?" Dr. Kubler Ross says that they will tell you. I found that many persons, believed not to be aware that they were terminal, answered with, "Oh, I am very sick," or, "I will never leave this hospital again," or, "I'm hoping to go home one more time to get things in order." They were aware that they had limited time and approximately what amount of time was left for them.

How do They Know?

How do they know? Possibly there is an intrinsic factor, some innate knowledge within the body, that lets the person know when the balance of nature has been overcome, or when the disease or trauma has blocked the body's ability to heal. This is true of some animals. Some animals will voluntarily separate themselves from the pack to go to a quiet spot to die.

Even if there were no innate biological knowledge of approaching death we think persons know as a result of cues given off by others around them. When I worked in the recovery department I usually asked the patient's family to accompany the patient and me into the elevator and back to their room. There was a great difference when I called a family into the elevator who had just received good news from the physician such as, "The operation was a success, after the normal surgery pain is gone your Mom will feel better than she has for some time," or when I called in a family who had just been informed that their mother's pain which they thought to be gall bladder, was now known to come from metastatic cancer. When they were told the cancer metastasized to vital organs and her life was very limited, they were in shock. There was a significant difference in the way these two families looked and reacted.

It was on this elevator ride that I did a great deal of patient teaching. To decrease the fear, I showed them the bandages and the bags. These were now an extension of the patient. The patient needed acceptance of them as a part of him. Families need to be taught how to get close to their loved one without interfering with the tubes and machines. I would say, "See the I.V. in this area? It is in very secure and will not fall out. Go ahead and hold the hand with the I.V." While I was saying this I would model by stroking that area and running my fingers along the veins of the arm that held the needle. I would tell them, "This hand has been insulted and assaulted. Hold that hand." I showed how to maneuver around the machines and tubes to get in close, hug and hold.

Not all wanted to see everything I showed them or hear the details. There was a difference in how the patient teaching was accepted. Those who had received good news were eager for information. They were vibrant and talkative. Those who had received bad news stood tightly against the wall of the elevator, skin and knuckles white. They did not want me to waken Mom. "Let her sleep," they would say, hoping to stave off facing each other with pain in their eyes. The same was true of the floor staff. The staff treated the terminal diagnosed patient in hushed tones, they were very gentle. Yet each patient, cured or terminal, needed to heal from this surgery to go back home to live life again.

Now, I ask you, if you should awaken from anesthesia tomorrow morning, do you know your family well enough to know when they are acting abnormally? Can you tell when your mate or children have been crying? Can you tell when they are too quick to give reassurance, saying, "It's okay; everything is going to be all right." Can you tell when they are too saccharine, too sugar sweet? You can, can't you? Our dying persons can, too.

Don't Know They are Dying?

Why, then, do some patients appear not to know? There are several reasons. It may be their life style. They may never have talked about deep matters and are not going to start now. It may be that they are smart people and know their family well. Do you know what subjects your family just will not tolerate? Each family has taboo topics. This dying person may not be willing to break the family mores. He will not risk having someone important leave the room never to return because that person could not endure the conversation. There is nothing the patient wants more right now than the support of family and friends. He will not cause a rift.

It may be the dying person's coping pattern to deny. Or it may be the family's coping pattern. When it is the family coping pattern not to talk about these issues, your support and listening is so valuable. Never hesitate to go to someone even though he has many visitors. You may be the only one who can listen. Dr. Kubler Ross said if we have only one or two persons to talk with about intimate matters, that is enough. You can offer to be that precious one.

Terminally ill persons often play a dual game. On the one hand they act as though they are completely accepting; but while alone in private, in emotional exile, they deal with their worries and concerns. They wonder, "How will the dying be? Can I get my affairs in order in time? What will the after life be like?"

Important to Share Life's Experiences

A dying person is often forced into emotional isolation. Yet, if he is of sound mind, been a responsible person and comparatively free of excruciating pain he will want to deal with his life's issues.

Part of knowing you are finished with a phase of life is the need to do a life's review. You have done that many times. Think of the times you have left one phase, school, job, or age group. You spent a lot of time thinking of what you had just finished, about the good of it and what you wanted to do to complete it.

When a person prepares to depart life they go far back to the beginning reviewing each phase. They look at their strengths and deal with regrets. Society has recognized this need in other periods of life and has developed rituals to help make that review. Special days mark religious passages such as baptisms, confirmations, bar mitzvahs, graduations, celebrations of marriage, births of babies, and house warmings. Now, at the dying time, that person must include each of these in his review of his life. His marriage, children, education, and religion are all affected and included in his dying tasks.

Yet, how does our society help the dying person make this review? Think of the lady who is gone from her social group for two weeks to have a baby. When she returns how is she greeted? Do they allot time for her to talk? Do they ply her with questions to help her talk? They ask, "How much did the baby weigh? How long was the baby?" Chances are that the questioner is not overly concerned about the inches of the baby, but more likely providing the Mom with an opportunity to do the necessary emoting and expounding. Customs like this give one an idea of how important it is to share our life's experiences with groups.

Contrast that with the absence of another lady from the same group. She was also hospitalized. A fast growing terminal cancer was discovered. How is she welcomed when she returns to the group? Does anyone even mention her absence? Quite often they do not. Is time allotted to talk about this emotional event in her life? Probably not. Does anyone ask the nonsense questions just to start her emoting? Can she make believe nothing has happened? No she cannot. When she thinks about this group she wonders how many more times she will meet with them. When she thinks of her house she wonders how many more times she can do her vacuuming. When she thinks about her finances she wonders if there will be enough money left to support her husband after her medical bills are paid. She wonders, "Can they afford that one special trip abroad before she gets too weak?" She thinks about her children and friends. She must assimilate this event into her self-image. Our dying persons are forced into emotional isolation to do this work. She must develop a new life style just as the young mother with the new baby does. If you can be the one person not afraid to listen, you are doing a beautiful deed.

Playing Games

Hiding news of imminent death forces families and visitors to play games. Whenever you hear that someone is not to be told of their terminal illness, it is usually prefaced by, "She is not well enough to take it yet." Or, "We don't want Grandma to know her son is dying because she can't take it." But Grandma will have to know at some time. It is difficult to hide the death of a son from a mother. How much more healing for all concerned if Grandma can be brought into the family communication, comforted, and given a meaningful part of the dying event. Seldom is the stated reason the real reason for the secret. Dr. Kubler Ross said when there is a secret surrounding the dying you will nearly always find someone who cannot bear to listen. It may be the doctor who cannot bear to face his terminally ill patient with the news. So he says, "I want her to be stronger." It is often the family who cannot bear to face the poignant grief of an aging mother as she sits by her son's deathbed. If you are working with a family who has this secret, look for the protectors who are afraid. They are most in need of your care. They need to be encouraged and supported to face each other's grief.

Secrets Cause Ineffectual Visitations

How do you feel when someone tells you "Don't let the secret out."? Aren't you uncomfortable in the presence of the patient? Aren't you afraid they will see your expression of hesitancy? Playing games with this kind of secret tends to cause visitors to do too much talking. They come to visit with the dying person and start talking before they enter the door. Then they talk nonstop. If the visitor pauses to take a breath and the patient manages to get in a question, they go right on talking as though they did not hear. The visitor tells the patient how nice it was to see them again and that they just have to run because they are so busy. The visitor brings a fresh face, new stimuli, perhaps a lot of love but not much conversational value to the dying person.

Usually what one sees when there is more than one visitor in the room, is people talking over the head of the patient, making believe he is not there, or that he cannot hear. Visitors are not comfortable with this behavior? When one is uncomfortable over several visits one develops avoidance behavior. Even though this visitor may care and love very much he will start to stay away from the patient. This not only is true for relatives and friends; it is true of helping persons as well. All are plagued with fear that they will be the one who let it slip. Then they will be blamed for letting the secret out. Everyone becomes fearful and develops avoidance behaviors.

Studies show that company tends to decrease the number of their visitations and the amount of time they spend when there is a secret of this magnitude. Nurses tend to take longer to answer the call light and refrain from going into the room except when absolutely necessary. Absolutely necessary means they have a task to perform. It is easy to become task oriented, focusing the conversation on bed making, bathing, eating, and the like.

Ministers and para-professionals tend to put something between them and the patient, such as the Bible, rote prayer, inhalation equipment, flowers, cards, or a wheelchair. Everyone talks at the patient; no one talks with the patient. The sadness is that in the time between the sad news and open conversations, there are many intervening conversations which include lies and cover-ups. This results in hurt feelings, missed opportunities and guilt. Eventually it will become apparent to all that this person is dying. Delaying news of this sort seldom does anyone any good other than postponing the sight of real grief in each other's faces. How much better it is when communication can be open from the beginning. Then the dying person and each grieving person can comfort, encourage and teach each other how to cope. Any decision to delay open conversation among all persons involved should be weighed very carefully against the repercussions of keeping major secrets.

Personal Death Awareness

Denial of Our Own Dying

We all will die someday and in time, we all will grieve. About half of us who have a mate will bury that mate. And even though we dislike thinking about it, the reality is that many of us will bury a child. Yet we can not imagine that if we eat right, sleep well, and exercise correctly, in time our bodies will just slow down, atrophy away, and one day cease to exist. That poses a very interesting philosophical argument. If there is no ability to imagine nonexistence, perhaps that is the strongest argument for continuation of the spirit in an altered form.

Therefore, when you find that people you are working with find it difficult to come to terms with their own finiteness, be understanding of them. It may not be natural to humans to understand life's limitedness. This may have to be experienced through personal losses in other arenas. Some of the persons you are working with may not have had a major loss in their lives before. What does happen is that as we grow older we develop an understanding of limited time left. However, that doesn't come until about the age of 35 to 40. If you listen, you will hear many of that age say, "I've got about as many years left as I've already lived."

It may be unreasonable to expect a person younger than middle age, to understand his finiteness. Most teens think they will live forever and therefore are willing to involve themselves in deeds of bravery. Some are willing to take great risks, while saying they know they can die as a result. Often they go on to describe the effects of their death as though they will be there to reap the result. They say words such as, "Others will know what I have been through. Mom will be sorry how she treated me. I'll go down in history. It is worth it for the cause." These teens show no indication of realizing that they will have ceased to exist. They can not imagine that they will not enjoy a benefit from this.

Middle aged persons express this denial by talking inappropriately about planning their own funerals. Often they will say, "When I die, I want everyone to have a party. Have fun. I don't want anyone to feel sad." This is not realistic. Family and friends who loved you must deal with their sadness at some point and the most appropriate time is at the funeral. Another way you hear denial is when you hear someone say, "When I die, I don't want organ music. It makes ME cry." Where does he think "ME" will be? There to cry? Some persons say, "When I die, I don't want an open casket; all those people looking down at ME!" Where do they think they will be? Looking up from the casket? They cannot imagine no longer existing. If one no longer exists all of this does not matter.

Understanding denial will help you when you listen to people voicing inappropriate opinions about their own dying and making foolish plans. Then you can encourage them to think, not of their own needs, but of the needs of others who must mourn for them. Sensitive thoughts of their loved ones will help them to carry out realistic pre-funeral planning.

Older people express their understanding of the limitedness of life by saying things such as, "I should have 20 more good years," or, "I won't live to see the tree I planted grow big. I planted it to shade someone else." Or, "That's the last-- whatever. My mother-in-law said, "Last roof I'll have to put on the house." When I went home to see my father he excitedly said, "Come out to the garage to see my new car. It's the last car I will be buying and I really like it." My enthusiasm waned instantly and I said, "Oh, no, Dad. You're not going to die. You'll have lots of new cars yet." Dad was 83 years old. Who was more realistic, my Dad or me? Though I had been working with the dying for many years I responded with denial when confronted with my own emotions about a primary person to me.

Realizing the limitedness of life can happen suddenly. When I was 39 years old I had been married 17 years. My favorite bed spread, a wedding gift had worn out. Two babies had been changed on it and later used it as a trampoline while jumping on my bed. The spread had served me well and survived many washings. Now I was shopping for an equal. Nothing quite appealed. Then one day I was in an expensive bedding store and saw on display the most beautiful bedspread with matching drapes. I stopped to drink in their beauty. Never did the thought cross my mind to even think of buying them. They were far too expensive. After this, every spread paled by comparison. Back at home I looked at my spread's threadbare material and thought, "My last spread lasted 17 years. I am 39 years old now. How many more bedspreads will I be able to have? Three, at most? Wow!" Suddenly I saw the limits of my life. Oh, yes, the expensive bed spread and matching drapes look lovely in my bedroom.

When you are working with families you will often see that they are experiencing this loss through the eyes of their own personal growth and development. They are viewing the loss quite differently, depending on whether they are a child, teen, 35 year old, or already into the limited life span years.

It is important to get in touch with your own personal reactions to loss, death, limited life span, and limited body function, because how you help others in their losses and their dying will depend on your philosophy of life and how it includes the possibility of loss. If you have never explored your feelings concerning loss, the naturalness of death and the limiting factors of life, seeing all this in others will cause you to be very frightened. If you are scared you will avoid talking or you will talk too much in order to crowd out the possibility of your fear surfacing. It is the mirror effect that is most scary about working with the dying and the grieving. When looking at another and seeing oneself in their position, in their story, in their situation, one is looking into a mirror of, "There, but for the grace of God, go I," to, "Oh, God, there I will go. I will grieve someday. I will die someday."

When this happens, deal with the reflection you saw in the mirror. Grieve your passing. Affirm your life. It helps to journalize your reflections. It is very important to talk with a debriefer about the mirror experience which is common to all helping persons who deal in the area of high loss.

Personal Experience is Not a Flag of Credentials

When making a therapeutic visit go with empathy, not with sympathy. Sympathy identifies with the sufferer and now claims the pain as one's own. Sympathy feels and tells its own story, not the client's. This means there are now two persons who are victims in need of assistance. Empathy is often very much affected by the other's pain but empathy does not become the victim. Empathy often shows tears, cries with, has shaking voice, cold sweaty hands, and sleepless nights. Empathy says, "This is tough, this is rough and alone it is too much to bear. Lean on me. Perhaps together we can see this through."

Personal experience is not a flag of credentials! Your credentials come from your knowledge base and your attitudinal approach. In fact, similar personal experience that has not been worked through can be a hindrance to effective support.

Filter the Patients Story

When I was doing pre and post operation teaching in a hospital, the patients often said, "You are so understanding; you must have had surgery yourself." I began to avoid a direct answer because the patients were incredulous when I told them I never had surgery, but I also never had been a patient in a hospital! The general feeling was that I could not be an effective helper if I had not gone through the pain myself.

So many persons said this that I believe the, "Man in the Sky" must have heard. My kidney ruptured, necessitating major surgery with a long convalescence and rehabilitation program. When I returned to post-op patients and heard them say, "I get muscle spasms." I groaned and leaned to my right side. They continued with, "Sometimes I get such sharp pains." I would say, "You do?" Instinctively, I leaned further over on my right side, protecting my very long incision. After the patient's third remark I listened in a fully bent position. One day the thought came to me, "Why does my surgery experience make me a better nurse?" Now I had to filter the patient's story through my own wound. I had to deal with my own pain. I had to separate mine from what was their pain. Often my patient's response to surgery and their need was very different from mine. A direct application was inappropriate. In no way was I a better surgical nurse after I had undergone surgery. I was a very good nurse before. I needed to validate that by going back to my work evaluations and the many appreciation letters sent to the hospital by my former patients.

In grief work I have found it is common for a grieving person to say to the helping person, "You can't possibly understand!" Or, "Your husband is alive and mine is dead." Or, "Your children are still living!" I have heard many a speaker at a grief seminar answer that accusation from the podium saying, "You are right. I can't understand. My primary people are still alive." The speaker would falter with survival guilt and fumble. In essence they apologized for having living folks. I have heard other speakers spend as much as 15 minutes apologizing for not having had the tragedy experienced by the audience. This is a significant factor in burnout of helping persons. It may be true that you have not experienced the same type of loss; however, you would not be in this work if you had not received the "Gifts of Grief." This understanding of loss can come from other types of loss. Human beings have the ability to extrapolate. Educators tell me that one of the best ways to receive emotional understanding is through novels. There you get to understand and empathize with a variety of feelings that you could not experience in your own life. You do not have to experience the same type of loss to be helpful to this family.

We need to look at this dynamic. The mirror factor in grief is often devastating. For someone who does not regularly face an audience of fifty parents whose child was killed, the impact is overwhelming. It behooves the helping person to take the time to prepare for the impact of the mirror on their own vulnerability. Then they need to prepare for the anger of mourners which is often displaced unto the helper. The helping person must examine the emotional cost of working in an area of high loss. After an event with an audience of mourners the support person must plan for the healing of their own grief and emotions.

Plea, Please Let me Own My Grief

When I first heard mourners challenge helping persons I thought they would be better comforted by only those who had suffered a similar loss in their private lives. In my years of experience with groups of bereaved I found that they also reject each other on the basis of, "But for you it is different, your child died after you were able to say good-bye, ours died of sudden death." Or, "You didn't have to watch your child die. You have the comfort of knowing he was well and lived life fully until he died." I began to see that what appeared to be a rejection of the helper was really a plea, "Please let me own my grief. I am not ready to see similarities with grief of others. Yes, their child died. I am sorry but I must own my own grief. It is this Mother's heart that is broken. This is a special little boy who is dying. He has a name and a birth-date and unique characteristics. Do not group me."

It is the task of the mourner to own his own grief before he can take in from others. We need to zero in on helping validate that personal loss. After being able to own his pain as his very own, the mourner will reach out to others who also suffer. From the richness of their own wounds they use their pain well to assist persons to heal. There is something very personal about grief, yet at the same time it is an expression of our shared humanity. This helping others is not automatic. Not everyone who has gone through loss is therapeutic. The mourner helps others, not by overlaying the similarities of their personal grief upon another but from the gifts of understanding, love, and knowledge gained through the experience of having loved and lost.

Rejected Their Story

When you find yourself saying, "I know. That also happened to me." Take a good look at what you have done. You have rejected the other's story in favor of your own. It is common to listen to a helping person foist upon a grieving person, the stories of a long litany of tests, x-rays, and interactions that occurred to someone unknown to the mourner. Visitors and helpers often seem impelled to tell their story. Do not tell your personal stories. Grieving persons whose family member is dying or recently died are in crisis. They cannot assimilate more than two or three thoughts at a time. If you tell them your story they are held prisoner to you. This only makes them nervous. All they can do is nod politely until you are finished. The helping person usually has good intentions believing all the wisdom he has gathered through his experiences will function as a model for the distressed persons. It won't. At the time of deep grief, pain, or fright, that is not the time to patient teach! The knowledge you carry with you is for you to enhance your therapeutic self as you support the griever in his quest to find his own path through his personal history.

You Get 2 Sentences

This takes a great deal of self mastery. Yes, it is helpful to share your pain at times. A simple, "Yes that happened to me also," is sufficient to let him know you are a kindred soul. Then if asked about it you may answer in two sentences. No more than two sentences. "Yes, my father died when I was 16. It was so hard for Mother and me." That's all. You have just used up your two sentences. Now, if the listener asks you to tell more, you have another two sentences. "Dad died of lung cancer. We took care of him at home for 14 months." That's all. If the listener asks you for more, which they seldom do, you are lucky because you get two more sentences. Persons in crisis cannot handle more than two sentences worth at a time.

Especially do resist sharing with them all the wonderful philosophical insight you have gained through the years since your experience. One mother said, "Oh, the awfulness of having my pain reduced to a philosophy!" Your philosophy is valuable to you to help you present a therapeutic presence to the sufferer as he struggles on his path toward developing his own personal philosophy. Perhaps later, he will ask you about yours. Likely he won't. If he does he may find yours edifying, seldom will it fit him exactly. The task of grief is for the griever to develop his own philosophy of life which includes living with the unanswered questions of loss. Your hope is that he can achieve this.

How to Make a Therapeutic Visit

Making the Visit

When going to make a visit, the first thought that runs through your mind is, "What can I say?" The answer is simple. There is nothing you can say to take away the pain so don't try. Rather change that thought to, "Can I bear to listen?" Accept your nervousness on approach. Dr. Robert Kavanaugh said the hardest thing he ever did was to go to the home of tragedy. He did this for eight years as part of his job and said it never got easy. Don't expect any more of yourself.

I had a busy day in Recovery. We had two patients that were in crisis and I was emotionally as up for crisis as I could ever be. On my way home I stopped at another hospital to visit a friend who had suffered a tragedy that day. As I walked up the sidewalk toward the hospital door, I could not stop my racing heartbeat. I could hear it pounding in my head and knew it was up to at least 124 beats per minute. My voice cracked as I asked the Pink Lady for my friend's room. My words came out backward. As I reached for the room card I realized my hands were wet with cold sweat. I recalled Dr. Kavanaugh's words and laughed at myself. I hate following sheep like in the normal growth and development patterns of humans. I should be able to educate myself out of some of the unpleasant reactions. I realized then, that if this was happening to me out of my control as a nurse, coming directly from giving crisis care, then how much more difficult it be must for our lay visitors to meet their friends after a tragedy.

Go Directly to a Double Touch

This is not the time to stop and wait until you have got it all together. It does not get easier. The sooner you can make connections with your friend the more natural and acceptable your nervousness will be. Waiting will not help. So take all of your beautiful humanness and go to your friend. When you are near the door, look quickly to where your friend is. There may be other people in the room. That is alright. If your friend is free, go directly from outside the door to a double touch with the person you intend to bring comfort.

Timing is important. Imagine, for instance, if you are going to a party and feeling very warm toward the host of the opposite sex. You may think, "I'd like to give him a big hug. I appreciate him/her so much. If when you go through the door you go directly to that person and invite him/her into a hug, chances are it will be acceptable, welcomed, and nourishing. If, however, you were to mingle, greet several others, in 20 minutes get up your nerve, and walk across the floor, give the host or hostess a big hug it might be disconcerting to the huggee, and confusing to the others in the room. The optimum timing has past.

Go to the person you wish to comfort and do a double touch. You can take hands in hands or one hand in hand and the other on the elbow. Perhaps the second hand can reach across to the opposite shoulder, giving the person an all body acceptance. Or you can invite the person into a hug, holding him in deep compassion, until he makes the move to be free, letting you know he has taken in all that he can.

Ask the Obvious

State or ask the obvious such as, "Judy told me Jimmy was killed." Or "I heard you were in an accident." And then SHUT UP!! Do not break the silence! They will break the silence. This will be the longest silence of your life. But don't you break it. Some people will just hold your hand tightly and say nothing. Others will hold your hand and the tears will drip, drip. Others will pour out their hearts saying, "I am so glad you came, do you know what happened to me? Everybody comes in and says, "You will be OK. I'm not OK. There is nothing alright about this!"

He could No Longer Talk

I was called by the ICU, saying a former student of mine had been asking for me during his conscious moments for the last two weeks. He was failing fast and could no longer talk due to progressive throat cancer but the nurse thought my presence could still be valuable to him. I went immediately. The nurse on duty told me he had not been conscious at all that day. At the bedside I took his hand and said, "Father Jim, this is Clarice." He opened his eyes, squeezed my hand with urgency and said, "I am so glad they found you. We have been trying for two weeks. I want to tell you before I go that this is such a good work you are doing. The dying and those supporting them need your work so much. I want you to know I support your continuing efforts in such a needed and worthwhile work. Keep it up and do write the book so that others can use your information. Do you know what happened to me? I am only 54 years old and have so much more to give to the Lord's people but He is calling me now. In December--," then Father Jim began his personal story of when he first felt the discomfort in his throat, the medical procedures, the emotional struggle to accept medical failure and the will of his Lord that he die now. He was ready and accepting of his fate even though he still would not choose to die so young with so much more to give.

This man, whose cancer had taken over his vocal chords had not talked for days, now talked nonstop and with energy for 25 minutes. He did not break his touch or his grip. And yes, as fascinated as I was by his story, my back pained terribly from the bent over position and my thighs cramped painfully but I did not break the dynamic, knowing the importance of timing and that timing can seldom be recalled. Then his story was completed. It had progressed as so many stories do, in chronological order from the first experience to today. I recalled Sr. Mary Jane Linn's words of how the dying need to tell their story and how so few ever find someone who will take the time to let them finish.

When Father was finished, he gripped my hand tighter and his eyes became very intense, demanding almost. He commanded, "Pray with me!" I was unaccustomed to doing that and he caught my hesitancy asking, "Won't you do that for me?" I said, "Yes, how should we pray, Father?" He clasped both my hands in both of his, brought them up to his neck and encircled it, saying, "Pray that I be cured!" As a nurse I knew this to be unlikely so I gently encircled his neck with my hands and prayed, "Oh Lord of Father Jim, grant him the peace of mind to be open to this experience. Give him the grace to accept what he must accept and the strength to go through what he must go through. Bless him with the warmth and support of friends as he moves along his journey. If it be Your will that he be cured, we are grateful. If the path must be otherwise, grant Father Jim peace and the warm feeling of Your presence. Thank you, God." The kind priest took a deep sigh that seemed to reach to the bottom of his toes and in a soft gentle voice said, "Oh, thank you. How good that was. I am tired. I want to sleep." He closed his eyes, never spoke again, and died a few days later.

When you pray with people ask their prayer agenda. Asking, how should we pray invites them to focus which is very helpful, then as you are praying open your hands to send energy to them. You can do this in an inclusive way as you sit in your chair extending to them across the room. If you are near and they have a physical concern it is helpful to place your open hands about one inch above the hurting area as you pray. People receive a lot of warm energy from you.

Watch as the person talks to you. People tend to center emotional concern in a body area or organ. As they speak they often worry, fidgeting hands over that area, or twitch the neck, or purse the mouth. It may be they have stomach, colon, back, or joint reactions to the primary disease. This may not be the injured or operative site, so you may want to make note of that when with patients. It may not be the injured site that bothers them the most.

The Little Heal

Always leave a visit with a "Little Heal." It doesn't have to include the prayer words but the message is the same. You need to take the time to verbalize it. When verbalizing your closing, do so in a gentle ritual voice tone as you would a prayer. This invites the recipient into a quiet state where he can hear and take in more of your message. All warm and successful people do this. Notice how this is done in your environment. It takes so little time and the effects are so long lasting. When I worked in the Emergency Department we often received patients who needed immediate emergency surgery. The team worked fast and efficiently putting in IVs, giving medications, or stopping profuse bleeding; yet, as several of us rushed alongside the cart being wheeled hurriedly into the operating suite, someone nearly always bent over the head of the patient, talking the, "Little Heal". No, this wasn't the chaplain. This was the anesthetist, doctor, nurse, inhalation therapist, or assistant.

It was not a religious hospital, nor was it in the Bible belt. It was a community hospital outside of a large metropolitan area. The point is that this is done every day and does occur in your environment as well. Look for the models that exist for you.

Affected Yes, Not Afraid of Your Fear

What you want non-verbally to say is, "I am not afraid of your fear of death, or your fear of living with this loss you are experiencing. I am affected by it. Yes, you can see that by the nervousness with which I approach you. You can see that your loss affects me by the trembling in my body as I hold you close and stumble as I voice words to comfort you. You can see I am affected by the tears that run down my cheeks unable to be controlled, though I would like them to be. But you can see that I am not afraid of your fear, I do not run, I stay with you, with my entire human inadequacy showing. I do not hide by over-talking or philosophizing. I am here. My compassion for you is available to you when you are able to take it in."

Much of the value of your visit takes place long after you have gone. The value comes in the months and years of remembering tragedy while assimilating the meaning of the loss into the new self image and life style. In that remembering is a source of strength that came in the form of hope from a helping person who had the courage to stand by and just be.

Set up the Environment

After the initial greeting, pull up a chair. If you are in the hospital or nursing home, get one of those little chairs which are against the far wall. If you are visiting in a home, get one of the little chairs from the kitchen and bring it into the living room or bedroom. If the patient is lying down, place that chair at his waistline so that you can sit hand-in-hand. If that is inappropriate or uncomfortable, you can lay your arm within an inch of his hand or close enough to let your energy pass to him. Avoid sitting in an overstuffed chair or couch if you are not a casual visitor. If you are making a therapeutic visitation you must take the time to set up your environment in order to be effectively received. Take the little chair in a home and sit thigh-to-thigh facing the person you are supporting. This position allows you to use an open body position of acceptance. You can easily hold hands, stroke an arm or thigh if appropriate and invite the person into a hug from which you can gently rock, coo, and stroke the back of the person you are comforting. Do take the time to set up the environment for a therapeutic setting.

Do this even if there are other people in the room if your role is obviously that of therapeutic visitor, such as nurse, pastor, doctor, hospice volunteer, pastoral visitor, Prayer Chaplain, Steven's minister, significant friend, or relative.

Interior decorators will tell you that if you want to encourage intimate conversation in your home you must put the chair settings within eight feet of each other. Anyone sitting out of the eight-foot range will be out of the intimate conversation. Often the personnel in the hospital realized how badly a patient needed a visitor. Their joy was great when the elevator opened with a visitor for that patient. How sad it was to walk down the hall later and see that much needed comforter sitting slunk low in the overstuffed chair way over in the corner of the room. Well, nothing very intimate is going to happen from way over there in that sunken chair, when the head of the bed where the hurting patient is facing the ceiling. He cannot see, hear or feel the visitor.

If you are a hospital worker or nursing home worker and you see this, do your people a favor. Walk in that room and say, "Here let me get this for you." Move the bedside table, put the chair at the waistline and invite the visitor to hold hands with the patient. Many visitors need to know how to get close amongst all that hospital furniture and equipment. Show them how to get around the machines, tubes, and oxygen masks.

Sit Down

Even if you have a very small amount of time it is important that you sit down. There is a strong message communicated when you place yourself on the eye level of the other person. Studies of persons visiting for five minutes have been done. One half sat and the other half stood. Later an interviewer asked the recipients how long the visitors were with them. Those whose visitors sat guessed 12 to 15 minutes, those whose visitors stood guessed the visitor was there from three to five minutes.

My husband and I waited five hours in an emergency hospital for a physician. We had a very needy child and had traveled scary hours for this specialized care. At one point my husband was sitting in line for his turn, the ER nurse came in obviously in a hurry, saw my husband, and said, "Oh my, are you still waiting for care?" She slid into the chair next to my husband and put her hand on his arm. Later as he recalled the hectic event he always said, "But the nurse was so nice, she sat with me." I know how busy she was at that time and that she took no more time than to say that one sentence. If she had stayed standing the comforting impact would not have been nearly as great. Do sit, especially if you only have a little time. Do resist the temptation to put something between you and the patient such as a Bible, rote prayer, a card, or medication. Greet, listen be fully there, be fully with, even if for a short time.

Always Touch

Always touch when you greet and when you leave even if there are many other persons in the room. If your visit was meant to be a family support visit then touch each of them as you leave. Do not forget the children. A pat on the head will not do. Stoop. Get on eye level and hear one sentence from each of them. To a teen, a caring punch on an arm, a shoulder to shoulder bump of camaraderie, whatever mode they can accept is meaningful. Hear the one sentence from them.

If you are not willing to touch you must take some time to examine your motives. Are you still overly influenced by a sexually sensitive society that says, no touch at all if not meant for sexual reasons? Do you carry some of that into the house of grief and fear when reaching out to touch a frightened member of the opposite sex? I agree, it is easier if they are elderly, young, or dressed in a hospital gown denoting their victim status. However, if they are in the prime of health, dressed beautifully and as intelligent as you are, they are still worthy of your compassionate caring, brotherly, sisterly, fatherly, motherly touch. It is not what you say that matters so much as how you say it. Did you place yourself at eye level, did you listen, did you let your feelings show, and did you touch? In the over-stimuli of tragedy your words are likely to be forgotten. "He touched me," will be remembered forever.

How Long Should You Stay?

How long should you stay when making a therapeutic visit? Not longer than 10 minutes. If someone opens up and wants to talk the visit should seldom last more than 20 minutes. Remember, we are talking about visiting persons who have just heard bad news and the stimuli is overwhelming. They cannot take in more. After 10 minutes most hurting persons can no longer take in new stimuli or new information. After about that length of time they use all their energies to deal with waiting for you to leave. They have reversed roles and have become the host or hostess to you. That takes simply too much energy right now. If they have been hurt in the accident, operated upon, or are ill, they are simply worn out after 10 minutes. For our hospitalized patients we have given them enemas, medicines, starved them, put them through agonizing tests, uncomfortable positions of pain in places such as the x-ray department. Now they need to expel gas, burp, snore, or whatever their bodies are busy about in the moment. Not many of us are socialized to doing body self care in front of and within hearing distance of outsiders. Please do not stay longer than 10 minutes when the patient is in deep grief, pain, or fright. Know why you came; know what positive outcome you wanted to achieve by your visit. Achieve that and leave.

Learn the High Art of Terminating

It is very important to know how to terminate a visit. The way to do that is to, leave! Remove your body from the premises! There is nothing so uncomfortable as to watch someone leave for an hour. In fact, it borders on cruelty. Because by saying they are leaving they cut off all meaningful conversation for everyone. So nothing happens as they shift from foot to foot and drag out closing rituals. Have a contract for time when you come in, say, "I just stopped in for a few moments." Then keep your contract. If something occurs during the visit to change that then you must re-verbalize your contract, saying, "Would you like me to stay longer? How long? Yes, I can stay until four o'clock."

Be sure to tell teenagers to only stay 10 minutes and tell them why. Tell them it is not the length of the visit that counts but the memory of the visit that is so very beneficial. This gives the teenager courage. They think, "I can manage 10 minutes." Let them know that there is no way a one-hour visit can take the place of five ten minute's visits. Saying, "I'll stay longer because I can't come often," is seldom valuable. It is the fact that you were there that means so much. Later on when the evening is so lonely, the warmth of your touch will still be felt on their skin. In the middle of the night when sleep just won't come, your smile or shared tears will be in their memory's eye. The colors you wear will brighten up their mental pictures.

You bring so much in with you when you visit and you leave all that beauty with them. The sound of your voice echoes in their mind's chambers to help them through confusion. They remember your smell. Ah yes, did you know you bring an odor that is peculiarly you and that it is wonderful? Please don't wear perfumes. If the person is ill or medicated, scents tend to make them sicker. Avoid using perfumed after shave, hair products, etc. You do not have to be overly concerned on a short visit unless the person is very allergic. But avoid all perfumed products if you're a caregiver who will be with them longer. Buy a set of hypoallergenic unscented products for your visitation days. Not because you are allergic, but because your patients are sensitive. How great is the natural clean smell of another, especially in a hospital, nursing home, or the house of a sick person where the nose is bombarded into amnesia by over stimulation. What a breath of fresh person you bring in.

You say, "Only 10 minutes?" but look what you have brought to that house of grief. You have listened, reflected, touched, made eye contact, offered your help, compassion, love, caring, smell, color and given YOU. If you have traveled to a distant place or hospital, 10 minutes may be too short. Make an assessment and say, "I am going down for a coke now. I will return in 30 minutes. Please rest while I am gone." You can break up a long visit several times in this manner and give the patient a needed reprieve.

Role Reversal Difficult

Sometimes as the primary visitor, you are the one who is going to sit with them through the night, or accompany them as they make funeral arrangements. It is a beautiful gift to another to be with them in their hour of pain, fright, or grief. There comes a time when you as the primary visitor see that the recipient needs to rest. Some hurting people have always been good hosts or hostesses and now that they are the needy ones they are still taking care of you while you are actually caring for them. You need to verbalize, "I would like you to rest now." At times you have to back that up with body language.

My mother was hospitalized for major surgery. She was severely allergic to many things and therefore a high risk patient. It comforted her and I suspect the medical team that I, a daughter and a nurse would fly up to sit with her the night after surgery. She had a rough 13-hour stay in the

Recovery Room and finally was brought down with episodic reactions. Needless to say she was worn out, but so kind. She was glad to see me. After greeting I told her to rest. She said, "Yes, I need that. Are you okay?" I answered, "Yes." She wondered if I should have some food. How about a pillow? Was I warm enough? This went on intermittently for two hours. Finally I had to be firm. I said, "Mom you are interrupting my reading. I want to read this book and I want you to get the rest that is so necessary. You can't rest if you are worried abut me. I promise that if I need something or go down for food I will wake you and tell you, I won't disappear on you." Then I turned my back to her and continued to monitor her breathing through hearing. She finally rested.

Patient is Sleeping

So often I came to take care of a patient who was extremely upset saying, "I am so sorry, my friend came to visit and I fell asleep on them. How rude of me. I hope my friend forgives me." I heard so many visitors say, "I am going to sneak out and let her sleep. She needs rest so badly." The visitors have good will but without verbalizing their intentions their, "Little charities backfire." The patient instead of being comforted by their visit is distressed and guilty. What to do? Verbalize! When you come in give a time contract. If you think they are going in and out of sleep. Tell them. "I will stay until ____pm. If you are asleep, I will touch you gently on the forehead, if you wake, I'll wave good-bye, and if you continue to sleep I will slip out leaving you to rest. I will call you tomorrow." For those patients that cannot handle your disappearing, say, "Go ahead and sleep. I will sit quietly beside you until ____am. I promise I will not disappear on you. I will wake you up to say good-bye." This now has become a sacred contract. Do not slip out on them. It is cruel. If you do that, when they awake they will have many hours of distress. That negates much of the value of your visit.

Countless times I have heard a visitor or pastor say, "I was in her room but left because she was sleeping. Please don't! They are likely to be in a twilight sleep, or just resting with their eyes shut. It comes with fatigue, drugs, over-stimulation, or boredom. They need your stimuli and the love you bring desperately. Do not leave. Walk gently to the head of the bed, saying their name quietly. Gently touch them and softly tell them who you are and that you came to visit. If they do not respond go to the nurse to ask their condition and whether it would be best to be more aggressive in waking them or to let them sleep. Most people benefit more from being gently aroused. They will doze again. They have nothing else to do in the long hours of loneliness. Your visit is a blessing they need so greatly.

Outpouring

There are times when you know someone needs to talk, yet they do not. There are many factors that contribute to readiness. One is that it takes time to assimilate an emotional impact. It may be days or weeks before the person can put feelings into words. That is okay. Another factor may be that he is slow to trust you for one reason or another. It may be two or three visits before he opens up. Many of our grieving persons are so startled by the intensity of grief feelings that they don't believe you can really take it.

It might help if you reflect gently what you think you are hearing. You can paraphrase the issues you think he may be struggling with. Be very sensitive to the effect you are having, do not tell him what he is feeling.

When someone does believe you care and that you can take it, you may get an outpouring. All the feelings that have been dammed up inside may come pouring out in a flood of uncontrolled sobbing and choking. What should you do then? Well, don't run down the hall and call the nurse. Don't yell for a sedative. Don't run for tissues and stuff them in the person's face. Rather, invite him into your arms and let out parenting sounds of, "There, there, let it out. Let it all out. You don't need that inside you any longer. Poor baby. You've been through so much. So much feeling all stuffed up inside you. Let it out. This is good. Let it come."

You know what to do. It is instinctive in you. You do know how to comfort that hurting child inside this crying man or woman. You know because it is built into your parent self. Just imagine if a little kid came running to you with arms outstretched crying his eyes out. Think, what would you do? You would gather the little one up in your arms. With one hand you would snuggle the child's head into the crook of your neck and with the other hand you would stroke the upper backbone, all the while making cooing sounds that bring out feelings. Why do humans do this? Because instinctively we know this stimulates the sobbing reflexes to stay open and allows the feelings to pour out. If a person juts his chin out or keeps a stiff upper lip the sobbing reflex is interfered with. This stops the processing. This is not the time to keep one's feelings in. This is the time to let them out in a safe place with a safe person; you.

Outpourings are Self Limiting

Most helping persons are scared to death of floodgates opening with outpourings of feelings. We have a multitude of ways to interrupt the person when this starts. Most often we tend to ask questions, subconsciously knowing that to answer they have to get into thinking and leave feelings. If you really believe it is all right for them to have feelings and if you are willing to be there for them through the expression and facing of these feelings, you are offering the rare gift of yourself. I think helping persons are so frightened because they think if the hurting person really lets go, the outpouring will last forever. It won't. Outpourings are self limiting. Only enough will come out to relieve the pressure. Usually these last about four to seven minutes. Some persons may need to cry with you for an hour. Talking, then crying and talking again. But this is different. Always use your mature adult judgment. If the patient is in traction holding his head in a fixed position and his teeth are wired shut--maybe this is not the time to encourage him to cry, choke and sob. Many grieving people need to express their disappointment in God at this time. They may curse and damn God. Do not hush that or try to defend God. He can take it. Can you take it?

Own the Territory

After hearing this lecture one student of mine said, "I think my brother may need to do this. He was in a motorcycle accident and lost a leg, hip and his male genitalia. He is still in the hospital and is depressed and won't talk about it." The class encouraged her to go to him and verbally invite him to cry with her. She went to him and said, "I know we don't ordinarily do this in our family, but let me hold you and rock you." She then cuddled him and cooed in parental sounds. "Oh, poor Jerry, what you have had to go through. Poor boy, you must have so many feelings inside. Let them out with me. I can take it. I love you and I care that this has happened to you." He started to cry in her arms and she said it was just as though all this was pent inside, bursting to come out. He cried for half hour. His crying was not the most difficult part for her. She was feeling her own grief at her brother's loss and was glad to grieve with him. What was hardest was keeping the nurses from stopping the outpouring. She was interrupted several times and firmly said, "We are okay. We are handling this. Leave us." Yes, you must own the territory and take charge.

After outpouring and finding a kind loving response, persons have told Dr. Kubler Ross how they felt about it. "It is such a relief not to pretend. To lie still when I feel like jumping out of my skin. It's hard to pretend I am getting well when I know I am not." They have said they need only one person to understand. Then they can play the game of, "Everything is going to be all right," with the people who need that and enjoy them for who they are. Be that one person for someone. Often we stay away because there are so many visitors or such a large family. You may be the only one of dozens who can listen.

Come Back

If someone opens up to you and lets you see the depth of their feelings of pain, hurt, anger, jealousy, consider it an important duty to touch base with them within 24 hours, certainly within 48 hours. Make every effort to let them see your face. If not, touch base with them on the phone. If that is impossible, send something; send a message with someone, or a flower, card, or teddy bear. When you do return, treat the person as you normally would. Do not bring up the subject. Resist the temptation to say, "You really lost your cool yesterday." That is a NO NO! If you truly believe that it is okay to have strong feelings and to outpour those feelings, show that by your actions.

Treat the person as being okay. Ask them how their day is. What is their greatest want now and how can you help them get that. Tell them of your love. Avoid doing what I hear so many helping persons do by saying, "How are you feeling today? Yesterday you were really upset. Is today better for you?" That sounds like something was wrong yesterday and sets an expectation to be better today. Be better means no outpourings. The connotation is that outpourings are not an all right or normal thing to do. If you show by your behavior that you treat people normally after outpourings, you let them know that they are safe with you. They learn they can share at that level again if they should need and want to.

Some persons will apologize to you after they have spilled their feelings. They are embarrassed. Answer them with what is in your heart. Say what you feel. You may take their hand and say, "You honored me so much that you would share your deep feelings with me. I am glad to have been here with you. I am a richer person because you shared with me and dared to be so open. I am really pleased you chose me to be with you when you decided to process that material. I would be honored if you would share again with me anytime you have feelings. Thank you. It was a privilege to be with you."

When Are They Finished Sharing?

The recipient will give you a cue when he has had enough talking about the sad subject. It will not necessarily be when the story is finished. Often you will want to know the, "Rest of the story." You must be willing to let that go. He will change the subject and ask about next spring. This is true even with a dying person. He will ask about next spring because he is interested in you and how it will be for you, even though he knows there will be no next spring for him.

Only after he feels he has been heard can he talk about the small things. Then his emotions will be freed to consider the weather, new car, politics, sports, a joke, or hear news about friends. If the visitor comes in with this material, or a joke, the grieving person feels it as a rejection of his personal suffering. If after he believes he has been listened to, he is then free to be interested in the outer world and may love your humor.

Remember that when you are working with a dying person that dying is living, too. There is a lot of the day left for him after he has thought about his dying. If his pain is not too severe he involves himself in life. Do ask advice from him and give him feedback on the next visit.

For those who can have an inner peace in their soul about the dying time and who can sit quietly by in love without words, these are the gifted people, for they will be privy to a view of the world that their daily busyness will not give. The volunteer who sits a half hour with the dying has entered an atmosphere where daily events do not matter. It is a time-less time. Here at this bedside the clock and calendar have no more meaning. It is a quiet time, a peaceful time, a time where the sitter can ponder the meaning of a poem, verse of the bible, beauty of the fading light, or shadows playing on the face of a brick wall. It is a piece out of a day. It is a reprieve from activity. It is experiencing the value of just being. This is a holy time.

May this information make your life and those you meet easier and blessed.

Chapter 4

Family of the Dying

"Stages"

In this section I am addressing slow dying not sudden death. The dying process can go on over a period of months to five or even 10 years of time. I am also talking about the dying person being comparatively pain free, reasonably clear of mind, and is a person with a fairly well developed growth and development structure. This presumes a readiness of the persons involved.

By the term working, I am referring to the growth and development work that is going on at the time of the dying. These are the residual effects of this dying experience for friends and family which are often referred to as the gifts of grief. They will be there for years after the death.

Dying is a Closure

Dying is a closure. It is an ending. For the person who is dying, it is the end of life. For the family, friends, community, and church, it is also an end. It is the end of an era; an era in which this dying person had a place. Dying is a process. It is a growth and development process. For the dying person it is his last growth and development process to achieve. In this respect the victims of sudden death or suicide appear to be cheated of a very potent time in their life.

We as helping persons want to encourage and assist the dying person to a successful outcome. To do this we must understand the tasks of the dying person and be unafraid to enter into the process with him. Family, friends, and community, also have growth and development tasks to achieve by way of this dying process of a significant member. The support person wants to assist so they can grow through this dying event to gather the gifts of grief.

Different Styles of Dying

There is no one best way for a family to support the dying of their loved one. There are many different approaches to grief. As a support person you want to assess the situation to see if it is in accordance with their culture, past behavior and congruent with their style of life. If so, though very different than what you would do, it is potentially acceptable for them. Your part is to appraise the situation for healthy communication and closures. Then, assist this communication and closures to come about.

When my students feel inadequate, I remind them that there are only two things we can do for the dying and the grieving. How we do these two things is a result of our level of knowledge. The two things are giving gentle permissions and facilitating forgiveness. Giving gentle permissions is best done in an echo voice and in a nurturing, motherly or fatherly tone. By facilitating forgiveness, I did not say, giving forgiveness, we can not do that for another nor falsely reassure the other that they are forgiven, rather we mean facilitate the forgiveness process. There is a high level of compliance during crisis such as the dying time. Most of the time people will do what you suggest. You can give the gentle permission to facilitate forgiveness such as saying, "Call your brother and tell him you really want him to come and be with Mom." People, who resisted calling a brother for years, will frequently obediently pick up the phone in the presence of a trusted objective outsider.

We help by modeling the words for feelings and intention. These are not used in every day life so it is helpful to model them. Helping persons become a catalyst to new behaviors by showing an expectation of, "I believe in you. I believe you will see this through in a healthy way."

Inadequacy is the Nature of This Work

Even though it is socially unacceptable to acknowledge these feelings, support persons often identify a gut feeling of, "I worked so closely, got so involved, the communication we developed was so deep, now look what he did! He died on me! That shows how much he cared." There is a sense of rejection when someone dies. We ask the question "Why should we continue to put energies into work that ends?" It all ends in the grave.

This thinking leads to burnout. Often this feeling does not come until 2 to 6 months after a death and arrives with quite a shock of discouragement. It is the task of the helping person to do two things; one is to develop a personal philosophy of caring for the dying. The second, it is that it is imperative to develop a conceptual overview of family care.

Helping persons need to prepare themselves for present time disappointments. Often you can see better ways of doing things. You may patient teach, help identify options, encourage, and yet the family persists in a negative fashion. Remember the overview; this is of the training ground for the next loss experience. They may benefit months and years later from the help you are giving now. At the present time they are in stimuli overload. They must use familiar coping patterns for survival. Sometimes the situation remains negative. That too, you must accept and continually love and support families even when you can't support their behavior.

Hills and Valleys

Family life goes on for generation after generation with many hills and valleys, the hills are peaks of joy, the celebration of successes, weddings and births. The valleys are experiences of difficulties and sadness such as death, illness, dysfunction, and the like. The family life will go on after this dying event to experience more family joys, and yes, more valleys of sorrow.

This dying that you are involved with now is only one valley. The family is moving ahead. They will handle each new situation with the benefits of healthy coping patterns or with the hindrance scars of unhealthy experiences. The quality of future family life will have this experience in it. If healthy coping patterns are developed and practiced now the family will bear the gifts of this grief and be richer for their love and healing. If dysfunction evolves out of this dying experience the family life will bear the scars and inhibitions of unhealthy experiences. It is at the time that the physician says, "There is nothing more that we can do," that real works of the last growth and development stage begins.

Many Gifts of Grief

Working with the family who has a terminally ill person among them is an opportunity to work at one of the most potent times of family life. The results of your work at the time of dying are likely to be longer lasting than work at other times in the family cycle. Therefore it is a wonderful opportunity for the helping person to make a difference. It is a time when behavior changes are possible. Instead of all your work ending with death and the grave, your efforts are likely to last for generations to the third and fourth generation. After that length of time new people coming into the family through marriages and births will change the family dynamics.

The person who is dying brought to the family a life of richness, interaction, intimacy, caring, and sensitivity. If the grieving family can enter into the dynamic that is going on, the family can not help but grow in positive ways. Those who have processed grief to healing grief are more developed, well rounded, sensitized, compassionate, empathetic, philosophical, conceptual and more gifted persons for having gone through that event. As with all stages of growth and development the persons processing need intelligent outside help.

Occasions of Behavioral Change

It is said that there are three occasions when people can change behavior quickly and easily. Generally it is very hard to change behavior; it takes constant vigilance and continuous practice. Yet there are those times when people seemingly quickly and easily change lifetime behaviors.

Love

One of those occasions is love. Persons fall in love and instantly change their lifestyle. Many even move to a different culture and raise their children in milieus that are completely foreign to them. It is not uncommon to hear of someone going with a lover to a far-off county to live and raise their children in a foreign language, with strange food, values, philosophy, and celebrations.

Conversion

Another time when persons seem to change their behaviors, overnight, is at the time of religious conversion. All of us who work at self-growth know the painstaking long time it takes to change behaviors such as smoking, alcoholic, overweight, drug addiction, and repetitive thought patterns. We likely have tried to change some habits for many years. Even with a health crisis, people often cannot give up the behavior. But in conversion it is not uncommon to see instant behavioral change. Something happens.

See Own Finiteness

The third time when people are often open deeply to their center and able to change behaviors quickly is when they become aware of their own finiteness referred to as the, "Mirror effect." They have a gut understanding, "I also can, and will die." That experience is akin to terror. There is nothing like watching a loved one die that makes one aware of the finiteness of life and therefore ones own vulnerability. The griever must reassess all of their life's values. If a support person gently encourages healthy coping patterns, great strides are made in self growth. It is a readiness period sometimes referred to as a critical period of growth.

Therefore the family is open to change behavior at a deep level. When a significant other is dying the family structure is unstable and new behaviors can be incorporated. At the time of dying the family is open to change in a way that they cannot and are not at more stable periods of their family life. The representation model of family is broken and the family myths no longer work. They are brought to light during crisis time.

Family Myths

All families have myths. We all think we know who will be there, who will avoid, who will be strong, who will be weak, who will need our protection, and who we can count on. Oftentimes, that is not what actually happens. Each person responds according to his or her life as it is up to that moment. It is likely to be different than anyone imagined. It may be that the strong one is dying, the, "always be there," person is avoiding, the, "unable to stomach it," person is the one who cleans the patient, and the one everyone protected takes over leadership.

With so many shifts, the family system is vulnerable. The family system is pregnant to seeds for family discontent or ready to take on new healthy ways of thinking and behaving. It is a time when new behaviors are easily integrated. There is a myth that grief pulls families together. That is not true. The greatest need in grief is for an objective outside helping person to give, "gentle permissions."

A New Era Begins

The point here is that this dying event is a mentorship for the next dying event in the family life of the bereaved. The work with the dying and their family is not an ending, but a beginning of a new era. Life of a family goes on in a continuum from generation to generation. Coping patterns both healthy and dysfunctional are passed down from generation to generation.

Beauties of the Father

You have all heard it being said, "The sins of the father shall be passed down from the father to the son to the third and fourth generation." Well, I don't know exactly what is meant by that but we know the, "Scripts" given by the parent, meaning the coping patterns of the parent, the way the parents think and act do affect the children to the third and fourth generation.

If the sins of the father, the disharmonious behavior of the parents are passed to the children's' children; if the negative characteristics can be passed on, how about the, beauties of the Father? Shall the healthy coping patterns also be passed on from generation to generation to the third and fourth generation? It passes on three or four generation because then the family actions and behaviors are diluted through new additions from marriage and new births.

Case Study

Let's say you are supporting a family. The dying person is an elderly man clear of mind and aware that he has only a short time to live. Let us say that you recognize a strong bond of love between this man and his son. Let's say the son is thirty 35 old, and has a son four years old.

After watching this family a while you realize they do not have either verbal or touch skills by which to express this deep feeling of love. Because these are inadequate does not mean the love is not there. You notice they do not hug, sit close, and do not put hand in hand. Because they have never done these things does not mean that they would not benefit from them. For some reason they just did not develop this in their family and culture.

This is an interaction that one of our hospice volunteers described. She recognized a strong bond of love between the 35 year old son and the dying man. Every evening after work the son of the old man came with his 4-year old grandson. They were a loving bunch, but no outward symbols or tender touch, no feeling words, and no heart to heart talks. There was a lot of objective talk about health, cars, and ballgames.

The volunteer sensed the dying father wanted to express the meaning of his love to his son before he had to leave. She asked him, "Are you proud of your son? Why?" In answering the dying man practiced saying out loud words for his feelings. This was new to him.

Then the volunteer asked, "How do you think your son feels when he hears you say that?" The man replied, "Oh, we don't talk like that." She went on to show her expectation that talking about this is good, by asking, "Would you like to tell your son how you enjoyed him before you have to leave?"

The dying man answered, "Yes." So the volunteer suggested a model by saying, "When he comes in today, why don't you greet him with--. Then she repeated the Father's exact words.

"Son, have I ever told you--. How proud I am that you are a good family man. How proud I am that you are a good Daddy. How proud I am that you are an ethical man. How proud I am that you are a good builder of houses. They are sturdy houses and you do not overcharge, yet you make a good living for your family."

Do you think it is difficult to speak this way and not weep? Let's say they do this and weep together. One of the first tasks a family has to learn in the grief period is how to weep with one another. Men need to learn to weep without losing machismo when saying feelings, hugging and touching each other. If they fail to learn this task they will use all their energy in putting on a strong front. They will appear hard even though they are not. If they can't fake it, they will avoid each other by simply staying away or being part of a crowd.

Do you think the 35 year old of this story will relate differently to his son because his Dad had the courage to continue growth on his deathbed? Will the son touch his boy more freely, might he be less afraid to weep with him and might he be able to express his pride more easily?

When the 4 yr. old boy is 13 years old and his best friend is killed, will his Dad react and relate to him differently because the old man had the courage to grow on his death bed? You see, grandpa dies but the gifts of his life and dying are there for the grandson and his children. And that is the rhythm of life.

And so it is that any gift and coping pattern that this family can learn during this dying process will be there for them when the next person begins their dying progression. We can project to the future, we know that this generation will have it's time and the next generation will come. Yes, the old man will die but the gifts of his life, even, and especially, those developed during his terminal period will stay with the family to the third and fourth generation.

Dying Fully Healed

Broken unto Death?

The impetus of the dying person is to work hard and diligently toward dying fully healed. The natural drive of the grievers is to utilize the dying process as a healing growth progression in their own lives. Neither dying nor grieving is a pathological happening. It is a natural process. Nature provides this time for the survival of the species and growth of individuals. Look at the efforts of a dying person who has a good growth and development foundation, is somewhat free of excruciating pain, and clear of mind. He works conscientiously at dying fully healed in all the components of his self. Yes, his body, broken unto death, ready for the transition, whatever that means according to the philosophy of the dying person. Let's look at the basic questions terminally ill people ask? In the following section are some of the concerns we hear patients asking help with and information about.

Stages of Dying

The following are some of practical approaches to the styles of dying. There are many different ways families have of dealing with their dying experience and each is appropriate if it is according to their life-style and background. You want to assess the situation making sure that there is healthy communication and that closures are being done and assist these to come about. If you see unhealthy coping you want to intervene to set the scene for healthy managing by verbalizing permissions, providing resources, and giving positive reinforcement when it is implemented.

When you see continued interactions that you perceive as inadequate, you may feel you have failed. However, that is the nature of this work. Often you may identify better ways of doing things, you may do patient teaching, help them identify options, encourage, and yet they persist in continuing in a negative fashion. This too, you must accept. Continue to show your love and support even when you cannot support the family's games, myths, and unhealthy activities. I always feel it is sad when volunteers judge themselves as being good or not good based on whether they get a certain type of response.

It is important that you continuously bring to mind that this is a learning stage where the actors, because of stress, are impelled to use their familiar coping patterns. But in the next dying situation they will have had the time to consider and implement the healthy ideas you are sharing now. The results of your work are months and years down the road.

The dying person and the family are likely to be in different emotional stages. Generally the dying person is further along towards acceptance than are the family and friends. The terminally ill person has thought this through more completely and understands better what the outcome will be. I think the dying person's body communicates some of this information which makes the seriousness of the illness more clear to him than to those who are not getting the chemical signals from the body. The family sometimes is still more hopeful for additional remissions than is the patient.

I think Kubler-Ross's description of the stages of dying is still the most helpful to use. Lay people are very adept at noticing the mood or atmosphere that is present in a room. For instance, can you tell when the depression is so deep that, "You can cut it with a knife?" Or can you tell when the mood is hopeful, and bargaining? Can you tell when everyone is acting as though nothing happened, yet, you know they just received bad news. Can you sense when you know there has been a big fight and everyone is making, "Nicy nice?" Yes, you can tell the moods in a house. That is the ability you want to sharpen in order to assess the mood at the dying time to work with that mood or phase in an intelligent manner.

Denial: No not Me!

There is a tendency to think of defense mechanisms as negative. Rabbi Grollman says that God made us beautiful, he gave us defense mechanisms. Often the news is too hard to bear. The meaning of the information is too great to assimilate in a short time. The human is given the ability to space and let the information sink in little bits at a time. Kubler-Ross said, "Just as we cannot look at the sun continuously, we cannot look at our death continuously." Be sensitive to this dynamic and do not look upon this as pathological.

During the period when the family and patient are saying, "Oh no, it is not me, this can't be true." There is a tendency to be busy with wasted effort the person may simply be busy for busyness sake. Many tend to do a lot of doctor hopping and or looking for natural remedies for cures at this time. They believe there must have been a mistake. Perhaps there was a mix up in the x-rays, or a new medicine or different natural remedy can cure. People often spend their family's fortune and we hear of those who spend untold amounts of money going all over the world for treatments for their condition.

What can you do while this is happening? Do not take their crutch away from them. If they need to use denial, fine, but try to buy time for them. After three reputable clinics or three reputable physicians who give the same diagnosis you may want to slow them down a bit. One way you can do this is to give them a future to pull into. Their future has been fragmented by their diagnosis. Whenever they think ahead they get scared because none of the plans they had are predictable. It all looks scary so they get very busy. This makes them feel they are doing something to save their own or loved one's life. In that way you do not take away a needed crutch but you provide them a safe person to explore a frightening reality.

What you can do is help them see a reachable future by saying, "Why don't you give this medicine a chance, lets say about two weeks. Do you think that is enough time to give the medication a chance to make a difference?" If they seem agreeable, say, "I will call you then, about March 17th. We can look at it together and plan what you will do next about another Doctor or remedy." Then when that person is alone and feeling scared they remember, "He said he would call me on March 17th." So even though now looks scary, March 17th will come." There is a theory that we are not pushed by our past but that we are pulled into our futures by our thoughts. The more stressful the situation, the shorter the future you offer them. If today is a high crisis day, say, "I will call you tonight." In crisis, two weeks is inconceivable. Then when panic hits them they will say, "But, he said he will call at eight tonight." We see people doing this thinking pattern all the time. They say, "I have to wait for my son to call at eight." If you ever make a promise in a crisis situation when they are under duress, keep it. They wait and wait. It is not like the promise you make to a friend or a business associate. Don't misconstrue the two. If for some reason you cannot make your time to call be sure to cover your bases. Call them before or immediately after with a reasonable explanation.

Talks About the Future

People are often confused by a patient or family member who talks realistically about a coming death and in the very same conversation talks about future plans as though everything is normal. They wonder, does this person accept their dying or are they in denial? I don't think it is either/

or. If they are talking realistic about their dying and the topic switches to something else such as buying a new TV or taking a vacation. It may sound contradictory, but I don't think it is. I think we all talk about things but yet, how many of us really go to Hawaii or Switzerland. I think the dying person is just talking with their normal manner of speech. They are thinking futuristic as they always did. They just are not thinking or talking about dying at the moment, they are talking about vacations. The brain is not designed to stop fantasying on a calendar date two months from now. The normal brain thinks in the future even if the body is dying.

It sounds like denial to you because you are looking at them and keenly aware they are dying. They have been looking at their dying for 24 hours a day for a while now, and your conversation is a welcome diversion. I suspect that if you asked them if they thought they were going to live to follow through on those plans, they would laugh at you. They would say, "Of course not, but we have already talked about that." If you think the person is using denial so they do not have to deal with reality, you might respond to them with, "That would be nice, wouldn't it?" That gives them the choice to respond with, "Yes, it is going to be nice." Which tells you they need to keep that crutch for a while and they want to stay with the dream? Or else they can say to you, "Ya, wouldn't it." That way you give them an opportunity to deal with it and explore reality.

Another situation is that many people are said to be in denial when the truth is that they have decided to die with their boots on. They intend to live as close to normal as is possible. They may have chosen not to deal with their dying until it comes. They feel there is time enough to deal with it then.

Remember that denial is not a negative attitude. It might be a God-given reprieve from facing the unbearable truth, or it may be that they lack information and need more education. It could also mean that they don't intend to ever look at their death because they never looked at any tragedy of their life realistically. For them, denial at the dying time is appropriate to their life style of never facing reality head on.

It may be they have chosen their confidants and you are not one of them. You want to ask, "Are you able to talk to someone?" If the answer is "Yes, my brother, or, the minister," you respond, "Good." Now your work is to support the family and be friendly to the patient. We need to ask ourselves, "How many people do we want to confide in?" Usually three is about the answer." Yet, somehow, when someone is given a diagnosis of terminal we think they want to confide their deepest feelings to anyone who carries a clipboard.

Anger: Why Me?

The patient is saying, "Why me, why not the other guy?" The relatives need more help at this time than the patient because the patient has energy and frankly-- is often a bitch.

Americans are afraid of anger and interpret all anger to be negative. Anger is all right. It may be an appropriate emotion for this situation. Anger is energy to get out of a situation. It is often the only emotion that can confront terror. Terror may be what the patient is feeling when considering the dying time. Often the sight of one's own death produces pure fear. The family goes through these phases also. Watching someone they love die by systems and the knowledge that someone they need so much and care about so deeply can leave, produces panic. Therefore anger is a good emotion providing the energy to look at what is left, to pick up the pieces and make the most out of what remains.

At the University of California, Berkley, when explaining this concept to us, they said, the usual manner of responding to an angry person is to get very calm and quiet. The tendency is to answer sedately. They said the dying person often desires someone to get in the mood with them. So when they say, "Dam it! Why do I have to go through this?" You might choose to respond in the same energy saying, "Yes, damn it! Why do you? It is not fair!" I think we all have had an occasion when a friend was willing to shout with us for a while. They were shouting with us, not at us.

Good or Bad, It is Mine

When I was at the Mayo clinic I called my nurse friend, Donna Kruger, and cried, "They told me my kidney has to come out and I don't want that!" She responded, "You grew that! You grew that all by yourself, and now they want to take it away!" She was so great. We kept this up for

25 minutes. I vented all my resistance and finally came to acceptance. It wasn't until I hung up the phone that I realized she was therapeutic. I felt so understood. I was in a dark, little, rented room and this was such a ray of light. It was so great to have someone get into the feeling with me and recognize, "Hey, I don't want to give it up! It is my kidney, good or bad. It is mine! This is taking my body and plans away from me against my will." At some point each person comes to, "I don't want to, but this is what is. I accept that and will work with it."

Family Needs You More

When the patient is angry the family needs you more at this time because the patient often is unpleasant. This means that it is embarrassing to the family. They need to know that that you understand his reaction, that you still love the patient even though at this time he is rejecting you. The family needs to be reassured they haven't lost status. They need to hear that this is a normal reaction not a reflection on their culture or morality.

Power in a Powerless Situation

Angry patients may exhibit the full range of behavior including biting the handle off a tooth brush as one of our patients did. He always said that he never wanted anyone to take care of him and he meant it. But a student nurse decided she couldn't stand that green stuff that was growing on his teeth, so she got the tooth brush in where everyone else had failed, and he bit it off. Now he would not spit it out. Two hours later he still had the brush inside his mouth. His family was extremely embarrassed, but he was obstinate. He had power in an otherwise powerless situation. The family needs you very much at this time.

Often the patient will exhibit the power they still possess and the only way some can do this is to throw things at you. That often happens. A nurse friend of mine had a soap dish flung at her so hard that had it hit her it could have taken her life. This was done by a newly spinal cord injured person. No one knew how he mustered the energy for the throw, apparently with his teeth.

Damn God

In the stage of anger many patients dam God. One minister student of mine said he learned not to take people's theology too seriously at times of high stress. His experience is that in about three weeks their theological thinking returns to about the same as before the episode. This is no time for stuffy proofs on faith or arguments. It is no help to show shock or reprimand by reminding them of the correct way to express this. It is not about theology, it is about hurt and pain of dealing with the loss. It is more helpful to acknowledge that it does not appear fair at all from our perspective either. It is all right to admit that what has happened does not look like the work of a loving Father. God does not need you to defend him at this time, but perhaps He does depend on you to show loving loyalty with your human presence when God's presence is hidden from the patients view by a dark cloud of tragedy.

The family needs your help in understanding this behavior. It is often frightening for them to see a family member mad at God; the real problem arises if the patient dies in this phase, and they sometimes do. Family and friends will need your help in understanding that God made us fully human including the emotion of anger. They will need help in understanding the purpose of anger is to provide the energy to get out of a dangerous situation. They need to know that anger is reasonable and it is right to have all the emotions and that our part is to be responsible in how we use emotions. Take into account the physiology of humans. Know that the fight or fight response means that sometimes feelings are chemically induced and not by choice.

When relating to the angry patient you want to say non-verbally, "I'm still coming back because I care." Don't we all deep down wish for unconditional love?

Trigger Anger

Anything can trigger anger. You may never know what you said or did. Just walking across the room may cause them to realize that they will never walk again, and that may trigger outrage. You may say, "I need to go home now to take care of my children and clean up my kitchen." That will make them realize that they will never walk again, take care of their children again, or clean up their kitchen. Perhaps that will send them into a tirade of anger. You may never know what you did to trigger that behavior. For the most part it is not necessary that you know. Do not run that over and over in your mind. The only thing is necessary is that you leave gently, and return with unconditional love.

You are Dismissed

The hospice volunteers as well as other support persons are often welcomed by a family at the initial intake. Some families begin to see the presence of an outside helper as representing the fact that they are failing and that they need assistance. It makes them acutely aware they are not succeeding in keeping their loved one alive. This is one of the usual points in time that a helping person is dismissed.

Another way they exhibit power is to dismiss you from the room or the case. If that happens to you, it hurts very much. If you stay in this caring role long enough, it will happen. All helping professionals, paraprofessionals, doctors, nurses, ministers, lawyers, nurses, social workers, and volunteers get to experience dismissal and criticism in one form or another. You must be willing to go through this.

The family may reject you when they are feeling powerful. They want to believe they can do it on their own. This often happens when there is a reprieve in the illness or when a relative or friend moves in to become a caretaker. They don't want your presence being a visible representation of their failure. They may hope that now they can do it on their own.

Right now you want to non-verbally to say, "I still exist but will not intrude on your need for control." This reprieve is good for the family. The duty for you as a helping person is not to take that seriously. If it is done in anger, you need to leave graciously and quickly. Even though you have been abused, leave with a little heal, perhaps it is a wave goodbye, a kind touch, an understanding sentence, but do not linger. Give an objective reason for your quick exit, such as, "I need to get my children from school," or "I have to go now, call me if I can be of further help."

Then call the group you represent immediately. Drive about two blocks to the nearest parking place and let the church, office, or supervisor know what happened before the family's phone call is placed. They will call. Your supervisor will handle it with finesse if forewarned. Remember, this is one of the variables that are built into the caring business.

After you are Dismissed

What should you do if that happens? Continue your contact with about the same rhythm as you had before, but by honoring their need for independence. So do not notice their rejection, touch base in a non-threatening way such as a short phone call or knock on the door to leave a flower or banana bread. Give a simple greeting, do not linger. If you think more distance than that is desired by the family, send a card. Your intention is to keep the door open a tiny crack so that when the going gets rough for them, they can easily call on you again. You do not want to impose yourself on them but you do want to keep the rhythm of caring ongoing in a non-obtrusive way.

Get Your Emotional House in Order

When ever you are abused or dismissed you need to go immediately to your supervisor and your debriefer. You need to examine your verbal and non-verbal behavior to see if you can improve your communication skills. You will question: did you bring this on, is there is a new approach or another response you can use, do you need to clarify something or rectify something to the family?

Before you go to bed that night ask your debriefer to help you get your emotional house in order. Do not re-run abuse in your mind. After you have talked to your peer and debriefer, you need to: examine your consciousness, rectified what you can, go over your priorities, evaluate again why you are doing this work and then let it go. Do not let it re-run more than two rounds in your mind. If a new idea has not come up in two rounds, do something to change your thought. You need to practice limiting re-running of stories in your mind or burnout will come too soon.

Bargaining: "Yes Me, But--"

Energy to do Closures

Bargaining provides the needed energy to do the closures that are necessary. The terminally ill person does have living to do. That means tasks to be done. For many that means a desire expressed as, "To live long enough to--." You will hear many people say, "Okay, I have to die but I want to live long enough to go to my daughter's wedding, son's graduation, and clean the tools. Many persons want knowledge about their disease passed on to those who might also be affected, especially the contagious or hereditary illnesses. They often volunteer for research.

They may be concerned about the travel of relatives. The dying person wonders, Will the children be here to comfort Mom? Does daughter have someone who will stay with the kids so she can come? Do they have the money for the airfare? Did anyone call Johnny in the air force?

What is soothing to the emotions? Do they: yearn to visit a place such as the mountains, ocean, Disney world, Hawaii, homeland or cemetery of Mom and Dad? If they cannot travel anymore one can expedite their desire with videos, tapes, and pictures. Do they yearn for news of someone– can someone facilitate that for them? Do they wish to take another trip?

My Dad wanted to buy one more new car, and my Mom wanted the certificate of deposits in the bank to mature so she could divide the money between her eight children. She told me this in August and died November 23, two weeks after the last certificate matured. A percentage of those who are dying mobilize the energy to carry out their wish.

Postponing the Dying Time

The more years I am in this work the more I take bargaining power seriously. We had a lady with cancer that had metastasized to all her major systems. She could not even turn in bed by herself. They began the 24 hour ritual of sitting around the clock. Her friends took turns because it was thought the dying time had come, she said, "No, I am going to go to my daughters wedding in June." Medically we could not understand how she lived. As the daughters wedding date came near in June, she mobilized energy, got dressed, had someone take her to the wedding, and she slept in her bed at home that night. The next morning she called seven of her friends to meet her for breakfast at a Holiday Inn. She talked and talked about the loveliest wedding she ever saw. After she had it all talked through she looked at the ladies next to her and said, "Would you take me to the hospital now?" They did, and she died two days later.

Another patient also left the hospital to go to her son's wedding. When she returned, the nurses at the desk couldn't believe their eyes as this sick lady came out of the elevator wearing a beautiful blue brocade dress. She raised her finger and said to the nurses, "Remember, I have two sons. There is another son to get married."

His Goal is Met

The patient's goal may not be the obvious one. It is common to hear that a son's plane lands at the local airport and the patient dies. People say, "How sad." Yet the patient hears the news of the landing and his goal is met. He may have waited for the son to get home to support Mom. When all the closures have been done and the goodbyes said, he has no reason to wait.

I often had patients say to me after receiving a terminal diagnosis, "I just want to go home one more time to go through my things and walk around my home." There is a desire to discard the skeletons in the closet. Everyone has them. Where are yours? Perhaps you need to arrange for their discard now.

We hear this desire expressed over and over again. Use the bargaining time to check to see if the closures are done, the will brought up to date, and the pre-funeral planning done. This is a good time for them to write a group letter to each of the family members so that everyone hears and knows of their wishes and hears the same information, otherwise there are a lot of mis-understandings.

Many parents and grandparents are afraid that their children will forget them or not know them as a personality. While they are bargaining is a good time to suggest they make an audio CD, or video to each child.

It is so nice for them to have a CD and hear Dad's voice talking to them. This is especially helpful to a grieving child in the years to come. At that time they can integrate the meaning of Dad's message at that new stage of growth and development. Hearing a message as a six year old is different than hearing the same message as a twenty year old. Much more can be assimilated at twenty.

Depression

Unfinished Business

There are two kinds of depression at the dying time. You need to detect which kind the patient is dealing with now. The first kind of depression comes from unfinished business, perhaps a business to be sold, legal papers to be made, or a will updated. Many dying persons are responsible for an elderly parent, dependent child, or an incarcerated relative that needs follow up with birthday and Christmas gifts given. As you identify these needs you may be able to facilitate making it happen. Not that you should do it, but you can connect the need to the people who can make it happen. Often the dying cannot let go to die peacefully until they hear from the person who will give the continuity care.

Some of the parents who are dying are the sole custodian of minor children. They want to make arrangements for their future care or adoption. Dying parents of sound mind and comparatively free of excruciating pain are still responsible parents. It gives them peace to know they have managed for their dependents. This needs to be legalized and completed ahead of time. There are many business matters to attend in the dying. Such as, many people have a private business or property to sell. The elderly often have this in place and pre-completed, however, a high number of dying persons are in the prime of life and these matters have not been part of their agenda. Enabling this is a wonderful thing to do.

There are social needs of the dying person. We want to ascertain: What does a dying person want from their relationships? Who do they need to say goodbye and hear farewell from? Are there particular loved ones they need to have near?

Permission to Die

Perhaps you will discern that many people are depressed because they do not have permission to die. They may be hanging unto life way past the natural time to relax and let go. Some mates beg them not to leave so the dying person hangs on. It is helpful to suggest to the survivors that they give them permission to die. Children who are dying often hear their parents begging them to live; they need Dad or Mom's permission to go. One nurse noticed a little girl just could not die. Her Dad came each day, held her, loved her and told her how much he would miss her. He begged her to please get well. She tried to obey. When the nurse asked her about that, the little girl said, "I am so tired, but Daddy says I should get well. I just can't get well." The nurse spoke to the Father saying, "Your daughter needs your permission to die and to leave you." They talked for some time. That afternoon the Dad went in and picked his daughter up and said, "I will miss you very much; I love you more than you will ever know. I know that you have to go away. I respect that, Honey; you do what you need to do. You have my permission to go when you need to go." This is the hardest task that any parent has to perform. It needs to be done. The little girl rested after that and appeared at peace. She died quietly the next day.

One lady was begging her husband not to die. She repeated over and over that she could not manage without him. After this discussion with the hospice worker, she said to him, "My husband, when Jesus comes for you I want you to reach out, take his hand and go with him. Don't you make Him wait one moment for you." Apparently that was their style of communication.

Forgiveness

Many people hang unto life because they need to hear they are forgiven or need to ask forgiveness from someone. Some are striving to accept forgiveness of themselves? It seems the real work of healing closures cannot be done until the forgiveness issues are quieted.

One social worker in my class heard this and said, "We have a lady who should have died long ago. Her body was overcome by disease. There is no apparent reason that she should live. Yet she hangs unto life. She doesn't seem to enjoy life but seems to be waiting for something. The students encouraged her to ask the lady why she was hanging on and couldn't seem to relax and let go of life. This was very scary for the social worker but she decided to contract with the other students that she would do it. The following week she reported this story. She said to the lady, "I noticed that you do not seem to be able to let go of life. You seem to be tensely hanging on when all your work appears to be done. Tell me, why can't you relax and die in peace?" The lady replied, "Oh, how I would like to die. I would like to have peace. I don't like hanging on like this. I would love to relax and let go. If I could hear my daughter tell me she forgives me I could die in peace." The Mom went on to explain that when her daughter was eighteen years old she got involved with a boy the Mother strongly disapproved of, so the daughter eloped and disappeared for two years. After that, without any phone calls or letters, Mother's doorbell rang. When Mom opened up the daughter was standing there. She invited her daughter in and offered her a cup of coffee. They talked as though nothing had happened and have never discussed it to this day, twenty two years later. The daughter was already in her forties. The Mom wanted to hear that she was forgiven for her anger at the girl's marriage.

The social worker went on to tell the class, that she was relieved. She knew the daughter well and that she was a fine lady. She came to the nursing home daily to feed her Mom dinner and was very supportive of her. The social worker found her an easy person to work with and talk to. She was excited and waited for the daughter's arrival that evening. She invited her into a side room and confidentially said, "You know your Mom is hanging unto life. She said she could die in peace if she could hear you would forgive her for her anger at your marriage twenty two years ago." The daughter looked at the social worker and said, "Never! Never, will I forgive her for what she did to me! How she ruined my wedding that I always dreamed of, how she made my first two years of marriage miserable. A dutiful daughter I will always be, but I will never forgive her. Oh, I will be good to my Mom and make sure she gets everything she needs, but I can't forgive her that. She ruined my life."

Did that Mother know? Now the social worker had her work cut out for her. After two hours of crying and pent up outpouring the daughter said, "Okay, I am willing to go in Mom's room and talk with her but I really don't want to be alone. Will you come with me?" Together they went in; the social worker took the daughters hand and placed it into the Mother's hand. She said, "Your daughter has something to say to you." There were many tears by both, many words, and finely hugs. Then Mom seemed very tired so they sat quietly by her side. Very slowly Mom's breathing became quieter and quieter. In twenty minutes the breathing stopped. Mom was at peace.

How Will the Dying Be?

There are unspoken emotional needs of some dying persons. They often ask for knowledge about their impending death. These are some of the questions they think about and ask a safe person: "How will the dying be? Won't I be able to breathe? Will it hurt very much? How much time do I have left? Will someone stay with me to encourage me through the dying?"

They want their favorite music, to hear the language, prayers, songs, church and popular songs of their youth. The want someone who will reminiscence the past with them, someone to talk freely with, cry with, and laugh with. Many dying persons are denied the opportunity of laughter because others will only be solemn around them when the family is too overwhelmed to deal with this. However, the dying person may need a reprieve.

Men are Jettisoned into a Female World

Dying men yearn for the presence of a man to affirm their masculinity. Men are jettisoned into a female world during their last months or years on earth. Caretakers are likely to be women and men hesitate to visit the sick so the dying man is seldom around his own sex.

Spiritual

Spiritual musings are very frightening for religious families to hear. They usually respond with quick conversation stoppers and reassurance. The dying person is forced into emotional isolation to ponder these momentous questions alone and in secret.

It is common for the family to refuse the minister the right to visit with the patient in privacy. Family and friends should step out of the room for a time when the minister is present. They often need to hear this suggestion from a support person.

All people seem to be impelled to ask the same basic spiritual questions as they look at their dying. They wonder: "Why me? Why me now? Why not the other guy? What did I do to deserve to suffer like this? Was I so bad? Is there any good that comes out of suffering? How can I reconcile dying when I have so much left to do? Was my life of any worth? Is there an afterlife? Is the afterlife really going to be like I always thought it would be?"

These questions worry many, "Religious families." They consider the investigation of thought to be doubting the faith. That is not what is happening. The dying person is impelled to consider the realities of what these answers might be, similar to questions that we ask before traveling to a foreign country. It helps him if you can listen to his thoughts and reflect back to him.

Real Sadness

Another reason for depression is real grief. The dying person is saying, "Yes me. I am finished." This is a great grief indeed! He grieves for you now as you will grieve for him when you stand at the open casket. But he also grieves for his life, his job, his wife, each child, each dear friend, each hope and dream. It is a great grief. At this time you will want to respect his quietude. The family needs you more than the dying person.

The dying person wants few visitors now, and tends to chooses only one or two persons with whom he is comfortable. Often the dying person prefers someone that was not close to him and rejects the child who was a main caregiver. This can result in long lasting hurt feelings. You will need to assuage the feelings of those who thought they would be chosen but now are not wanted near the bed.

You can do a lot now to salve injured feelings. To help them understand, to forgive and grieve openly. Often feelings are so hurt among family members during this dying time that the family splits apart after the death. Perhaps you can ameliorate this just by your presence. They need to know that the one chosen to sit the last days is often someone who is less agitated by the dying. They are chosen for reasons not measured by love. Perhaps the one who is closer to them is grieving so heavy that the dying person finds it too disturbing. Also some people just have quieter inner selves and both animals and sick people like being near them. This is a matter of therapeutic presence not a measure of love.

Rejected by the Bedside

Ever once in a while a dying person will ask that someone be kept away and not allowed in their room. The family member or friend may need to be by the dying person even though he does not want them there. This is delicate. In holistic care, I think we have to consider the survivor as well as the one who is dying. For those not wanted in the sick room for an extended time you might suggest they go in for a few minutes. This is for the sake of the grieving person, not necessarily for the one who is dying. The mourner may need to do this for their healing. Ask them to stay a short time. If they are very disturbed and upset give them a gimmick, something they can do, such as give them a wet washcloth to sooth the brow or gently rub the patients arm. Perhaps they can comb the hair, gently massage the shoulders or feet. If they can help with the bed it often is enough to lighten the hurt feelings. Suggest that while they are there they say their goodbye and express their forgiveness.

Activity in the Family Room

During the dying time when the end becomes near, it may be good to have an activity in the family room or kitchen. That is a good time to put together a photo collage and make individual photo albums for each child. It is good to write and place in a ring binder the history of that person. Some of this can be completed after the death by including the poem, song, and prayer cards from the funeral. It is good to have these binders on the family bookshelf so those who feel called to review this information have access to it in years to come.

Part of grief healing is to put the life of the dead one together in a meaningful form. Sometimes it is fulfilling to involve the dying person previous to the death. In long term dying it gives an opportunity to take pictures of the dying person with each child to add to the child's album. The mourners will use this as part of their grief work in the following years.

The binders are also helpful for visitors during the dying time. They can flip through the photos, or memory book and that gives them meaningful bits of discussion at the bedside. They might say, "I saw pictures of you fishing in the north woods with Bob. You two had some great times, didn't you? I am so glad that you had that and I am glad for Bob that he had that time with you." Or someone may say, "I didn't know you had your picture in the paper for the Lions club."

It is good to have pictures of the patient present at each age level, as a baby, two year old, eight, sixteen years, a new bride, new Mom, mature lady. It is a lot easier for visitors to tune into the dignity of this person who lies in a wasted body if they can see pictures of the meaningful life they lived. The realization that this is a closure of a full life with meaning becomes evident with the photos and mementoes.

Notice how at times the home of the dying is a very active and busy place and at other times it is quiet and subdued. See how at times your support is needed most by the dying person and other times you are needed most by the survivors. It depends on the task the family or the dying person is working on.

This is where you are potent with gentle permissions and facilitating forgiveness.

Acceptance

Physical

Ah yes, body broken, broken unto death; ready to leave the body for the transition.

The Dying Time

It appears that we do not have a choice whether or not to die. But it does seem we have some choice in when to die. This may not be for all people but it does seem true for many. We have all heard of people who sit with a dying person round the clock for days. Then they leave for a much needed shower and the person dies while they are gone. Or, they will go to the dinning room for a much needed hot meal and their person dies while they are eating. The family needs to hear from you that possibly the person who died chose to spare them that experience. It may be they have been waiting for an opportunity to die in private. Dying persons are often smart persons who wonder, "How will the dying be?" They wonder if there will be choking and gasping for breath. They want to spare their family that last scene. So they wait to utilize the opportunity when the family leaves. The family needs to hear from you that it could be an act of love.

I see a lot of families hurt by not being present at the death. Dr. Glen Davidson refers to this 24 hour watch that goes on as the waiting vulture syndrome. He asks, "Would you like to be watched 100% of the time?" He asks, "Would you like all your body sounds and activities being observed by your friends and family?" then he asks, "Why do we think the dying people do?"

He thinks that if we appreciate our periods of privacy, dying persons do also. He thinks families need to be educated that when all the goodbyes have been said, forgiveness's given and received, and all the closures are done, the friends and family ought to be able to kiss their loved one goodnight saying, "I will be back in the morning, if you are still here I will see you then, if you have gone I will see you in the hereafter, whatever word expresses that for the dying person. I love you and I wish you well, goodnight." Then if the person dies during the night the friends and family should have peace of mind that the closures have been done. It is different if the dying person begs not to be left alone. Not all dying persons want someone there around the clock. It is a percentage and you need to assess which it is. It is dictated a lot by culture as well as the emotional needs of the dying person.

There are some people that feel this is more important than others. Kubler-Ross kept emphasizing that no one should ever have to die alone. I think this is true about the dying process but not necessarily about the transition moments. When you do cross-culture studies you will discover a number of cultures that are very private people and turf conscious. You need to find out which one it is. In one of the areas I lived the waiting vulture syndrome 24 hour watch was a very high value, while in another place I lived that need was not even perceived. Someone stayed close to the sick room so if the patient struggled or called they would hear, but nothing was made of the fact that when they checked on person he was found dead. If he slipped away it was called a peaceful death.

Not a Happy Time; a Time of Acceptance

It is important to realize this is not to be mistaken as a happy time. The patient is saying, "If I must go, I bend my will to the greater force," whatever that may mean to him. The family needs to say this also. They need to say, "If you must go, if you have to leave me now, I bend my will to this greater force and join you in this transition phase. We will see you when--." In that way, they can sit quietly at peace during the dying time even though this is not their choice.

During this time some people like to quietly sing songs known to the family or from church. Others gently recall life's experiences saying, "Thank you Dad for--." Others just prefer to be quietly near. Each family has its own comfortable atmosphere during the sad times. Encourage the people to create this atmosphere so that it is positive for them.

For those who can have an inner peace in their soul about the dying time and who can sit quietly by in love without words, these are the gifted people, for they will be privy to a view of the world that their daily busyness will not give. The volunteer who sits a half hour with the dying has entered an atmosphere where daily events do not matter. It is a timeless time. Here at this bedside the clock and calendar have no meaning. It is a quiet time, a peaceful time, and one where the companion can ponder the meaning of a poem, verse of the bible, beauty of the fading light or shadows playing on the face of a brick wall. It is a piece out of a day. It is a reprieve from activity. It is experiencing the value of just being. This is a holy time.

May this information make your life and those you meet easier and blessed.

Chapter 5

Sudden Death Crisis

When I was asked to present nine hours of material in the Superdome of New Orleans, Louisiana, for The Combined Emergency Dept. Nurses Assn. & The American College of Emergency Physicians Scientific Assembly of USA & Canada, I went to the consumers of health care at death scenes to do my research. I visited many chapters of The Compassionate Friends in the Chicago area.

I asked them to tell me what they wished Nurses and Physicians knew and would do for the next set of parents that had to see what they had to see, hear what they had to hear, and do what they had to do. I promised to take their suggestions to the International Convention.

I had a tape recorder and went from one to the other. They talked with me as a group and then stood in long lines to tell me what is helpful around the care of an injured and dying child. The Compassionate Friends and local Emergency Department Nurses and I condensed their message to this presentation which I shared at the Convention. It was published in three condensed forms, in the Journal of Emergency Nursing, Critical Care Update, and "Emergency Medicine A Comprehensive Review" by Aspen Systems Corporation. This information became the general protocol for managing families around death by the emergency care services.

Sudden death is a part of everyone's life. Once in about every 20 years we will deal with a sudden death event. Knowing the normal dynamics that occur at the scene and following the death will take away some of the unnecessary fear.

There are typical ways in which people react. You may react in one way at one death event but later at another death you may find yourself in an entirely different emotional state. This is appropriate. Please prepare yourself to accept yourself as the person you are at that movement. There is no judgment on the reactions, they just are. As the support person, friend, family, work, or church community, you want to know the best way to be supportive when you stand by the victims of sudden death.

The most important thing to remember is that grief will take a long time. The foundation for healthy grief work is being made in the moments of this crisis time. Much of what you orchestrate around the body at the scene of the death, what you facilitate, what the mourner hears from medical and spiritual people, what is done with and to the body at the scene, hospital, and the place it is pronounced dead, is the substance that the psychic will use over and over again as the person tries to make sense out of life, death, and spirituality. From this the mourner must develop a philosophy of love and loss that enables them to gather all the gifts of having that dead person in their lives but without their physical presence.

Sudden death happens fast. The person may die over a period of hours or days but the onset is fast. It happened to me when I watched a 49 year old man jump high into the air to spike a volleyball and come crashing down in death. It happened to my husband when a 42 year old man he was bowling with threw a ball down the bowling alley and followed the ball in death. It happened to several of my friends who came home to find their mates dead in bed, on the floor, or in the bath room. It happened to my high school son when he drove to work following a car that crashed into a tree in front of him. My son crawled into the car and held the eight year old boy as he took his last breaths. Later my son was on a lonely police patrol far out in the country in a western state when he came upon a crushed car. The responding crew was an hour away while Craig held a 17 year old boy's head to his chest stroking and talking with him as he slowly bled out. The boy was crushed between the car and a steel bridge. The car was embedded into the bridge. It happened to my friend as she followed her husband's truck and saw it hit and burst into flames. She watched her husband through the window of his truck as the flames engulfed the area. Death happens fast.

This is life. This is what happens to all of us. We do not talk about this. It brings up our greatest fear. It is helpful to know what is normal and to augment that which is useful. For the survivors this makes all the difference in how they manage their grief in the years to come. People never forget these scenes; they are impelled to go over and over them to make sense out of their emotions, and to integrate the experience into their self-image. If you can stand by and just be a loving presence you are doing a wonderful service.

Who is the helping person and how should a helping person act? I will address a helping person as anyone who is helping the griever. It is not necessarily a professional. The person who is physically present is the primary caregiver at the time of sudden death. Who provided help in your times of grief? It was probably a neighbor, often a stranger, a friend, or a relative. Everyone who cares is a potential helping person.

Typical Reactions

Reactions to the news of death are many and varied. There are two typical reactions an individual experiences when he or she hears of a sudden death. The first reaction is to run, to get away from the tragedy. When the crisis happens people run very fast; some run toward the scene and some run away. Those who run toward the scene do so because of discipline and training, but the natural reaction is to get away from the tragedy as fast as possible because of fear or personal safety.

The second reaction to sudden death is to get away from grievers. One can observe a group of grievers huddled together on the street where a sudden death has taken place, a restaurant, theater, or hospital, but rarely is a helping person with them. Most bystanders become concerned with everything except the psychological needs of the mourners. It is a normal reaction to be afraid of the grievers. Robert Kavanaugh, in his book Facing Death, says the hardest thing to do is to approach someone who has just lost a loved one in a tragic death. Even though some people often experience this situation as part of their work, no one really gets used to it. You are probably reading this document because no one knows when this information will be needed again, and you would like to be knowledgeable when it happens. You want to know what to do when the next time you are the neighbor, co-worker, church member, person in the car behind, or the listener to those who grieve sudden death. Remember this is a taboo subject, so your gift of listening is a wonderful gift.

Shock and Denial

What happens to a father, mother or friend after a child has been struck by a car? What happens to the woman who is beside her husband in a restaurant when he collapses from a heart attack? The first reaction is shock and disbelief. The response is, "Oh, no! It can't be true! This can't be happening!" There is a reason for this denial; it is too great a stress for the psyche. The mind cannot cope with so many stimuli at one time, so the mind uses denial as a defense mechanism and assimilates information at a slower rate that differs for each individual. If a person is forced to face a tragedy too quickly, there is a possibility he or she may flip out. Many cases of amnesia occur after people see members of their family being mangled, struggling and dying in front of them. The resulting amnesia occurs because the scene was more than the mind could bear.

Numbness

Some grievers act numb and show no reaction. It is difficult to know if they heard the message or if it had any meaning. When asked if they understand what has been said they often answer, "Yes." They give the impression they do not care about the person who died. Gently reinforce reality with, "I'm so sorry. It's hard to lose your husband." They are less likely to deal with a tragic message if they are not given adequate time at the scene or if they leave without viewing the body.

Mechanical Reaction

Shock may be followed by a period of numbness, during which responses become mechanical. Perhaps the person just sits and stares, trying to regulate the amount of incoming stimuli. They may respond to little or nothing at all. Sometimes when individuals first learn a loved one has died their only response is staring and saying, "Oh is that true?" This is because they cannot cope with the reality of the news or the magnitude of the stimuli. A number of families told us they did not know they were being told that the person was dead. They heard the term expired and filled out the paper work. They said they were half way home before they realized expired meant dead. That realization is too difficult so they put it off. These are automatic responses they are not choice responses. As helpers it is important for you to realize they may not have understood the enormity of the information yet. It will hit them later, and you may want to prepare for that.

Numb actions are very mechanical. These people are putting off activity to survive overwhelming stimuli. Information is needed, such as a social security number or the name of the funeral home where the body is to be sent. Newly grieving people have no idea how to respond to such a question. They may answer like a robot, simply and without feeling. They may reach for their billfold, and if the information is not in the usual pocket they may have no idea where to look. Grievers need simple suggestions. Give regressive care by putting a coat around them. Bring them something warm to drink, do not fill the cup too full or make it too hot. They need gentle, caring support from you. Lightly reinforce reality by saying, "I am sorry, this is so sad." Don't worry about what to say because they probably will not remember anyway. It is all right to be quiet and say nothing, but if talking helps either you or them, go ahead and talk. Anything said in a parental tone is comforting. Some voices are soothing to frightened people. They may not remember what you said, but they will remember you were there, you cared, and that you touched them.

Loud Scream

Some grievers react with a loud cry. They may throw themselves on the body and try to breathe life into it. They may scold the body or beg the dead one to wake up and tell them it is not true. Give them all the time they need to deal with the message they have just received. Do not try to silence the griever or be concerned about other persons hearing them. Rather, let the others know you are with the griever and will help see this through. Show by a calm and accepting attitude that this is the natural. Let your own tears flow if they come.

This scream comes from the very bottom of their belly. It is often referred to as a primeval scream. This release is an important psychological need and should never be stopped. This is a normal response. Can you imagine yourself walking down the street with your child or friend and suddenly seeing that person hit by a car? Would you stand there and calmly say, "Oh my goodness, he is dead." You would want to throw yourself on the person and shout. If there were no response you might try to breathe life back into him. When you realized he was dead you might want to shake him in anger and frustration and say, "This can't be!"

When this happens let it continue. Grievers must do this if they are to accept the reality of the event. They must confirm this tragedy really happened. Always think of the mourner first, not the other people around the grievers. This is the time when death is given the top priority. Screaming results in a tremendous emotional release and grief work begins sooner if the griever is allowed and encouraged to express emotions freely.

A Parental Arm

After this class a 22 year old woman was returned to her room from Recovery. Suddenly she died. Her young husband threw himself on the bed with her, holding, crying, begging, pleading, "Please do not leave me!" The staff was relieved to have this material to reassure them that; yes, it was okay to let him grieve actively and loudly. After 20 minutes they wondered if he was all right, 30 minutes passed, at 45 minutes they said, "But Clarice didn't say how long."

People need as long as it takes. However, sometimes it is too hard to walk away alone. A man on the team recognized that need. He put a Fatherly arm around the young husband's shoulder saying, "Come, now is the time to say good bye; I will stay with you while you do that." Then he said gently, "Come with me now; we will walk out together."

There are many ways to react to bad news; none are a measure of love for the dead person.

Appropriate Activity

Other persons engage in activity at bad news. They say, "Oh my goodness, he is dead. We must call 911, direct traffic, and notify the relatives." Then, "We need to give a police report, talk to the ambulance personnel, we need John to come with his car to take the passengers home, this is the name of the insurance company, call this funeral home, call the church, someone has to call Grandma, she lives alone, send Jim to go over and be with her." These are helpful people to have around. They make phone calls, fill out papers, and give information to authorities.

People hear and say, "He has it all together." Don't kid yourself. These individuals are looked on as being mature. They are not denying the death but they are denying the meaning of the death to themselves. They are not accepting the reality of death any more than the person who is sobbing out of control or the person who is sitting in stunned disbelief. They are delaying the acceptance of the death by occupying time with appropriate activity. Eventually they will need to talk about it and then they will do their crying, often alone in the quiet of the night. Many of these people experience delayed grief. It is not surprising to hear that someone is, "Going to pieces," six months after a death when they seemed so accepting at the time it occurred. This indicates they are just beginning the process of overcoming their grief.

Developing Awareness

After the initial response comes a developing awareness of the meaning of the loss. Within minutes to hours the griever experiences an increasing awareness of anguish and loss. It may be expressed as physical pain. In the beginning it is most commonly described as a pain in the pit in the stomach. As time goes on the pain moves to the place of the body that caused the death, such as heart, neck, head, etc. These people present at the emergency department describing pains that fit the exact symptoms of the grief event. Often the physician can only tell by lab or diagnostic results whether it is a grief reaction or an illness. That is why it is so necessary to have a physical six months after a loss and again at a year post death. Encourage these individuals to accept this as normal grief and to talk about their concerns and about the pain they think their loved one felt when dying.

Physical Grief

One of my students who was a nurse said, "Now, I think I know what I have been experiencing. My brother was killed in a car accident. He had no external injuries; his neck was broken by the whiplash." For 11 years after the accident Anna suffered from an extremely painful neck. She held her head carefully and tense for fear of increasing the pain. It became chronic. She had the all medical tests and was under chiropractic care for years. Now it was apparent to her that she was surrogate suffering her brother's injury. This is common.

I watched a nineteen year old boy hitting his fist into his stomach as he ran from his crashed vehicle. Then he rolled on the ground and did seventeen summersaults before he stopped. The physical pain of seeing his beloved car smashed caused that much pain in his stomach. Grief is physical. Grievers bring to the emergency department complaints that are difficult to evaluate by clinical tests. It is wise to ask a grief history whenever the symptoms seem inappropriate. Ask them if any major losses have occurred during the past year. For example, did the person move, lose a primary person, break an engagement, or lose a job? Ask if they know anyone who had similar symptoms. Often they will answer, "Yes, just like Dad experienced when he had his heart attack." This is a clue that the symptoms may be a grief reaction or triggered by grief.

The impact of grief on the elderly is often misunderstood. It is said that the elderly can take grief in stride. Do not let their calm exterior be misleading. A calm exterior is not a measure of the depth of their grief. Be gentle and if possible call someone to be with them. Even with your best efforts they often give up on life after a major loss.

Anger

Anger is part of every grief reaction and sooner or later it will surface. In the beginning feelings of anger at the dead are unacceptable so these feelings develop into free floating anger. It is commonly directed against persons they perceived as needed at the death time but now are expendable. Typical targets include police, ambulance personnel, emergency department personnel, morticians, and ministers. Each is necessary initially but is expendable after the crisis is over. Such anger helps to disperse the intense feelings without jeopardizing the primary support group.

Outbursts are very common at this time. Newspapers print pictures of someone at an accident scene berating a police officer or attempting to beat up the driver of the other car. It is normal to feel intense anger when you see someone in your car killed by another. Anger is an important emotional response and should be expressed.

What can a helping person do in this situation? The principle concern is to protect others from the angry individual and to protect the grievers from themselves. Grievers have a need to pound on something; a common reaction is to put a fist through a window. That is why there are window-less quiet rooms in hospitals. They need to be restrained if that is necessary to protect themselves and others from injury. Reflective feelings are helpful, such as, "That's a good reason to be angry." When anger is directed at a dead person, grievers are usually hushed and quickly removed from the area. Intervene and let them express this feeling. At times the dead person did something to cause the death that the survivors meet with disapproval. This is a terrific emotional experience for the survivor. As a support person protect yourself and others, but otherwise allow the griever to vent feelings.

If they scream and curse God or anyone else, let them. This is a very intense emotional strain that must be relieved. One minister said the greatest lesson he learned was not to take the theology of a person too seriously during acute grief. He found if mourners were permitted to express their resentment of God they later returned to the same spiritual relationship that existed before the death. Guilt is part of grief and the griever is impelled to ask himself all those torturous questions, "If only," or, "Why didn't I." There is a desire to re-run events leading to the death. Guilt is especially severe in certain types of dying, such as when the mourner was the driver of the car, made the mistake, owned the gun, or took mind altering substances resulting in the accident.

Professional Feelings

Later, anger can turn to criticism of professionals or others who were somehow involved in the death scene. You will hear stories of insensitive police who would not let a family member through a yellow roped off area, paramedics who were too rough and emergency departments that had no physician trained for the type of emergency care the dying person needed. Do not take these stories as the facts unless you go back to these departments to check on the real thing. In time this anger must be directed at the source which is the dead person for causing this havoc and pain. You will hear the beginnings of this reflected in remarks such as, "My husband died and didn't leave me a penny's worth of insurance." Or, "He knew better than to drink and drive."

Be sensitive, knowing that the professionals at the scene are human too and are dealing with their own emotions. The EMT, paramedic, police officer, nurse, minister, or physician is affected by seeing a dead child or a mutilated body. They must be concerned not only with professional role but also with their own feelings. If you are a friend, neighbor, or relative at the scene, perhaps you could say, "My friend is very upset, he doesn't mean what he is saying." Although professionals are trained to function at death scenes, they have the same emotional needs and responses as other people and it is considerate to think of their feelings. The helping professional will usually respond, "That's okay, I understand." However, deep down they appreciate the kindness. Feedback that is critical comes back quickly to professionals, it is rewarding when someone cares enough to give positive comments. Sending a thank you note to these departments is a thoughtful action.

Tears

Tears are likely to be seen during the stage of developing awareness. The sooner tears come; the sooner grief work can begin. All cultures provide a socially acceptable form of regression by which to elicit a response of comfort and tenderness from others. This makes it easier to reach out and touch the mourner. During the time of extreme pain, fright, or grief there is implied permission to enter the private turf of another, even a stranger can put one's arm around a crying person to soothe them.

When crying the reality of loss begins to sink in, grievers are no longer denying the death but instead are saying, "John is dead and will never come back." There is not much denying in crying. Tears are also a physical equalizer. If grievers are to heal from grief, they must be able to cry out for help, they need to be able to elicit responses from others, and they must have the inner resources to heal. The sooner after a death that reaching out happens, the better.

It is considered the most important work of those giving comfort to evoke tears so the process of healing can proceed. That is why cultures of old have had professional criers, poets, sonnets, and sad music at the time of grief. Old cultures knew that the grief must come out or cause chaos within.

If there are no tears, find out why. Perhaps the dead person is not really missed. Perhaps they had withdrawn their emotional support years ago and the grieving has already been done. There may substitute emotional support persons already in place. Perhaps they never did attach to the one who is dead. Sometimes we think people should have attached when in truth, they did not.

Sometimes there are no tears at the death time because the news of sudden death is not a surprise. It was expected and a plan was in place. When might that 3 a.m. call not be a surprise? In many cases such as death involving an alcoholic, drug addict, criminal, or someone in dangerous work such as Special Forces, police, or test pilots are situations were the survivors have been alert to the possibility of tragedy for a long time. The sorrow is still there and grief work needs to be done, but it is not a total surprise.

Viewing the Body

How should we relate to the body of the dead person? It is important that the primary grievers view the body. Doctor Kubler-Ross emphasizes that if the body is not viewed, it may take years longer for the grief to heal because it is difficult to realize the person is really dead. Many helping persons think that by preventing the griever from viewing the body, they can eliminate the image of deadness. Unfortunately, this is not true. While resolving the death, the mourner spends hours visualizing the accident scene and imagining what might have happened to the body of the loved one. If the body is seen, resolution can begin immediately.

There is a need to see the body at peace. Most cultures have methods to accomplish this task. Regardless of the magnitude of an illness or accident, seeing a body at peace brings solace to the grievers. Even when the body is fragmented, cultures have usually placed the body parts in the anatomical correct position. There is a need to honor the body with the respect that the dead person gave to it in life.

Many in grief have said they wished they could have spent some time alone with their loved one. If possible, give the family some private time with the body and then each member individually. Be alert to the fact that one person's "no" does not speak for everyone present. There may be others that need to be with the body for awhile.

Prepare the Body

One never gets used to death and it often helps to go in first to straighten the clothing or do other chores. Then return to the family and say, "I was just in with your mother's body." Then say something appropriate about what you saw. This shows your acceptance of the body, helps them acknowledge the death, and gives them permission to view the body. They think that if you were there and are alright, they may survive the experience also.

In crisis, medical people cut the clothing off to quickly evaluate the entire body. When the person dies they are personally affected and upon receiving the order to quit life saving techniques they sometimes walk away to hide their tears and busy themselves with the next patient. When it is a child you may be sure that some of the team has children or grandchildren the same age, and this identification is very difficult for them.

Though not intentional, sometimes no one stays behind to put the body in a position of peace. One father received the call that his seventeen year old boy was in the emergency department and he should come right away. He had the three younger girls with him and took them along to the hospital. They were told the boy was dead and they could go in to be with him. They ran to the room to discover the boy was lying nude. The father localized his grief and anger at the death on this incident. For months he repeated, over and over, "My son always respected his little sisters, he would never have been nude in front of them." Of course the medical team felt terrible; but nudity is not a bad thing when you are saving the life of a person, just check the area a second time before bringing in visitors.

I was surprised when I thought I had prepared a woman's body with great dignity to have her daughter scream at me, "Put a nightgown on my Mother!" I had the sheets clean and nicely placed. I was soon to be preparing the body to send it to the funeral home. A nightgown did not compute to me, I understood and gladly complied.

Another woman angrily yelled at me, "Put a pillow under my Daddy's head!" Often anger is the first response when they see someone they love dead and whoever is there is going to receive it.

Tubes and Equipment

Immediately after the death, slightly raise the head to prevent pooling of blood in the face and head. Tubes and equipment may be removed but need not be put away. Sometimes equipment may need to be left for later paperwork to be done. Some of those interviewed said the presence of equipment was comforting because they knew extraordinary efforts were used in an attempt to save the life. Others focused and saw nothing and no one other than their dead beloved.

Always explain the black and blue marks that are frequently seen on infants and the elderly. Their skin is thin so that when the blood settles to the lower parts it looks as though they are bruised. This is normal. When it is not explained but seen, the family seldom says anything. Each thinks the other beat the person and caused the death. They think they are protecting someone from the police and keep this secret for years. It affects their relationship.

Go With the Survivors

I go in with the family unless it is clear that they want privacy. If after a short time they seem comfortable I step aside or just outside the room where I can hear if they need help. Encourage them to touch the body, to talk to the body, and to tell the body how they feel. Suggest that before they leave they say, "Good-bye" Families said they wanted to say these things as well as to scold or love the dead one but they were embarrassed. It is very important to verbalize these permissions. It might be helpful if you show your acceptance of the body by touching it. Some families do not like a stranger touching their loved one but most do. Stay very alert to their reaction as you gently caress the cheeks and arms. If it is a child, show your acceptance by cuddling the child and then offer them the option to cuddle the body. If they are waiting for transportation from the scene, ask if they would like to hold the body. These nonverbal permissions will do more to comfort many families than any words. Keep very alert to see if this is unacceptable to some of the family members. If so, step back quietly and immediately.

Permission to See the Body

People are ill-prepared for sudden death and really do not know whether they should view the body. They need permission, but often think it would be unacceptable. Verbalize the permission by saying, "Would you like to see the body? I will go in with you." The normal response, especially in sudden death, is, "Oh no, I don't want to see the body." If someone asked me if I wanted to see the body of my dead child, I would respond with an emphatic, "No, I wish to see him alive and running." It is important not to hear the first "no," but to wait a few minutes and then return.

When someone feels scared to go near the body and you know that a minister, friend, or other family member is expected, you can suggest that they wait until the other person arrives and then they can go in together. Families are often reluctant to call their minister, thinking it will be too much of a bother. They tend to see a minister as a participant in the funeral but not as a grief support person. Yet, the minister may be the only professional who will continue to relate to them into the post grief period. The minister's effectiveness will be enhanced if there is personal involvement from the beginning. There is value in the minister's mere presence. It is not that he or she has to do anything. Being with, praying with, and standing by is an incredible support.

Some grievers insist that they do not wish to see the body. In that case the supporting person should use sensitive intelligent judgment about how much to encourage them. This may not be right for this individual at this time. The objective is to give those who are hesitant every opportunity and support they need to make their decision.

Show an Expectation

Show an expectation that the family will want to view the body. Most persons who do not view the body at the time of death or in the emergency department are sorry later. Until they see and touch the lifeless body the news is too unbelievable to accept. Once the body is seen and touched, death is hard to deny. Then the family can muster the courage to do what must be done. They can bury their loved one and eventually let go. If the death is not accepted, then letting go is impossible and the family will be condemned to a lifelong search. Many hours must be invested in fantasizing about whether the person is really dead. Whatever the mourner sees at the scene of death or in the emergency department is real. It is a picture that may be dreadful but is still reality.

She Just Walked Away

A young woman, was called by the hospital and told her husband had been electrocuted and she should come in as soon as possible. She lived nearby and was at the emergency department within 10 minutes after the call. A nurse met her and said, "I am sorry, your husband was dead on arrival. Would you like to see his body?" The woman answered, "No." The young woman said she could not believe that the nurse just walked away. She said her insides just screamed out to the nurse yet she could make no audible sound. When asked what she wanted from the nurse she said, "I wanted to tell the nurse I was afraid to go in alone. I was afraid I would faint or vomit. I didn't know what it looked like to be burned. I thought maybe he was all charred. Later, I found there were only two little marks on him. I felt so cheated. I wanted to hold and caress him. I wanted to weep on him and run my fingers through his hair and his eyelashes like I always did. I couldn't believe the nurse just walked away. Didn't the nurse understand I meant I don't want to see him dead? I want to see him alive."

Her whole being was crying out for the nurse to say, "It is okay to scream and express your feelings. I will help you see this through; you will not be alone." She wanted someone with strength to reach out and help her say goodbye; but the nurse just walked away. She said her husband had an open casket; however, it was not the same as when his body was still soft and smelled natural. She regretted her quick response to the nurse.

Some families who chose not to view the body did so because they were afraid of what they might see. Countless others were angry because they were advised not to see the body because the injuries were too severe. Later, during the searching phase they questioned firefighters, coroner, police, and the mortician as well as every available bystander and found that they were denied seeing the body because an arm was missing or there was a large gash on the face. In reality, these injuries were minor compared to what they imagined. They were angry because they were denied the right to see the body of the loved one and were given misinformation about the extent of the injuries. We have arranged for many mourners to see the Coroner's pictures when grief is delayed for this reason. This has been a great help to them.

If, after a suitable time, the grievers are unwilling to view the body, honor their decision. However, be certain one person's refusal does not speak for the entire family. The brothers, sisters, or children of the deceased may need to spend time with the body, and they should be encouraged to do so. Later grief work is facilitated if even one member of the family or perhaps a minister sees the body. That one person can share what they saw and reassure the other grievers it was indeed their loved one who was dead.

I will never forget my mother's experience when her baby died. My baby brother died unexpectedly and suddenly at home. As was the custom in that area, my parents were going to transport his body to the funeral home themselves after he had been examined and pronounced dead at our home by the physician. Dad brought the car to the door and Mom carried the baby. When she got to the car she became confused and said to my sister, "Should I put him in the back seat?" My sister responded by touching Mom's shoulder saying, "No, Mom, why don't you hold the baby?" Mom cuddled the baby for the entire 15 mile trip. Afterwards when she talked about the incident she said these memories gave her so much comfort knowing that she cuddled her baby boy on his last trip. Even my mother, who loved babies so much, needed this permission and I am thankful my sister was there to verbalize it.

Mutilated Body

The family can understand that the body has been through a great deal. Usually at least a portion of a mutilated body can be uncovered. For example, the hands of a loved one are readily recognized by the family. Bandage or cover any mutilated parts and place the least injured side toward the door. Check to see that the hands are in a restful position. The head is on a pillow, and the sheets are neatly arranged. Explain to the family what has occurred and the condition of the body. Describe what you have done and what they are about to see. Take time to let the vision sink in. Usually they will not disturb the coverings, but if they remove them, remember it is their right. They have a right to the body of their loved one.

Headless Body

What about the headless body? That often happens in certain types of car accidents. Can it be shown? Yes, the families say they want to be near the body. They say they know their family member's hands and body very well. They want to spend time touching, talking to and loving on the body. Just prepare the family well about the extent of the injuries. Put a pillow at the head area and put clean towels over wounds.

The only part of my son that was intact was one arm with a tattoo. He was taken directly to the funeral home where they prepared him according to this protocol. His wife was able to stay a long time with him while stroking his arm. That is good. Think of someone you love. Is the face the only part of them that is recognizable and meaningful to you, or are there other areas of the body that have meaning? For example, what about the hands? Do you trace the veins and know the shape of their nails? Are they not an important source of nonverbal communication? The family who views the mutilated body will also recognize and find meaning in that part of the body that can be shown. Most grievers seem to benefit from that viewing of the body.

When you are aware of the normal dynamics of grief you realize that in time these extensive injuries give comfort to the grievers because it gives a reason for the death. Death is often more difficult to accept when the body is perfect and there are no external injuries. This may sound very difficult, but remember the grievers must develop an acceptance of the death of this person. If they understand the nature of the injury, it helps them accept the death.

Bed to Crematorium

Body Donated to Science

It is interesting to note that many individuals donate a body to science to escape the need for dealing with the remains. The final disposition of ground, sea burial, or cremation brings a sense of completion to the family. When the body is donated, this completeness, this finishing, this sense of the elements returned to nature from whence they have come, or placement in a final resting place is missing. When this occurs, there is a tendency to wait for the dead to return; therefore the grief work is delayed. Those who choose bed to crematorium disposal are also affected in a similar way.

There are ways to help the family in such instances. For example, the body can be viewed in a natural position in bed for a few hours. They can even hold a simple religious or memorial service at the bedside. Such activities greatly facilitate grief work.

Body Cannot Be Shown

A severely mutilated body, such as burned, submerged in water several days, or falling off a mountain can complicate the grieving process because the body is not intact enough to be shown. However there are things that can be done. The principal need of the family is time. Spend as much time with identifying material as you would with the body if it could be shown. It takes clock time to come to grips with the reality of sudden death.

For example, a lock of hair might be given to the family. Identifying dental films of the autopsy and from the person's personal dentist could be shown to the family for comparison. Show exactly why they are the same. Spend time looking at identifying jewelry. Explain where it was on the body, what the trauma did to the jewelry, and any other information that you can share with the family. That is all they have now. I have two friends who were invited to sit with the body bag closed. Both feel very comforted by the experience. One lady spent four hours with her husband's remains in a body bag and remembers that as a most intimate time. That memory was comforting to her as she grieved in the months after.

Families who do not see the body find it difficult to believe it was their loved one who was dragged from the lake or who was in the airplane when it crashed. Somehow, their gut feels that it is all a mistake and a part of them waits forever for the return of their loved one. Their fantasies are fed and encouraged by news articles about people who were given up for dead and then returned years later.

Too Bad To Be Shown

The family has to make friends with the death wound. The death wound gives reason why he cannot return home. Mothers told me, "I always took care of his wounds in life, why would I shrink from his wound in death?" The mind does not exist in a vacuum. When a family is told a body is too bad to be shown, their mind conjures up every image they ever saw in movies, pictures, and in their personal fears. Reality is often much less gruesome than imagination. Reality has the courtesy to hold still in time and space.

Criteria for not Showing Body

When I did the consumer research for this document the parents who's children died a mutilated death said they wanted the criteria to be the same as if their child had lived for a couple of days in the intensive care unit. In the ICU they know they would be expected to see their child and participate in his care. If he died they want to be well prepared as to the extent of his wounds and encouraged to be with his body to say farewell.

One Father said, "I had two sons in a car accident. I came running into the emergency department saying, Where are they?" I was met by crazy people who were saying crazy things. They were saying unbelievable things like, "Bobby is here. His body is too bad for you to see. Dan is upstairs in the intensive care, go up there and be with him." The Dad protested, "No, I want to be with Bobby first, then I will go upstairs." The personnel were adamant. The Father continued, "In frustration I ran up the stairs into the Intensive Care Unit. Immediately I was escorted to my boy Dan's bedside. There he was with his head completely bandaged and he was gurgling through a tube." He looked terrible. My anger flashed and I was mad! Who were these crazy people who thought I could not be with my boy. I ran down to the emergency department and said in a determined voice. Get out of my way. I am going to be with Bobby." With what appeared to be great relief the personnel said, "He is gone, the funeral director already picked up his body." The Dad said, "I ran to the parking lot, speeded across town marched into the funeral home and demanded, I am going to spend time with my son!" To the Dad's surprise the funeral director said in a fatherly tone, "Of course. Come with me. I will bring you a chair." The Father told us, "I sat with my boy and we talked. First I talked and I talked until it was all out of my system. Then Bobby talked. I heard him. Then we talked together. Finely I could do what a Dad has to do." I asked, "What was that?" "Put him in the ground. How else can a Dad put his child's body in the ground unless he knows at his gut level that he is dead?" Yes, parenting tasks continue after the death of one's child. There are burial tasks, funeral tasks, memorial tasks, and closure of estate tasks, as well as the task of internalizing the love and bond in one's heart that will remain there forever.

The Father went on to explain that Bobby had only a small cut. His living son's injuries were much worse than the injuries of the boy who died. Remember that yearning and searching last for months. Grieving people are still intelligent people. They are impelled to be good fact finders. They will later discover as so many have that, "I was denied the right to be with my child who only had an arm torn off, or head disfigured. I could have held his hand for an hour and we could have talked. I know his hand as well as his face. I put band aids on his little hurts many a time and trimmed his little finger nails. I would have gotten so much comfort tracing the veins of his hands, and putting my hands against his for a high five. I was denied that."

Families usually take about an hour with the body, many like to wash and comb their hair. There are extenuating circumstances where people need to take longer to let the enormity sink in. Do bring them a chair or a rocking chair if it is a child.

Too Much Loss

A four year old was playing beside a swimming pool where her many cousins were swimming. No one noticed her slip into the water until it was too late. It was 9:30 pm at the emergency department when her Mom was told that her daughter died. Mom became extremely active and verbal, talking, crying, and refusing to accept that she was dead. The staff stayed with her. As the hours went by they put the family in a private room, brought a rocking chair where the Mom rocked her daughter, scolding her, loving on her, begging her not to fool Mommy anymore, saying, "You are fine, I saw you get off the school bus, you were playing, I know you are all right. Wake up now!" The stomach contents came up and she did what every good Mom does; she wiped her daughter's mouth and cleaned her face. Mom aggressively refused all sedatives. It was 6:00 am when the totally worn out Mother permitted the funeral director to take the body. She quickly regretted that decision and wanted to pursue him across town.

The chaplains went with the Mother to be with the family at her home. This is the story they came back with. Mom and Dad, both professionals, escaped Cuba on a boat. They left with four children but were discovered by the soldiers as they waded through the dark waters to the little boat. All four of the children were shot and drowned at sea. Mom was pregnant and this was the little girl she birthed. Sometimes there is too much loss. It takes a long time to have the enormity sink in.

Death often takes place in the home. At one of my rural conferences a paramedic said he found the Father collapsed between the sink and the toilet. His little four year old son was calling and actively trying to wake his Dad. The paramedic said he knew it was going to take about forty minutes for the coroner and others to arrive. So the paramedic sat on the floor and cradled Daddy's head in his hands. He asked the little boy to help him talk to Daddy. Together they had a cherished forty minutes. The little boy needed to be active so he was in and out. But he always returned quickly. I asked the paramedic how he knew what to do? He answered gruffly, "It just seemed right to me."

Needs of Grievers

Understanding Treatment

Grievers often do not realize how much is done to help a patient who is brought to the emergency department. I remember a case where a man was brought to the emergency department still breathing and in great pain. His heart stopped almost immediately and after a time the physician went to the family and told them the man had died. He said, "I am sorry there was nothing more we could do." The family accepted the statement and left. About a month later a representative of the family came to the emergency department and asked about the circumstances surrounding the death. He said the family was distraught because they thought nothing had been done for their loved one. The family interpreted the physician's statement, "There was nothing more we could do," as meaning nothing was done. They felt our hospital was too small and wished the patient had been transferred to a larger hospital that could have done more.

In grief, many mourners do not have the ability to reflect. It is helpful if they can return to the scene and talk to the same personnel who were present at the death. They can clarify things that are bothering them. Misunderstandings are common because of the intense emotions experienced at a death scene. Be aware that such misunderstandings are likely to occur and make every effort to put the mourners' minds at ease. In this case the head nurse was able to pull the patient's chart and show the test slips and all medications that were given. The family was reassured when they realized that everything possible had been done and transfer to another hospital would not have benefited the patient. This realization helped the family to cope with their great loss.

Need to Return

Grievers have many needs. They need acceptance that their reactions are okay. Give privacy but do not restrain their outburst because of lack of privacy. They need permission to react and permission to cry. They may feel very embarrassed if they have outbursts of emotions, they may even feel ashamed. Perhaps they are self disciplined professionals and their emotional outbursts catch them by surprise. They need someone to approach them and say, "It is good that you verbalize your feelings, go ahead and cry, it is all right that you screamed, you have good reason to loose your cool, this is very sad, this is very hard to bear."

If they have acted out, they need to hear, "It is perfectly normal to lose your cool. Sometimes the pressures of life are just too much; you are not expected to be in control all the time." As a support person you may be thinking it; but grieving people need to hear you say it. Touch them whenever possible. Put your arms around them and give regressive care. If you offer them coffee they will probably say no. Bring something hot or cold anyway. Bring a chair and ask someone to sit with the mourners. It is particularly comforting if the same support person can be with the family throughout. Express your concern and sympathy when you are ready to leave. Tell them you care and would like to hear from them again. Give them a card with your phone number and the best times to call you.

In three weeks they will have many questions that did not occur to them at the time of the crisis. Those questions, if unanswered, will haunt them and greatly impede the grieving process, such as, if only we had gotten to the hospital quicker. Facts are better than circular thinking. Facts hold still in time and space. Then they can be dealt with. Encourage the mourner to go back to the scene, talk to the paramedics, police, and hospital personnel and mortician. Their questions should be answered simply, honest and factual. Typical questions are: "Was he in a lot of pain? Did he open his eyes? Did he ask for me? What did the doctor really do for him?" This kind of psychological emergency care does so much to relieve anxieties. The time and effort you spend as a helping person do much more than medication to help the mourner adjust to the loss of the love one.

There seems to be a compelling need to return to the scene of a death wherever it may have occurred. Some mourners may want to pace off the skid marks, drive over the stretch of road reliving his last trip over and over again. There is a need to return to the emergency department where the loved one was taken and a need to talk to the helping persons who cared for them. It takes about three weeks for the reality of sudden death to sink in; that is a good time to make a return visit.

Needs of the Helping Person

The support person also has many needs. If you have been through a sudden death with a family, you will be emotionally drained. You have a need to show your tears. Many grievers say the greatest comfort they received was seeing tears in the eyes of a helping person. This reassured them that the immense grief they felt was justified. It lets them know the person who was so important to them is recognized as being important and worthwhile to others. Therefore, do not be afraid to show your tears.

When you are alone again, it is important that you refill your emotional needs by finding a supportive group or person. You need to talk to someone who will listen to your feelings about what you saw and experienced. It is hoped that each of you has someone you can go to and say, "I just need to tell someone what has happened, or I need comfort from you." It is normal to be emotionally drained; be kind to yourself; be gentle with yourself.

Appendix A

Hope & Faith

In the Person Beside

Bear in mind that this Hope and Faith needed so much by the griever is often, "Only in the person that stands beside." If you have the courage to be there *with*, that alone is enough.

Hope and Faith are not something you can give away. You cannot give that to another nor demand they receive Hope or Faith.

When we look at those Moms and Dads in the emergency department standing at the side of their child's body, their future is fragmented and shattered right before their eyes. How can we say to them, "You must have hope, you must have faith." Nothing looks very good to them.

Often someone came to them saying, you must have Hope, you must have Faith. I saw the grieving person stiffen and struggle; but, let me tell you that when someone came into that emergency department from church, neighborhood, workplace, or a relative, and stood beside them quietly caring; when that someone had the courage to be calm, wept with them, and gently said:

> "I will stay with you,
> I will go to the funeral home with you,
> I will come back again tomorrow to see what you need.
> I care about you and
> I care about what you have to go through right now"

That is what made the difference for those grievers.

This is what you do for others.
You bring the light with you and
You let the light shine through you into their space.
You cannot give the light to them nor can you demand they have it in themselves.

If you believe in your friend, in the Process, in a Higher Power that provides the light in this period of darkness, then you must go stand beside your friend and let the light shine through you to bathe their space. No words are necessary for this to happen. It just does. It is the magic of communion.

Since mourning is a long time, you must be willing to redo this often. Resist the urge to allay your nervousness by talking at them. In the time of deep grief, "Talking at" makes them too nervous.

It is so much easier for you, the helping person to go to the mourner when you have a bit of knowledge. Remember their volatile emotions, and lack of future images scares them.

Just knowing that you believe they have the inner resources to proceed day by day is incredible to them. You can encourage them to be aware each day, to observe the organization that is coming into their new life style. When the disorganization covers so many facets of life as it does in the loss of a primary object, the little order that is happening day by day tends to go by unnoticed. This is part of what you can affirm on your visits. You can be a mirror and reflect the little successes back to them. Warning, be truthful, do not exaggerate or you will lose their trust; the griever is still smart.

Neither you nor the mourner knows what their future will look like. If their child has died, if their mate was killed, their style of life will look very different two years from now. You don't know what their future looks like and neither do they. It is a process. Your part is to provide the belief that what looks like disorganization will evolve into a healthy style of living which includes the memory of, and the gifts of the lost object but without that person, place, body function, thing, job, profession, or fantasy.

Appendix B

The Chancery office of the Archdioceses of Chicago asked if I would present an all day seminar to parents whose children died by suicide. Preparing the material caused me to deeply suffer the parent's grief. I had two teenagers at home, one hyper daughter who repeatedly said she was going to kill herself if a boy did not look at her in a prescribed way. I did not take her too seriously, but now was soon to meet parents whose children followed through on that thought. I had such sympathy and empathy for them, that to comfort myself I sat down at the computer to allow this meditation prayer to flow through my mind. I printed it out and took it with me to Chicago in the early hours of the following morning. I drove to Holy Angels Cathedral on Superior St. to present the seminar. Near the address, I found a restaurant and read for the first time the inspiration I received the night before. It comforted me.

We started the conference with eighty Moms and Dads at 9:00 am and finished at 4:00 pm. I gave the conclusion to the seminar, but no one moved. I then did an extended summary, blessing, and conclusion, saying, "Now you are free to leave." No one moved. Then I said. The seminar is over. They answered, "Give us more. You have more." I said, "No," pointing to the piles of outlines that were already used. They responded, "Yes, you have more," pointing to this manuscript. I explained that it was private, a personal prayer that I composed to prepare myself for this conference. They answered, "That is okay. We want you to read it to us."

Not one member of the audience had moved. Befuddled I picked up the manuscript, walked to the mike and read my prayer. In that mental zone I was unprepared to instantly have a dozen hands pulling on the manuscript. I griped it tightly saying, "No, no, it is my only copy." The priest came quickly to my rescue saying firmly to me, "I will take it." He walked to the microphone and announced to the group that he was having it duplicated and they could wait for their copies. I couldn't believe it. It was as though I was a bystander watching. I really wanted to re-read the manuscript in the quiet of my home to see if I could understand the intense reaction of the audience.

Since that time I have been invited to use "A Meditation on Suicidal Grief," as a closing for several seminars on Suicide Loss. One minister did criticize the theology expressed in the meditation.

A Meditation on Suicidal Grief

According to the
Seven Last Words of Jesus on The Cross

In the area of death and suffering, our bible tells us very little in answering the question "why?" However, in many places our Bible does share with us "how" to go through the experiences of suffering and death.

There is a thought that in dying, man is to die fully healed, not broken unto death, but fully healed, ready to leave his body for the work of the transition. Perhaps then, the traditional last words of Jesus on the cross were not just accidental words spoken at the last minute. Rather, as with all of His life, these last words were teaching words helping to show us how to pray when faced with suffering and death. Since dying is a loss, perhaps these last words were appropriate to grief work also. Following is my mediation on suicidal grief according to the last words of Jesus on the cross.

O God, We Pray For Healing Grief.
Father into Thy Hands I Commend My Spirit

Resignation: I will give my grief to you, oh God; how can I do that? Jesus did that by surrendering. Let us look at how He did that.

Father Forgive Them for They Know Not What They Do

You say your loved one knew he was taking his own life.

Those people also knew that they were murdering a man by putting him on a cross.

Jesus still prayed, "Forgive them they know not what they do." What did He mean by that? He was teaching us that many do the undesirable act but do not know the completeness of what that act means.

Suicidal persons don't know the whole story of the reaction to their death. Their world is narrowed to their own pain and they are seeking peace, release.

Father forgive them, they really did not know about all of this grief.

This Day You Will Be With Me in Paradise

Jesus had to give away all that He owned before he died, his robe was gone, and He owned no earthly possessions. But He did own paradise and He gave it to a thief.

Give your grief to Jesus. He gave His paradise to a thief. He can give it to a suicide person. Give your grief to Jesus.

Your loved one had an earthly paradise. To heal, Jesus showed that we must give away what he owned. Take that which you want to keep from your loved one's possessions. Let his relatives and friends take what they need and turn the rest over to whoever can be blessed by your loved one's paradise.

Mother – Behold Your Son; Son – Behold Your Mother

Part of dying is to give away our loved ones. Your loved one did this in his death by suicide. Jesus showed us that that is part of the work in order to come to healing grief.

He meant for his Mother to look to John for the, "Sonship", she needed.

He meant for John to look to Mary for the, "Mothering," he needed in his grief.

Jesus shows us that part of the grief work is to get our, "Mothering, brothering, and our parenting," needs met.

Go out and find your social family, build one if you don't have one.

A tremendous flow, of energy went into that person who is now dead.

You must find a recipient for this love flow or it will bottle up in you and you will, "Explode." Find someone to receive your love-gifts. Jesus showed us that this was necessary.

My God, My God, Why Hast Thou Forsaken Me?

The aloneness that Jesus felt to cry out like that must have been terrible. The aloneness someone felt to commit suicide must be terrible! Terrible!

The world does not understand. We know that Jesus understands that loneliness. My God, My God, Why hast Thou forsaken Me?

When you are ridden with guilt, with which all survivors must deal, when you are saying, …. "If only, …. If only, …. I had foreseen, reacted, done this or done that ….," just remember,

Mary and John were at his feet when
    He cried out those forsaken works.

Think of how they felt. They too, were helpless in the situation.

I Thirst

Jesus thought of his body needs when he was dying. He lets us know that is part of the work of being fully human.

You thirst. Take care of your nutrition, liquid, social, rest, and exercise needs.

There is another kind of thirst ... a thirst for spiritual water ... for hope.
Yes, you thirst for hope ... take that hope wherever you find it.
Hope for meaning in all this suffering.
Hope for forgiveness for others and for yourself.
Hope to assimilate this loss into a total life that will have love, joy, and happy excitement in it again. Even though that is not for now.

How to heal?

Jesus said, "I thirst."

It is Finished

Yes, at sometime all the mulling over, grieving, begging, and questioning of why ... will be finished. Just as Jesus saw that his struggle, physical and mental was finished .... So will your struggle have a finish to it.

That finish does not come when the answers come.

No, it comes one day when you know that you are willing to live a full life that contains unanswered questions.

It comes by an, "Act of Will."

It comes that day when you give your grief to God to worry about. When you say, I have grieved my two years; I have taken my time to grieve. I have examined my conscience and have rectified all that I can rectify in my human state.

Now, I accept this. I give the rest to You.

Then, my friend, you will have acute grief at intervals, but the rest of the time you will invest in life.

Not yet, Lord .... but in time. In time.

Father, Into Thy Hands I Commend My Spirit

Jesus showed us how to give up by an act of will. He could have just withered away. He made an act of will. He had no choice to die or not to die. But he could choose how to react to his dying.

You too, have to die. That part of you that had your dreams, hopes, and ideals of yesteryear needs to die before you can have rebirth.

Jesus shows us how to die …. by surrendering.

There is a beautiful hymn that starts with, "I surrender you, so that God may use you." There is some thought that the dead are tied to us while we grieve. That is their work in the afterlife. When we surrender them and give up our grief, they can go about the work of the afterlife.

"I surrender you so that you may be free."

The last stanza of this song is

"I surrender you, I surrender you, So that God can use me."

Think of that. It is heavy. Take your two years to grieve …. more if you need. Then at some point make an act of will. "I surrender you, so that you can be free. I surrender you so that God can use me." Yes, I have a life to live for God on this side of your grave.

Take a deep sigh of relief and say:

It is Finished

Father, into your hands I commend my loved one's spirit.

Father, into your hands I commend my spirit.

Chapter 6

There are some repeats because this lecture was often given without the supporting content of the other chapters.

Dying Event

"Being There When"

We in the caring professions know that the dying time is one of the most difficult times a family will have to live through. My approach in all matters affecting you the caregiver, friend, or family during the time of dying is to be as honest and straight forward as possible. In this way you can begin a trusting and open communication relationship with the person who is dying and also with the members of the family for which you are concerned. This sets the map for healthy resolution of the changes that occur after loss of a significant other.

How will this come into your life in the future? Many times you will be in position to support a friend who has a dying member in their family. Perhaps it will be your neighbor, a member of your social group, church, or work families. What happens so often is that when listening to them talk about the upcoming dying event, you will find yourself thinking. I'd like to say, "Call me. Don't be alone at that time if you do not wish to be. If I'm m not at work or otherwise obligated at the time of your call, I will be there." Be sure to build conditions into the promise because at the time of deep grief, deep fright, or deep pain, the listener is literal. Much pain is caused by a seemingly careless promise to be available. So, realize you are an adult with adult responsibilities and wish as you might there are times you cannot respond to a call of need. That is why you should encourage your person to have at least five persons on that list, perhaps more. Then you will wonder, "What will the dying event be like for him? What will it be like for his family? How can I possibly be a help to either the dying person or the caregivers who are supporting him?"

Purpose

I know that dying is a part of all lives and the dying time will happen in your life someday. That is why I have a firm personal and professional belief that information belongs in the hands of the user, not in the minds of professionals. For that reason I share with you this material.

I offer this information to help you prepare and anticipate symptoms which are indicative of approaching death. Only a few of these symptoms I will discuss will occur in each dying situation. However, I want to relate each possible symptom to you for the purpose of decreasing your fear if an unexpected symptom in the dying event should appear suddenly. All the symptoms described are indicative of how the body prepares itself for the final stage of life.

Sometimes you will want to use this information as a primary caretaker. That means at some time in your life, statistically speaking, you will be personally giving care to a dying person.

Sometimes you will be a secondary caretaker, meaning you will be supporting your sister or friend as they give care. You may not even go to the house of the dying person. You still are effective as a support person. If you do go to the place of the dying person it may only be a couple of times. Perhaps the dying person actually lives a long way from you and you can only fly there two times a year, as was the case of my Dad. Yet my knowledge could support my brothers who were primary caregivers to him. So while you may not do anything in the house of the dying, you can be a very instrumental caregiver to the caregivers.

Then there will be the times you find yourself using this information in a tertiary care mode. That is you will be providing therapeutic listening to a person who is recounting a deathbed experience of some time ago. Your responses can make a difference in how that person assimilates the death experience into their self image.

This chapter is a focus on long term dying not sudden death. Long term dying can take place over years. The actually dying time can go on for weeks. Admittedly this is hard on the families, however with this in mind you can see why we say that dying is living too. Dying is living until death occurs. The quality of life for the dying person, as well as the quality of life and communication for caregivers is the highest priority of the support person, which is You.

Historical Setting

The great anthropologist, Mandelbaum, said that the first responsibility of a society that has been dispersed and reassembled is to define how each member is to be supported during times of dependency. It must be decided how one is to die, how to support the dying and how to dispose of the body. Society must decide how it will support the grieving during the long grief process when they are vulnerable to attack, accident and illness.

Our society has been dispersed by its mobility, working women, diversity of religions, races, ethnic groups, multi-marriages, quickly altering value systems and changes that occurred in church traditions. The family with a dying person has no idea what to do, what they can do, what is healthy, helpful, or appropriate. They do not know who in the relationship, church, or community can be counted upon or to whom can they can go for resources. It is a culture taboo for families and friends to talk about the dying event and they find they are quickly ostracized if they repeatedly attempt to emote or ask for ideas.

There are no models to follow. Each family with a dying person becomes a pioneer as if they were the only family to plod through this experience. Because of increased longevity many families have never cared for a dying person. Or, if so, it was in another community where, "Things were different there."

It is the responsibility of the culture to provide models that protect, support, give form and rituals that encourage growth through the experience of grief. Our past healthy coping patterns for the dying event do not work in today's world. Neither the community nor the church's function and response to dying are the same as it was a few years ago. The old ways are no longer the best ways. Yet we do not have a substitute model developed for those that no longer work.

The family with a dying member cannot wait. With or without meaningful support they must talk to their dying person, stand by as he dies, and dispose of his body. Many persons feel insecure and unsupported in the days of knowing the irreversible event of death is happening. The result often is guilt feelings and complicated grief with compensated lives. There is no need for this waste of human effort and functioning. Our task is to bring into open conversation and easy access to healthy, helpful information about the dying event. The experience can then be a supported occurrence for those who die and for those who must continue with life.

The Caring Objective Outsider

Without a known cultural ritual to guide persons at a time of so many differences, a knowledgeable caring objective outsider is the most effective way to help the family. Who is this support person? It can be anyone who cares: a distant relative, neighbor, co-worker, pastoral visitor, hospice worker, visiting nurse, counselor, health care provider. It can be someone who cares enough to share knowledge, give permissions and promise continuity of support through the dying process. Usually this contract is made nonverbally by persons close the family. However, it can be a formal contract such as with hospice, health care agencies or a profession counselor.

If you choose to be that supportive person make your promises clear. Either promise nothing and be there when you can, or define clearly what you can do. Nevertheless, be aware that persons in crisis sometimes count on you when you didn't promise. So be clear about what you can do and what you cannot. Some persons will cling to you and ask you to promise to be there when the dying takes place. Be clear. Say, "Sometimes I cannot come such as when I am working, with my baby. Please call me when the dying happens. I want to come if I can." Make your limits clear, if you are a person who can't stomach the sickroom but will run errands, cook, guide funeral plans, then say that very distinctly.

Prepare the Family

Preparation of the Family

Some families are most anxious for information surrounding the dying event and cannot wait to ask an experienced person. I went with the hospice nurse on a first time visit to a home of a dying man. His wife met us at the door. She was waiting for us. She had put on company clothing and the house was ready for visitors. The patient was well cared for. The lady had taken care of her sick husband for several years and now that the dying time had come she asked for hospice visits. She had thought about his dying for so long and couldn't wait to ask how it would be. It was the first thing she asked us after the greeting and continued her questions until her concerns were answered.

Not all families are alike in their reactions. Some say, "Don't tell me anything, then it will just happen and I'll get through it somehow." You want to respect the coping pattern of each family and recognize that one member of the family may need information and the other not want it. The resistant person is often an excellent caregiver. Help them to respect the differences in each other. Often the one who is resistant to information about the dying event is comforted to know that someone else has it.

I think that in the case of the resistant persons it is still our professional duty to provide access to information for when they might be able to accept it. That means we have to let them know there is information available about the dying event that may be helpful to them and that we are a resource when they want it. I think we can go a step further and in casual conversation present patient teaching in a manner that is palatable and helpful to even the resistant persons. I often leave a handout saying, "You do not have to look at this now, but you will have it if the time comes that you or someone else would like to check on what is happening."

How Will the Dying Be?

One man, a fifty two year old engineer was nearing his terminal phase. I visited his home with the home health nurse. That day dying was on his mind. He was sitting in a rocking chair and looked fairly strong. He reached his hand up to take the nurse's hand and said, "Nurse, how will the dying be?" And then he wept awhile. Then he said, "I want to talk about it. I want to know. Is it all right if you tell me?" She said, "Yes, what do you think about when you think about dying?" He said, "I wonder what it will feel like? Nurse, won't I be able to breathe?" She answered simply, "No, you won't be able to breathe. That's what dying means." He cried for a while. Then he asked, "Will it hurt?" The nurse answered, "Persons who have your disease usually do have some pain in the dying process. Would you like to talk about that and make some plans that may help ease the pain?" He said, "Yes, let's make some plans, tell me. I don't want to be a baby about it." And he wept again. The nurse quietly waited for his next overture. He said, "I am so sorry that I am crying. I don't want to be a baby now. I have always been a strong and responsible man." The nurse responded, "It is all right if you cry. Tears are okay. I want you to take all the time you need to cry with me. But first I wonder if anyone has explained the nature of your disease as it relates to your tears. People with your disease cry a lot because there are a lot of tears made as part of the disease. Many times the tears are from the disease, not from crying." He was amazed and had her explain the physiology over to him several times until he understood. He was much relieved. The nurse went on to explain that in addition to his disease, tears were easily present as a result of general weakness and sometimes because of medication. Then she encouraged him to cry real tears when they were appropriate.

They then began the plans to prepare for his dying. With great joy he told us he had found someone to stay with him until after he was dead so he could die at home. This man had only one relative, an 88 year old mother who was senile and for whom he was the caretaker. They lived in a beautifully kept old home with original woodwork, china and crystal. It was hard for him to accept his dying because it would leave his mother without support. The lady he found not only promised to stay with him until he died but to get his mother settled in a good nursing home after his death. His happiness at being responsible was beautiful to witness. The nurse asked for the caregiver so she could participate in the plans. He said he would call her but wanted us to know that she was the prostitute he had frequented since he was a young man. His mother did not know this. The lady came from upstairs at his call and I was amazed. She was made up appropriate to her former role. About his age, she was wearing a see-through nightgown and told us with pride, that the boxer shorts she had under it were his. Other than that she wore only heelless 3 inch spiked, high heeled shoes. Her hairdo and makeup were extreme.

I took a step back and worked at my external composure. I thought, "Too bad this is a lost cause. We will have to have him moved to a nursing home." The visiting nurse, on the other hand, was a model of non-judgment. She asked the lady her commitment. Checked it out in several ways, found her to be sincere and capable, and then proceeded with the plans for pain relief and comfort during his dying phase. They practiced with her lifting him up in bed to put extra pillows behind his head, ways that he wanted to be touched, use of medication, and who to call for advice at the time of dying. They went over it several times because he wanted to help and the nurse kept reminding him that he would be solid weight at the time of his dying and unable to help. I've rarely seen a more motivated learner, or a more loving, considerate caretaker than that prostitute. Finally they were filled and both looked so relieved knowing there was something they could do to help when the dying time came. I gathered the courage to ask her why she would be willing to help him. Her face and eyes glowed as she told how wonderful it was to be needed by someone. Over and over she said, "No one has ever needed me before in my entire life." I asked, "Not even when you were a child?" She enthusiastically stated, "No, never, but I am needed here. He needs me and his mother needs me and I can do it for them." I left a wiser and richer person than when I arrived.

Reactions to Death

Give Yourself Permission

There are many ways to react to the news of the dying event or death. None of them are a measure of the love the griever has for the person who is dying or for the family of the dead one. As an observer we are sometimes puzzled by the reactions of family and friends. Sometimes it appears there is no emotion, love, or consideration, but that action is not an indicator of the love. Many relationships are jeopardized because of misinterpretation of performance at this time. All that the behavior tells us is something about where that person is emotionally now, his coping patterns, and perhaps his culture.

When you are anticipating the death of a loved one please give yourself permission for a full range of reactions. It is common to be very surprised at your reactions and you say, "I didn't think I would be this way." As a helping person you can say to others, "No one is ever prepared for a death. It never happened to you with this person before. You go ahead and be exactly the way you need to be."

Regardless of how expected the death is people invariably are not prepared for the finality of the death event. In fact, long term dying death may have many of the characteristics of sudden death. The close members of the family become so used to the dying, that may take place over a year or more. When the breathing actually stops, it is a shock. Our child grievers taught us this. Everyone around them thinks the children will handle it well because they knew Mom or Dad was going to die and were involved in the care. They were given all the information; yet the children seem to grieve deeply. In counseling they say to us, "Momma was always there. Whenever I came home she was there. Momma always had time to let me talk or to look at my school papers or to let me read to her. As long as I can remember, the house was never empty except when she was in the hospital, and then I was so lonely. I want Momma to come home again." Yes, Momma always came home again. We need to realize these children of dying parents often have more continuity of care than those of the working parent.

Mechanical Reaction

Some people react in shock and disbelief. The reality of the dying is too much to let into the psyche at one time. They may react in mechanical ways. They are numb and are putting off all activity until later. They will do what they have always done but if that activity requires a new choice, they may have no idea what to do next. Serial judgment making ability is gone. You may gently reinforce reality with, "This is difficult. This is sad. It's too bad. I'm so sorry." They may not remember what you said but they will remember that you were there and that you touched them. That memory will stay in their minds forever. For these people you may want to give regressive care, bring a cup of soup, fix their hair and put an afghan around them. Let them do as much as possible for themselves. That helps them orient to reality. Your part is to observe and gently help when nurturing is needed. Let them dress themselves, but you finish the button they missed. If there are phone calls to be made, let them do the call. If they can dial, let them; if not, you dial. You may want to talk to the person on the other end of the phone call, identifying yourself, explaining that their friend will talk to them now. You may want to add, "When you are finished don't hang up until I talk to you." After the grieving person has talked, you can take the phone and clarify or ask for questions. In our good will we make these calls for the grieving denying them a much needed opportunity for reality testing, centering, and receiving strokes. These experiences and memories become the building blocks for the grief-work that must be done in the months to come. It is wrong to deny them these interactions and participation in the dying process and funeral events just because they are deeply grieving now.

Crying

Some persons cannot keep the tears from dripping as they continue with activities, others need to stop and just cry. At the news of the death, some persons let out a loud scream that comes from the very center of their being. This cry should never be stopped. It is an important emotional release that affirms reality and allows for the beginning of grief-work. Some persons need to take a cry break every couple of hours; you will find them in the chapel or in their room. Children go to the playhouse or the woods and farmers to the barns or chicken coops. The working person needs to find a safe place for their, "Cry breaks." Some wail and weep; others read the Bible and pray. It makes no difference. The important factor is that they find a way to express this emotion.

Crying is considered very important so that healing can begin. In many cultures evoking tears was considered to be the most important work of those giving comfort. Some persons cry immediately and some have to wait until their unfinished business is done. If there are no tears it is considered a serious sign and the duty of the helping person to find out why. Ask, "Are you able to cry? Do you cry when you are alone, perhaps in your bed at night?" Possibly the griever feels they should not cry. Give them permission. Perhaps they are not crying because there has been preparatory grief and the tears are all cried out long ago. That doesn't mean there is no sadness now at the time of the dying, nor does it mean that the grief work is finished. They will still have to mourn the absence of a primary person and the life that was.

Perhaps there are no tears because the loved one who is dying was a not a nice person. Perhaps he was a person who detached his or her affection from the family a long time ago and the mourning was completed then. Yes, they receive family loyalty in their dying and death but their affection has been long dead. Perhaps the griever is not crying because the only legitimate feeling at this dying event is, "Thank God, it is finally over." Our society demands grief and tears at the open casket, yet in reality the only real feeling at that time for many mourners is relief. Later they will have to deal with the absence of that person in their future, but not now. You will be doing a very helpful thing if you can listen and encourage them to express these socially unacceptable feelings. At the same time give them permission to grieve real losses as they are feeling them in the months to come.

Crying is very important. For one thing, it is a physical equalizer. Have you ever felt so emotional you got a headache or thought your head would split? And then have you cried and found a relief of pressure? That is a physical happening. When you cried, tears came out. You can measure tears. There was that much less water and chemicals in your body, lowering your blood pressure and easing the pounding ache in your head.

Crying causes reality to sink in. There is not much denial in crying. Listen to a sobbing person and what are they repeating over and over, "He is gone, he is dead, oh, my God, I can't believe he is dead!" Never hush a griever; this is exactly what that person must come to terms with, no matter how awful it is.

Crying is important because it provides a socially acceptable form of regression by which to elicit a nurturing response from others. Think, "What is your instinct when you see someone bent over crying their heart out? It evokes a Motherly or Fatherly feeling in you and your instinct is to put your arms around them making cooing parental sounds of concern, comfort, encouragement, and love. Yes, even in our culture one man can put his arms around another man in such a situation. It is very important to elicit the tears of a man before the body of his loved one is put in the grave. Our society tolerates the tears of a man if the body is still above ground but as soon as it is in the grave a man is expected to hide his tears and be adjusted to the death, therefore he receives little or no comfort.

Anger

There may be an outburst of anger at the death. All the pent up feelings of unjustness for the event and unfinished business may burst forth. Some of this anger may be at the dying person for, abandonment by dying or for causing such pain. Anger at the dying person is usually personally and culturally unacceptable to voice at the death scene so they project that anger on someone else, a friend, relative, medical, or other professionals. When you see the behavior is out of proportion to the stimuli always look for baggage. See if you can get the angry persons to express their feelings and reflect on the feeling not the stated issue. Then if there is a real issue with the care that is given, he can talk it out with them in a mature way.

Many families and friendships are split at the dying event. It is common to experience feelings that are different from each other, feelings they did not know they could possess. These feelings are often more intense than the mourner ever imagined they could feel. Many of these feelings were previously unacceptable to them, such as jealousy, and shame. There is great value in the presence of an objective outsider to facilitate healthy communication, to model forgiveness, give permissions to feel, and to feel deeply without judgment.

At a conference in Berkeley, Calif., Dr, Garfield said that when someone gets angry the tendency of the helping person is to get more and more calm. He said he wasn't sure this was helpful. He asked us, "Think of when you are angry, don't you wish someone would get into the energy field with you?" He suggested that instead of being super calm, we might answer with same energy. "It is unfair! This is awful! There is nothing nice about this! I agree!" Do not escalate, just reflect and echo to let out the energy and gently lead the verbosity to a solution of the problem or ideas about how to co-exist with the problem.

Anger at the dead person for dying is often transferred to another person. Often it is transferred to an expendable helping person. In long term illness one can hear persons anger, by their saying, "If the Doctor had made the correct diagnosis earlier, the nurse could have been more careful when inserting the needle, if his son had cared enough about him to help him with the roofing, if Pastor had been more considerate, visited earlier, or not said that in a sermon." These may be legitimate problems but likely if the listener attempts to rectify this present situation they would find it was only a symptom and the anger would still be there.

The anger is at the dying person for causing all this pain, expense, havoc, and loneliness. The dying person is breaking the contract they had of future fantasy and is leaving the survivors in the lurch. They feel rejected and abandoned. In time they will have to face this anger. This is when you hear the widow say, "John left the papers in such a mess! If he really loved me as he said why did he under-insure us so badly?" These are clues that healthy processing of grief is beginning. However, this is all to be gone through in the future.

Appropriate Activity

Some persons react to the news of dying or death with appropriate activity. They immediately set into motion activity that is good, needed, and useful. It is not only adults who respond in this fashion but commonly when a child is killed, it is the teenager that performs many of the duties. This person's response to the news with, "Oh, my! Who is with him? Let's see, he has a son in high school that is close to his Uncle Joe, we'll get Joe to go over to the High School and tell him. His old Mother shouldn't be alone now; I'll call someone to be with her. We'll need a funeral home, that family has always used the services of the home on the west side. We'll need drivers to go to the airport to pick up relatives, and there will need to be plans for food." Everyone looks at this person and says, "Oh, aren't they mature!" Don't kid yourself; they are no more dealing with the meaning of the loss to the dying person or to themselves than is the one who is numb. They are accepting the reality of the duties and postponing dealing with the meaning of the death until some time after the funeral, perhaps when they are alone in their beds at night. Look out for the welfare of this person. Make them a teammate now for that is the role they have chosen, but be aware of their time to break. It will come after the funeral in the weeks or months to follow, long after the world has expected them to have adjusted. Theirs will be a lonely, unsupported grief. They will not have the arm around them as the one who is crying now has. If you will check on them and support them when it is their turn you are doing a caring action.

Many of my students say they know what kind of reactor they are. They will say, "I know because when my Mother died, I did this." Or, "When my Dad was dying I did that." I think you come to each dying, each death situation the sum total of the person you are up to that moment and you need to give yourself permissions to react in whatever way you need. Perhaps at one death situation you need to scream, another to weep uncontrollably, another to engage in appropriate activity being the pillar of strength for the other people, and at another death situation you may need to lash out your anger in a responsible manner, and at some events you may be numb, having no feelings at all. Any feeling you have is okay and while it may not be pleasing to others, feelings in themselves have no value, they just exist. It is possible to act responsibly while having any feeling.

Panic

As the dying time comes close some persons panic. Please give yourself permission for the full range of emotions. Some things are just too much. Perhaps watching a loved one take their last breaths is too much for you. Be who you need to be, get help for that dying person and then when help is there take care of your needs. Some persons who have been ever so faithful leave the room or the house at the dying time. Teenagers have told how they helped with the body but then had to leave the house to drive, swim or ski. Take care of yourself and do not let the last moments behavior be the criteria by which you measure your faithfulness to the one who has died. Often my heart has broken for a wife or child who could not progress in their grief because of guilt for panicking at the end. I would elicit this beautiful story of faithfulness over months and even years taking care of a dying loved one. Sometimes the dying person begged, "Please don't leave me," or "Promise I won't have to die alone." Then something comes up in the end, the caretaker leaves and sees only their human frailty and negates all the good work they did with that dying person.

This is very sad. It impedes assimilation of the mourner back into life, and puts an unhealthy weight on the last moments of life. One mother of three teenage sons took care of her husband over several months of invalidism with cancer. He was very large and she was very little. Her care bordered on heroism, but she was determined he should be able to die at home. Over and over he begged her to promise not to take him to the hospital and she reassured him. Toward the end he was on IVs and oxygen.

He began bleeding out, she panicked, called the ambulance, they took him to the hospital, performed all kinds of procedures on him, exactly what the family didn't want, and he died three days later.

In her grief she cried over and over for forgiveness. She knew it was the end; yet, she panicked and did not keep her promise. Encourage persons to make realistic promises. To say, "I'll do my best," or, "If it is at all possible." We need to recognize that the dying person is often clinging and will not rest with such a promise. Yet, grievers must be realistic. Reality is that we do not know ahead of time what the end will be like for the dying person or for the family. Sometimes a family member or caretaker needs respite care at the time of dying.

Fear of Haunting

One man's greatest fear was that he would not die at home. He asked for repeated reassurances from his daughter and wife that they would not take him to the nursing home. As the dying time became close the hospice nurse noticed increased tension in the daughter and mother. It seemed there were always insurmountable problems to show they could no longer take care of him. When hospice would solve and eliminate the problem, the daughter would find another reason to prove their care was inadequate and they would have to send Dad to the nursing home. Yet the stated desire was to fulfill Dad's request to die at home.

One morning the daughter called to say they had moved Dad to the nursing home during the night. She sounded relieved and defensive. The hospice nurse said, "You don't have to make any excuses to me. You are doing what you have to do and that is what counts right now. I know your Dad doesn't want that but you are saying that right now your Mom and you cannot handle it any more so that is the way it must be." Yes, it is important to think in terms of family care. The desires of one should not be met at the unreasonable cost to another. After the daughter felt the nurse's acceptance she said, "I don't think either Mom or I could stand the thought of him dying in this house. We could never live here again if he died here.

Sometimes we forget to check where the people are at emotionally. Part of the helping role is to define with the family, "How would you feel if he died in that bed? Could you sleep in that bed again?" These thoughts are in their mind. We are not planting them and it is healthy to bring them out in the open. Albert's wife died in a hospital bed in his eight year old son's room. The first time I came to the house I checked to see if the son was involved in the plan. Yes, he had been and was very proud to give his bedroom to his Mom as a last gift for her last days. We need to assess how each affected person feels and help them come to terms with their feelings and to get their needs met in healthy ways.

Do at the Time of Death

Time to Call

At the dying time someone needs to call the primary persons and the pastor. When you make this call convey an expectation that, "Of course they will want to come now and that their presence is valuable." Many persons in our culture are very concerned about breaking the privacy of a dying person and family. They hesitate to be comforters and need to be specially invited. In long term dying the persons who need to be there are known and this discussion ideally has taken place previously. The information of who needs to be there is part of the assessment made by the helper. Take the time to elicit this information. This is how a support group is developed for this grieving family. There is a bonding that occurs among those present in crisis. Later on, in the months to come these will be special persons in the mind of the mourners. It is important that the social family or support group have as much shared experiences as possible.

The personal Pastor should come and be present even though there may be nothing for him or her to do. You may want to do some encouraging with the pastor ahead of time. Many want to be part of the crisis experience. However many pastors voice their personal queasiness around death. It may be helpful for the pastor to hear they are free to leave the bedside and be available to family and friends in the kitchen with a cup of coffee. All persons involved need to be keenly aware never to underestimate the value of their mere presence.

It is sad that many dying persons and families who have a relationship with a personal pastor do not call him at the dying time. There are many taboos about the pastor's presence and as helpers we want to bring them out long before the dying event occurs. One taboo is that the pastor is the, "Death Face," and seeing him will cause the dying person to know it is time and he will become frightened. If this is not the role of the pastor then that has to be talked about openly. The patient should be asked if he would like the presence of the pastor at his dying. In those cases where this is inappropriate the pastor still should come to the hospital or home and be present in the adjacent room for the support and sharing with the family. What happens most often is the patient expects the pastor to come, the family has never talked openly about this and do not notify the pastor so the patient dies without this desire met. It is important to ask the patient their desires in the presence of the family so the family is confident they are not, "Scaring the patient to death at his dying time," but rather are providing a real important comfort service.

Role of the Objective Outsider

The helping person who is assuming the role of the objective outsider needs to consider the needs of the family who has a dying person among them. In this society, the family is defined as the social family composed of primary persons who may or may not be blood related. The personal pastor and mortician are part of the family and part of the care team so they need to be included in the care of the volunteer. The pastor and mortician need to be brought up to date on the condition of the patients and family as it pertains to their work and they need to be supported in the work they are doing with this family. So often we forget they are humans as well as professionals and we forget to prepare them. They are often not ready for what they see when they come to the sick room. Sometimes the condition of the patient has deteriorated and they are unprepared for that and sometimes the family dynamics are a surprise to them. Much of the personal pain, fright, insecurity, and grief suffered by the pastor, mortician and other helping persons could be ameliorated with a little communication, love, and encouragement from the objective continuity caregiver.

Knowing the balance between being assertive, directive, a shadow, and a silent caring presence, is the meaning of empathy. Generally be quiet and just observe. Be there to assess needs, give permissions, listen, love, encourage, and support. Asking questions such as, "What would you like to do? What would be important to you right now? Have you said what you wanted to say? What would you say ordinarily that you wouldn't say directly to the one who is dying? Would you like to say that to me? Be sure to include the teens and children in your one on one interaction. Donna Kruger who has been at the bedside of so many dying persons says, "I don't ever remember being aggressive in a dying situation. We have to remember we are dealing in a crisis situation and we are not there to tell them what to do. The diplomacy it takes is tremendous, yet it is the essence of compassion."

I was in Bob's home five hours after his wife died. I purposely kept track of how often I initiated conversation. It was three times. My students find it difficult to believe I can be quiet that long, but it is easy when the dynamic is heavy. Once I intervened for the presence of a child, another was in making funeral plans. I forgot the third episode. I floated from room to room; there was always someone beside me. One person would come to talk or just be there, they would float away and I'd move a few feet and another apparently watching for an opportunity would come to talk with me. Just knowing that a helping person cares enough to be there is incredible to most families. That you are there telling them who you are, that you intend to see them through is not too much for you to do. Most persons can do that even if you cannot stand to watch the patient vomit or help turn him. If you are not orientated to nursing stuff like that, you may feel sick. But you can be there and give continuity to the family. Go in and out of the sickroom or the house. Stay in the kitchen or waiting room if that is where you function the best. Go in when you can and go out at the point you get a little queasy. Then come back again to say, non-verbally, "I am here. I love you. Thank you for all you have meant to me."

Use that time with the family around the bedside or the table to reminisce about the person. Go back over the memories. Hopefully they have done this prior to this point. You can be a catalyst saying, "I wish I would have known him." Or, "I bet he was really special or I think I missed out on her sense of humor." That gives them an opportunity to tell what the dying person really was like. This is so helpful to the family. Encourage them to sit and reminisce with the patient in spite of not getting any obvious response. Just encourage them to tell the story. "Remember the time when we did this?" Husbands and wives can go back to the beginning of their relationship and over their many years of marriage.

Is the outside helper in the way? Is the dying a private event? Or is it a communal event? If it is a communal event, is the helping person part of the community and their quiet presence a support? I always ask "Would you like me to leave? Would you like me to stay? Would you like me to go in the other room? Would you like time alone?" Most often they don't really know but they will say, "Oh, please stay." Sometimes they will say, "Yes" to the offer to stay in the other room. That is still being there for them."

Oxygen and Suctioning

In long term dying, respiratory failure is often the cause of death. Families want to know whether they should continue with care such as clearing the throat and administering oxygen during the dying process. For the most part it will be more comfortable for the patient if the equipment is removed. They are no longer benefiting from the additional oxygen. In the cases where the patient has been on oxygen for a long time, he may be comfortable with the mask or nose piece. Removing it is sometimes difficult for family members to understand. They see that the dying person is breathing unevenly and think that oxygen will help. You may gently explain that the lungs are not able to take the oxygen into the blood any longer and oxygen equipment is therefore not necessary. For many families this is too difficult. In that case leave the oxygen on. It helps the family more than the dying person.

Suctioning is quite uncomfortable. In the dying process the patient is no longer able to bring up secretions, when suctioning is done it is usually unproductive. You can hear the mucus in the throat but secretions rarely come out when you suction at the dying time because they are down too deep. There are exceptions to this depending on the cause of death. A few patients may have a lot of secretions. Explain gently to the family that part of the dying process is that the lungs fill with fluid. If there are secretions, it helps to turn the patients head to his side to let secretions drain. Put a pad under their head to absorb the secretions. Check to see if the nostrils are opened and not flattened against the pillow or bed.

Have your emotional house in order. If you truly believe it is all right to die regardless of age, when the balance of nature has been overcome, you will convey a calm and accepting manner of the dying activities to the family.

How Does A Dying Person Look?

As the blood flow slows the normal pink color recedes. Some become pasty white. Most become very gray; some with liver disease look bronze. The hollows of the face become sunken and a few perspire. The family often wants to open the window or blow a fan over the patient thinking they are hot. This perspiration is from parasympathetic and sympathetic nervous tension relaxation and not because they are hot. In fact, they are cool because of slowed circulation and you may want to encourage the family to keep a light blanket on them.

Are They In Pain When Dying?

Are some people in pain while they are dying? Yes, some are, and even if in a coma you can tell they experience pain. Let the physician know and be sure to continue the pain medication according to Doctor's orders. Except in unusual cases of pain the patient benefits from touch. We believe they can hear even though they are in a coma. Hearing is the last sense to leave so continue to reassure and encourage them.

What Is Helpful To the Dying Person?

Many patients say the most reassuring thing is not being left alone, so unless they are adamant against it, provide calm, loving company. If the patient is not alert they need to have this presence communicated in some other way, by firm handholding, voice, talking, and singing.

I presented a workshop to nurses and ambulance personnel in Pella, Iowa. Several of the nurses explained how they had to get familiar with the fact that when they heard beautiful singing floating down the hallways it was an indication that a patient's dying time had come. This was a part of the culture of the people but new to the nurses who had just come to that hospital from other parts of the country.

I told this story at one of my classes and a hospice volunteer came back the next week to say she visited her 29 year old patient in an oncology ward at a large Chicago hospital and found her dying. The young husband seemed weary, lonely and faithful as he sat by his wife's bedside. All the talking had been completed long ago. Just the loving presence was needed now. The volunteer asked what would comfort him and he said he wished he could hear a song that was going through his head. She said, "I can't carry a tune, I've never sung, but I know the words and I'll try." She started and sounded awful. The husband joined in quietly to help her and the aide came in to straighten the bed and joined in a full and pleasing voice. A nurse came in to find out what was happening and joined in singing the harmony. The nurse then started a second song and the room began to fill with everyone singing. The nurse and aide left to continue with their work and other visitors and staff came in and started new song after song. This continued most pleasantly for three hours. The hospice volunteer left the room several times and said the sound coming down the hallway was tender, gentle and beautiful. The other patients and their visitors came into the hallways to listen. Some went to the room to sing a while. They all knew Emma's time had come and seemed so glad she was receiving love and comfort.

What Is Helpful To the Primary Caretaker?

Often the caregiver is exceedingly tired. The care of a dying person is demanding with its round-the-clock concerns. If the death results from sudden happenings and the patient has been in the hospital, the family members may have had little or no sleep for days. Primary caregivers often are exhausted. It may not be helpful to articulate to the caregiver how tired they look. Many persons like to think they are fooling everyone including themselves; they want to think that they are making it just fine. Think of how you feel on the days you are very overtired. Yet want to appear in control. Do you find it helpful for someone to tell you how exhausted you look? If someone tells you how tired you look it takes the wind out of your effort. We must realize that their rest may be a high priority to us but it may not be on their priority list at all. Therefore it is not terribly helpful to dwell on that fact with them. Ask, "What is important to you right now? Is rest important?" Then honor their response.

Sometimes the caregiver cannot bear to be away long enough to sleep. Often a volunteer will offer to sit with the dying person and the caregiver will lie down only to be back ten minutes later. That couch or that bedroom is just too far away from the dying person. Kubler Ross said the bed of the dying person should always be large enough so that the caregiver can lie next to the patient and rest. The only real rest they get is lying beside the one who is dying. This is especially true of a Mom or Dad of a dying child. As the helper, give them permission to crawl into the bed and rest. Help them find a way to do this without causing pain to the ill person and to find a comfortable position for themselves. Many persons never think of crawling into bed, even with their mate once they are in a hospital bed, so you need to verbalize permissions. Then, if they awake and the person beside them is dead, they have the comfort of knowing it was a peaceful death because if there had been any struggle they would have awakened. The warm presence of the caregiver is often comforting to the dying person as well.

For those of us working with the dying in the perimeter around metropolitan cities the lonely caregiver is a norm. Our dying persons have moved away from their place of origin years before. Their children live in distant states and now in their dying they have only the mate or if the mate has already died, they may have a caregiver who is a friend. The loyalty of these friends amazes me. We really do need to reach out and support them. One of our patients wanted to die at home. The only person left in his life was a man from his former work place. This man was slightly mentally challenged and his care was loving but not always adequate. It was a difficult decision to leave the dying man surrounded by inadequate loving care in the home where he wanted so badly to be. Love became more important than impeccable care. The temptation was to place him in a nursing home that would guarantee sterility and anonymity. He would have died alone without a primary person but he would have died very clean.

As the dying man became more dependent, this poor caregiver was afraid to leave the apartment to get groceries. Hospice coordinated food for them and help with the care. The caregiver's greatest fear was what to do with his friend's body if he should die during the night. He focused his fears on having the neighbors see the hearse come to pick up the body in the middle of the night so he came to the decision that after his friend died he would go into his bedroom, close the door and wait for morning before calling the mortician. The hospice volunteer encouraged him, that when the death occurred he could stay with his friend's body as long as he wanted. She invited him to call the volunteer to be with him that night and together they would plan calling the mortician. She said she would help him pre-plan with the mortician and coroner today. There is so much value in the presence of a caring objective outsider. Many people are going through all these concerns, fears and worries alone.

The Dying Event

A Peaceful Dying

Some people just sleep away. There is no indication of struggle. For the most part dying of a terminally ill person appears to the objective observer as peaceful. There are breathing changes that can go from 40 very rapid breaths to very slow. There are periods after this that the person does not breathe at all. That can last a few minutes and then the person may start to breathe again. Sometimes they will do this for a while and then go to regular breathing for another day or weeks. At other times they simply do not take another breath. The family may have a tendency to shake the person and say, "Take a breath John, breathe!" As the helping person just gently put your arm on them and explain, this is what needs to be happening now. His breathing will get slower and slower and then stop. This is the body's natural way of slowing down."

The objective observer who sees many deaths may describe it as a peaceful death, but the families rarely find it so. They are unaccustomed to dying and usually think the worst is happening to them. They need your kind reassurance that things are progressing normally and they are doing what is right. They will need to debrief this event with you, because very few people will want to listen to them rerun this incident over and over. Yet that is the nature of grief work. They will dream about this and redo this occurrence in their minds. With your help they can gain confidence, own their strengths and grow through this experience.

The Fighting Death

Some persons put up a real fight in their dying. They are restless to the very end. Something in them seems to fight what is happening. They sometimes get a wild look in their eyes and the eyes roll back in the head as the end draws near. If spoken to, the eyes may give a slight flutter, but usually they stay back, showing the whites and about half of the color. In the deaths where someone fights the eyes have a look of struggle and families say they will never forget that. This is a case where medication can play a role to help in the struggle. Some families take comfort in the fighting death and say, "She was a real fighter in life and she was a real fighter in her dying." Others wonder if this means the person did not accept their dying. Some persons think fright and fear are part of facing the unknown, the dying.

We know that some persons are not accepting and choose to fight but in other cases the reaction may be purely physical. I think one can speculate. Sometimes these speculations bring comfort, but much of what we see may be physiological. The chemistry of their body has changed significantly. The patient may have been very accepting. They may have been emotionally calm and spiritually ready. When the body is deprived of sufficient oxygen and is not totally compensated, the muscles will struggle and twitch. This may be a normal, physical reflex reaction. Anxiety is always present in an oxygen deprived patient. Perhaps some patients are completely unaware of this physical struggle happening.

Bleeding Out Death

The bleeding out deaths seems to be the hardest deaths to watch and cause the most flashbacks and later dreams. They are not, however, necessarily the most difficult death. Often they can be fairly quick and pain free. It is okay to die in that way if it is appropriate to the disease, as in the case of some tumors and cancer. The growing disease tissue absorbs the tissue of a large blood vessel and the blood trickles or gushes out. This can take place anywhere in the body. If it is in the lungs they fill with blood and often blood will come out of the mouth. If it is in the stomach or throat it may appear as bloody vomit. If it is in the bladder or lower intestines it will look like bloody discharge. Remember that a little bit of blood appears to be an enormous amount to lay persons. There may be only a little blood or in some cases a great deal. Just protect the bed with pads, continue to talk to and encourage the dying person as you would in any other death. Yes, it is all right for them to die a bleeding out death and you want to convey it to them. After it is over and again in the weeks and months to come, be aware of other professionals such as the pastor and mortician's need to debrief as well as the friends and family that were present or heard about it.

One young man had a tumor on his jaw. The doctor forewarned the mother saying, "When you see blood trickling out of his jaw which has the open tumor, that is a sign the end is coming." What happened is that the tumor infiltrated into a major blood vessel and he bled out in a few hours and died. Sometimes it is just too hard to watch someone you love slowly bleed out. In this case the mother called for the paramedics. There are some expectations that are just too hard for any of us. The sad thing is that the boy was then moved, lifted, poked and examined. He was hooked up to machines and IVs. This was a discomfort the Mom had hoped to spare him. She needed comforting to know that it was okay to be overwhelmed and that it was mature to take care of her needs in a responsible fashion by calling 911.

Here, too, the value of an objective caring outsider can be easily seen. This is a case in which the mortician had a very difficult time. Morticians are a forgotten profession. He had a son the same age as the boy and was unprepared for the massiveness of the tumor and condition. Those who were close to the family were aware of the need to prepare friends and relatives and could have prepared the mortician for the emotional component of this care. He, too, was a father. It is just that some professionals are not recognized as having personal feelings.

When the death occurs the valve at the top of the stomach relaxes and allows the stomach contents to come up as vomit. The valve on the bladder relaxes and lets the urine flow out. The sphincter relaxes and may leak fluid. Again just protect the bed if appropriate. Many parents tell of the peace they have known when they were holding their child while he died. They say the vomit is no problem whatsoever. They never minded cleaning it up when he vomited in life, and it was a parental privilege to clean it up when he died.

Reactions of the Family

Usually families and friends are controlled, controllably sad, perhaps weeping. Most people are surprised when you tell them they can have time with the body. Most people expect that it will be a hasty move of the body out of the house or hospital room. They usually respond positively and say, "Yes, I would like to stay with him a while. I would like to take my time now." Watch for a natural finishing of the group at the bedside and then set up an expectation that each person including the children will say goodbye in private, while the others gather in the waiting room, hall or other part of the house. There is no need to hurry the body away. You can comfortably wait a few hours for a child or friend who has not yet arrived and would like to say goodbye. In the case of bed to crematorium disposal of the body, there can be a bedside religious ceremony with the pastor and primary persons present. Even in this type of body disposal the body can be released with dignity.

One twelve-year-old's Mother died at 5 a.m. She and her Dad were with Mom. The plan was to take the body immediately to the crematorium but the little girl was not yet ready to release her Mom. She got out her Mother's pretty fuchsia nightgown and put it on her. She brushed and combed her Mom's hair into a pretty hairdo and then put on tasteful makeup. The hospice volunteer arrived and the little girl said she wanted to make her Mother pretty like she always did for her when she was ill. The daughter was unhappy with Mom's nails. By this time the fingers were stiff in a curled position so the hospice volunteer held them as the daughter painted the nails to blend with the gown. Then the little girl heaved a sigh of relief and said, "Mom is ready to go away now." As an afterthought she got a rose from a vase and put it in her Mom's hands. A finishing touch. At that time many friends who had been notified of the death began to arrive. They held a visitation and a beautiful spontaneous service for the Mom at her bedside. At 11:00 A.M. they called the mortician and said, "We are ready." How beautiful. Can you see the value of preplanning the death event? And you can see the value in not hurrying the removal of the body?

If the body is going to be kept extra long, do call the mortician and let him know. Tell him you will call him when the family is done. In the case of long term dying, ideally you would already have been in communication with the mortician and had an idea whether or not they would stay with the body for an extended time. Some morticians want to come immediately and stay nearby but not hurry the family in any way. They feel it is part of there responsibility to be there. There may be some legal concerns as well. This can be managed.

Preparing the Body

Sometimes the family will not be at the bedside, especially in unexpected death. Even though the person is known to be terminal, they are often found dead unexpectedly or it may be someone has called an ambulance and they die in the hospital. I like to make friends with the body before I go in with a family. It is easier on me if I have been by the bedside before. While you are there, place the body in a position of peace. Put a pillow under the head. Put a shirt or gown on. Put the arms in a comfortable position alongside. Cover the lower body with a clean sheet or blanket. You don't have to have everything clean but you may want to wash the face, if appropriate. The room doesn't have to be spic and span. If life saving measures were done there may be a lot of equipment or wrappings around. You don't have to get rid of everything or to wash each drop of blood if that was part of the dying. Families understand this was part of what their loved one experienced. If the body has been mutilated by injury or disease, cover those areas. Some persons like to bandage them and turn the bed or cart so the good side is toward the door

When the family or friends arrive, greet them. Prepare them for what they will see. Answer questions truthfully and honestly and show an expectation that they will want to see the body and say goodbye. Tell them to talk to their friend even though he is dead to give forgiveness or to ask for forgiveness. To give him permission to die now even though you would rather not have him go. Tell him what you appreciate him for, what you will miss him for, and say goodbye. This is the work of grief. In cannot be short circuited by not seeing the body. In fact, not seeing the body can make all of this very unreal and the saying these things very difficult. We are holistic persons and hearing someone is dead does not take the place of seeing they are dead. Until we see their deadness a part of us waits for their return. Seeing the body and doing the initial grief work in the presence of the body is very important and should never be skipped even and especially for children. Make sure the refusal of one person to see the body doesn't mean that is the refusal of each one. Some parents refuse to view the body of their dead child and plan a closed casket. The siblings, however, may need to see the body and say their goodbye. They need an advocate to find out if they wish to be with their dead brother or sister. Go with them. Guide them and debrief with them. The parents are overcome right now and will do delayed grief work.

I always go in the room with a family and model touch and talking. I touch the cheek, stroke the hair and hold the hand and then invite them to do likewise as they talk to him. Then I tell them I will be within calling distance, in the kitchen or at the nurse's desk and for them to take all the time they want. Remember you do not have to be comfortable with all of this. Let your own feelings show and if you have tears, let them fall. But do take your entire beautiful inadequate human and be there for them. Your main task is to give permissions for them to do healthy grief work and to facilitate forgiveness.

Do take the time you need to debrief yourself after you have worked this intimately with a dying situation. Tell your debriefer the story before the night dreams set in. Seek out a peer to check your work and put your emotional house in order by reviewing your motives as a helping person. Get in touch with your higher power. Be kind to yourself. Be gentle with yourself.

Note:

North Central Florida Hospice, Inc. has an article called "Preparing for Approaching Death" that is excellent. I recommend you get a copy of it.

Chapter 7

Pregnancy Loss

When I was asked to be a speaker at the national meeting of NACOG the National Association of Obstetric, Gynecological, and Neonatal nurses at the Hilton convention center, New Orleans, LA, I went to our local chapter of The Compassionate Friends. They put an invitation in the local newspaper explaining my speaking assignment and requested the presence of Father's whose children had died a peri-natal death.

I asked them to come tell me what they wished Nurses and Physicians knew and would do for the next set of parents that had to see what they had to see, had to hear what they had to hear, and had to do what they had to do. I promised to take their suggestions to the National Convention.

We hoped to have at least four in attendance and arranged to use the kitchen table at one of the member's home. Men began to arrive, they filled the kitchen, then the living room, and then the outside porch and others were on the lawn. I had a tape recorder and went from one to the other for a couple of hours. The Compassionate Friends and the local OB department nurses and I condensed their message to this presentation which I shared at the National Convention.

Our purpose as health care workers is to provide a framework wherein the grieving persons may process the emotional injury of pregnancy loss towards healing. The most difficult task of pregnancy loss is to make that loss tangible in a society that does not permit the time to be with the product of conception in order to validate its existence. It is a society that does not provide a ritual by which to mobilize the pent up emotions of the mourners toward healthy venting of free flowing grief. in a society that does not allow liberal opportunities to talk about the hopes, fantasies, confusion, feelings of guilt, and betrayal, as they attempt to move toward a philosophy of life that gives meaning to suffering and loss. They grieve in a society that does not provide realistic hope for their healing, does not provide a belief that these mourners of pregnancy loss will incorporate this experience into their representational model of self and be willing to see themselves as bereaved parents who can realistically hope to invest in child-love again.

We as helping persons are in a potent place to encourage healthy mourning for these grievers who are unprepared by coping patterns to know how to mourn. In our death-less society, many parents of peri-natal loss have had no previous experience with death. Many had never attended a wake or a funeral, much less seen, or touched a dead body. They do not have the ingredients to make healthy decisions for themselves, for the grandparents of the baby, or the siblings. They are persons in crisis, ill equipped to make informed decisions even with verbal and written material given to them. They cannot handle more than a couple of concepts at a time. These parents say to me that they wish in retrospect, that someone had set up an expectation for them. Letting them know what has been healthy to other parents whose baby had died. They wish someone had permitted and encouraged them to take time in their decision. They wish they had opportunities to change their mind after making decisions hastily without weighing all the variables.

A Real Event Has Occurred

With an understanding of the normal dynamics of grief and the tasks that must be done by peri-natal grievers, the helping person can be a significant instrument toward healing grief. Reality must be affirmed. A real event has occurred. The lives of this woman, man, siblings, and grandparents have changed drastically. Yesterday their world was sunshine, hope, full of nesting activities. They were in the mainstream of life. Everyone on the street smiled knowingly, sales people chortled, friends gave showers of clothing, hope, and teasing, fantasies played with the children of their mind. These families were busy yesterday re-arranging houses, rooms, and decorations. Mother's body was stretching to widths she could not fathom, their sex life altered with meaning and purpose of pregnancy. She was learning strange ways of walking, sitting, clothing, sleeping, and eating. Yesterday he was reveling in the father-hood that had already changed their lives even before he had seen his child's face. So many parenting chores had busied their lives, money had been allocated, neighborhood carefully chosen, relatives were involved in anticipatory fantasy concerning real, live, baby in utero.

Suddenly Shunned

They were welcomed everywhere, friends, salespersons, relatives, and work associates, all welcomed them. Suddenly within minutes their world changed. Nurses shun them, come in to do their duty and leave quickly. Doctors speak in medical-ease, relatives say, don't talk about it. Work associates act as though there never had been previous conversations about changed-lifestyle-with-baby. Everything is so distorted now, money still allocated but no product seen except confusing pain, casket, and cemetery lot. Gone: The constant chatter of "When the baby comes," replaced by empty silence of the womb-tomb. Persons speak to them in unfamiliar, hushed tones, saying unfamiliar things as, you may have anything you want in a funeral. They feel confused wondering, "How can I know what I want? None of my thoughts were about funeral style." All of their preparations for this event are inappropriate, all their dreams, fantasies, reading by the volume, patient education courses, classes attended, notes carefully written and categorized, no help to them now.

They wonder what to do now? "How can we change thinking within minutes, thoughts blend while awake and asleep, come all mixed together with funerals and cheery layettes." They have no coping patterns for healthy mourning. Their former coping patterns no longer work. They have not yet developed ways of coping with this unexpected foreign way of living with death. No one wants to listen to their attempts to make sense out of agony.

They struggle to change their thinking from, "What about the nursery? To what do other parents do for a casket?" They wonder, "Do other parents hold their dead baby? Can we give her a name? Will she be in heaven when I get there? Will Grandma take care of her in heaven and give the parent love that I so long to give. Will a funeral service be silly for a person that lived outside the womb for so short a time? But she did live so close to us that she shared in our bed and lovemaking."

Need a Cultural Ritual

Every part of the parent's being cries out for a cultural ritual to provide a healthy framework to know this child that has no face. They need a ritual that reflects the wisdom of a society to develop a framework in which to heal. Now they need societies care because they are grief injured and need Mothering and Fathering for their own hurting self. They need options, yes, but within a framework that has been developed, tested, and evaluated by a society whose minds were unencumbered by personal grief. Those who evaluate could therefore think with objectivity.

Newly bereaved parents think, "You tell me that I can choose? That it is up to me, that I can have it any way I want. What is it I want? Oh, I want to run away, to get away from this tragedy. I want to scream so loud I drown out the awfulness of the words you are saying. I don't want to hear, she is dead. I want to hold my hand over my ears and scream, No more. Leave me alone, please. Don't come with more pain of deadness, mutilation, contractures, hypos, IV needles, incisions, cold little body, casket urns, funeral. No I don't want to see that. Who would? Really if not looking is a viable option, then I will take it. Too much is just too much." These parents are crying out for loving guidance through a healing ritual.

They need you, a loving, caring, person unafraid of the intense feelings they are feeling now. They are persons in crisis. Persons in crisis cannot do serial judgment making, they cannot keep more than a couple of thoughts in the forefront of their mind. These parents ask, "What do you mean weigh options, I can't remember what they were. When you said, bring clothes to bury her in, I thought of the dozens of diapers I have. I didn't hear the rest of what you said. What do other parents whose child died do? I never talked to parents of a dead baby. You see, I followed the culture's mores and evaded those conversations, I avoided those parents, I thought they needed privacy, really I didn't want them to confirm my own fear that babies die sometimes."

Parenting a Child Who is Dead

How does one parent a child who is dead? If the dead child were 16 years old we would know the task of parenting. Parenting tasks are, to treat the body with dignity in death just as we treated it with dignity in life. Parents must ascertain the deadness of the baby in order to be sure that burial is the best parenting they can do now. Deadness must be confirmed in order to go on with life while neglecting parenting tasks such as feeding, clothing, and fondling the child. Only the surety of this Child's deadness can make this neglect okay. Parenting the dead child means to give him a physical place, it might be an urn, a grave, or a memorial plaque. Parenting the dead child means to close that child's life, say goodbye to him, forgive him and ask forgiveness of him, to say the regrets.

Need to Concretize

The parents need to say the hopes and fantasies so that they may be concretized and laid to rest with the body of their baby. The laying to rest of the fantasies and hopes takes a long time and is part of the grieving process. It helps them to put together a photo album, collages of memorabilia and tapes of special messages, songs, and funeral services. Journaling is also very helpful, it is good to put into writing the story and worth of baby's life, the gift of his presence, and the value to them because he came and was with them for a little while. This helps them process toward making meaning of the loss.

Reality starts to take concrete form once they are able to verbalize the parenting words that make sense out of what they are feeling. Healing for them is to hear their own words, such as, "My daughter had the cord around her neck," or, "My son died one hour after his birth." This helps them affirm reality by taking ownership of their parentage and loss. Only after they have identified what it is that is lost can they begin the difficult tasks of developing a philosophy of life to make meaning of loss. Then they can incorporate the meaning of the loss into the representational model of self and say, I am a parent of children who have died, I am okay.

If the pain is only a floating sensation of non-descript agony, it is very difficult to resolve. But if the pain is a result of a known loss confined to time and space, it is much easier to process it and in time to let go.

Grief Healing Takes Time

Grief work takes a long time. This journey of grief work takes years. It is a high risk journey of many pitfalls and causalities. For those who make it their lives are richer, more developed, and more beautiful. They have a zest for love and life that can only be obtained through an acknowledgement of the reality of death and the value of life. Our tasks as helping persons to those who mourn is to assist them through healing grief.

What do I mean by healing grief? I do not mean getting over missing those children of pregnancy loss. If they have bonded to their child of unknown face, they will always miss that child. The acuteness of that missing will be at times throughout their years as they go through their life's changes. And it will still be there when they are old, old, ladies or old, old, men. If the culture insists that they not speak it out loud, the parents will obey, but at the significant times of life they will remember this dead child. In five years they will be saying, "Ah, he would be going to kindergarten now." Or later on they will say, "Now, it is 18 years and he would be considering college." It is not uncommon to hear a dying patient mourn, "My daughter died when she was two days old. She would be 41 years old now and she would help me with my infirmities if she were still alive." The dead are always with us and that is okay. The task of these parents is to learn to live with their dead in a culture that is alien to the dead. Pregnancy loss is a culturally unworthy loss. "It is in secret I love, and in silence I grieve."

Then how do we define healing grief? If forgetting the dead child is not the objective of healing grief, what is? By healing grief we mean to develop coping patterns to live life fully with the memory of and the gifts of the pregnancy experience but without a physical presence of the child. Healing from grief includes a willingness to invest in love again, not instead of, but in addition to the love of the past. That is why there is no such thing as a replacement child. Just as in marriages, there is no such thing as a replacement marriage. There is then a second marriage. The same is true of one's parents, you do not have a replacement Father, you have two Fathers, the second Father is a step-Father, an adopted Father, or a foster Father. Parents have subsequent children, they have a second baby, their first living child, or a fifth child, their fourth living child, the third child died at birth.

Tangible Symbols

Because we are physical beings we need tangible things in our grief. That is why a donation to charity doesn't do the same thing for us as a dish of food, mowing a lawn, driving the children to the funeral parlor, praying with someone, or a gift of flowers does. As support persons we instantly recognize the mourners need to feel, touch, smell, and taste the symbol of their community's empathy. The symbol also validates that something serious really did happen to cause this confusion.

The very most difficult aspect of pregnancy loss is making it tangible in a world that is totally, unaware of the intensity of that loss. The world has never seen this child; the world didn't know his name. They never experienced the child as life, yet, the parents have. Parents and siblings of the peri-natal griever wonder, "What died? Which dreams and hopes died? Who is it that has gone? Why all these changes in Mommy's body and emotions? Why do people treat us differently now?"

The parents wonder, "How do we mourn someone whose personality was only a hope? How do we incorporate the meaning of being parents to this dead child who has no face? Yet, we were parents; it did happen. Our lives have changed. There is nothing to show for this change that was so central to our being that even our sexual response has been affected. How can we rectify all of this while complying with societies demand that we wash our faces, design nice hairdos, dress stylistic and respond to inquires with, I am doing fine, thank you?" Or "It is really for the best. Hell, it is."

How Can We Help?

How can we help? We as lovers and helping persons can help in the most potent of ways. It is as simple as giving permissions to mourn in a way that is most helpful and meaningful to this couple and their siblings. The first act that parents have to do is to concretize the realities of pregnancy product. They have to do this in order to give meaning to all that has happened to them. It is necessary to bond with the dead baby so they can lay the baby to rest in a grave or an urn. One cannot say good-by to that which one cannot find.

Fathers Present At Difficult Births

The Fathers want to be encouraged to exercise the option to be present at the birthing even when the birth is difficult, even when the Mother will be under anesthesia, even when the baby is known to be dead, deformed, or mutilated. They say that not to be given the option to be present at birth is a denial of their Fatherhood. They want to have clear information about what to expect. Fathers tell us they want the option and the time to change their decision. They tell us the opportunity to refuse is very helpful and later if they did refuse; they know they were given a choice and that helps them in accepting what is. Providing them the option is a way of returning power to them in an otherwise powerless situation.

Hold the Dead Baby

Both Mothers and Fathers want the opportunity to hold their babies when they are born dead or die in the delivery place. They need to be encouraged to call the baby by name and to feel it while it is still warm and pliable. They want to know all of its body, to know their babies good and normal features to reassure them as potential baby makers again. They want to know the deformed parts well so the night dreams and fantasies can be checked against reality. The task of these parents is to make friends with the deformity so as to give them reason for the death. They need to know the deformity well so they can check this out when considering future baby making. Reality is never as bad as fantasy, remember we are all products of our society and we have all seen many horror pictures.

Show the Dead Baby

I show a baby that is dead in the same way I show a live baby. I hold it and cuddle it. I touch all parts of it and help the parents to get comfortable with the baby who is dead by my own modeling. The parents need to be encouraged to take the time to be with the baby after it dies. Sometimes there are medical reasons to hurry this up, but in that case they need a clear statement as to what the reason is. They want it explained simply, a sentence or two at the time of need and re-explained in greater detail later. They would like the later explanation in about three weeks after the death takes place. Parents tell us they cannot remember details, they cannot assimilate the necessity of what to do and the expectations that are set forth. Later they want the details. These are intelligent persons and grief work must be done at the growth and development level of each individual. Therefore they need data to make sense out of what happens. They need a return visit to ideally be with the same helping person that was involved in the incident. This is imperative for healthy grief work. In about three weeks they have the questions they were not able to formulate during the crisis time. In three weeks serial judgment begins to return and they begin to assimilate more than a couple of thoughts at a time. They can take in more information now.

Parenting a Dying Baby

If the baby is known to be dying the parents tell us they want to be given the option to hold the baby in it's dying, even when it is attached to apparatus. They would like the option of being with the baby when it dies. One newly delivered Mom told of how she sat with her baby for seventeen hours as her baby was dying. In this way she mothered her baby as completely as she could until her infant died. Then she mothered her baby in death and through burial. If the baby is in the dying process, the parents say they would like us to take the baby out of the apparatus to die in the arms of it's Mom or Dad. They say they want to fully parent that baby through its dying, death, burial, or cremation. This is a bit foreign to us to think of parenting our children when they are dead. But there are parenting task for dead children. The great anthropologist, Mandelbaum speaks about the tasks of all societies to decide, how to deal with the dying, how to support the grievers and how to bury the dead. The task of burying a child is a parental responsibility over-shadowed by a community responsibility.

The parents need to hear permissions said out loud, such as, "You may stay here with your baby, but if you are tired you may go back to rest. Would you like us to call you and have you come if the baby dies while you are gone? Would you like to say good bye before you leave? Do tuck your baby in." Have both parents tuck their baby in before they leave the nursery. Say to them, "Give your baby permission to die while you are gone if that is necessary for him to do." Call your baby by name; tell him you will return and that you will see him later if he is still here. Tell him if he needs to go in the meantime that you will see him *then*. Then represents whatever eternity means to the parents. Use their word for it. All of this is necessary to concretize pregnancy loss. These are concrete memories by which to re-affirm their potential positive parenting in what looks to all the world like failed parenting.

Photo's of the Dead Child

Photos are so precious to these parents. They treasure them and often keep the originals in a locked box. Parents suggest the following as helps for newly bereaved parents. "Do take pictures, always." They tell us that no matter how bad you think the child looks, even when it is attached to machines, they want pictures. One parent told of her prized picture of her a-cephalic son, David. She brought to the hospital a little suit and a bonnet. The nurse put the bonnet on him and took pictures. She told me emphatically that it was her son! That she gave birth to him and it is her belief that she will be with him in heaven. She needed to make peace with his existence and the fact of his deformity. We cannot take away that task from her. Mourners are impelled to spend hours and hours thinking and remembering to make sense out of this tragedy. While she is doing this she has a picture to show that she was indeed a good mother to her special child. She feels that she gave him birth, baptism, and clothing. She knows that she treated his deformed body with dignity, and she gave him a proper burial. This is the task of good parenting.

The parents tell us they would like us to give them the option to see the pictures and if they refuse to please give them time. Let them know you will keep the pictures and other memorabilia for six months. Tell them they can call to claim these at any time. Many of the parents said they refused at first but returned to collect them and are very grateful that they were kept. Remember this is a grief where so little is retrievable. If we can give them anything, it is wonderful. The parents who talked to me said, "Please don't wait too long to take the pictures. In a pre-mature baby there is a big change in two hours. Some of the pictures show the baby as skeletons because the liquid has drained to the bottom of the body." The parents prize these pictures very much, but they also remember the child as more plump immediately after birth. One lady talked of her triplet sons wrapped in cuddly blue blankets. Someone took pictures of them in the nude. These are the only precious pictures she has. She wishes that someone would have thought to take pictures of them cuddled in their blue blankets as well. Pictures of babies in life-threatening distress should be taken while they are on the machines. It is a good thing to suggest to parents that they bring their cameras to take pictures before the baby is transferred to a specialty hospital.

Funeral

When the product of pregnancy is not seen, there is nothing tangible to affix one's vision in order to understand the changes that occurred in their household, the way people treat them, and how they feel emotionally. The value of the funeral service as a ritual of passage is noted in all societies. It is important that we do not inadvertently deny these parents the ritual of this passage in their lives.

Parents have suggested ways that the funeral can be made more meaningful to those who have suffered pregnancy loss. First of all, they want both parents to be part of the funeral preparation. The funeral director can come to the hospital. The parents can dress the baby at the hospital for its trip to the funeral home. If the Mother cannot attend the wake or funeral the casket can be brought to the hospital to be placed in a special room or the chapel. There is no need to hurry the funeral. The casket may have to be closed, but the funeral, memorial service and internment can be delayed until the Mother is able to be part of the activity. Many times you can bring all of the activity to her in the hospital and wait the interment until she can be dismissed from the hospital. There are times when a Mother is able to leave the hospital for awhile to attend the funeral and then return to the hospital for her medical care.

Parents Want Us to Know*

Fathers need to have the option to stay over night at the hospital. Siblings need to have a meaningful part of all rituals, they need to have the situation explained and re-explained in their words. Parents need to draw the siblings close and share their grief.

Official notice that an infant has died for this Mother in this bed should be very obvious. Parents tell of receiving happy-mail of congratulations and samples for the baby. Advertisers have been given their mail address and keep sending to their houses. Sometimes congratulations arrived six months later.

These parents need loving, gentle teaching about the long term grief dynamics of peri-natal grief. They need to know about: phantom crying they will hear in the night, their chances for future successful pregnancy, how long to wait before they begin another child. They need to know how to deal with their own response at seeing pregnant Mothers and hearing babies. Many felt that this was difficult. The reality is that a part of the female population will always be pregnant and there will always be babies in the world. This is true in the personal lives of these parents as well.

What they need to do is not use avoidance unnecessarily but learn to cope with their strong feelings. They need information on how to process loss while getting their own needs met. Some times avoidance may be helpful for a short period of time and only under guidance. They need to hear from you hope of their future enjoyment in life and their future ability to share in the happiness of other people.

Memorabilia Parents Want Collected.

Provide and gather as much memorabilia as possible to confirm the life and death of the baby in order to enhance comfort, communication, loving relationships between parents and children.

- Lock of hair
- Arm band bracelet
- Name tag
- Blanket the baby was wrapped in
- Footprints
- Birth certificate
- Baptismal certificate
- Death certificate

- Hello and good-bye letter from parents, siblings, and grandparents
- Toys bought in anticipation for his birth
- Special flower--the rose bud is the most often used
- Clothing special to this baby
- Baptismal dress
- Funeral card
- Memory book
- Marker for the grave
- Member plaque or urn
- Collage with other memorabilia

When these are gathered together and time is given to go through the rituals of saying good-bye, looking at the body, holding the baby, attending the funeral and internment ceremonies, the event is concretized. It affirms that something intense actually did take place in their lives. Now they can separate this feeling from subsequent pregnancies and birth. This experience can be dealt as a separate process and healed.

The effects of pregnancy loss are long term. If this loss is incorporated into the representational model of self in a healthy way parents and siblings can re-invest in love again. If the loss is not resolved, ominous fear hovers over their heads and colors all their love-actions and thoughts. If the baby's existence and death is not thoroughly assimilated the family cannot let go. Sexual activity is paired with loss and pain. Subsequent children are raised by grieving parents who confuse feelings for the dead child and the live child. It is important that the dead child be known, have a clear identity, and that its own name be specific to that baby. Then other loves can remain distinct.

Being comfortable with your own feelings in a death setting, showing expectancy that others will process the grief in a healthy manner, giving the permission to feel and grieve in the way that is best for them, is a beautiful gift to give. The benefits of your intervention are helpful now and can provide the family with a basis that they can use to invest in life and love fully again. This is indeed a potent position for a helping person.

The Compassionate Friends

At this time I would like to express how deeply I appreciate the sharing from the members of The Compassionate Friends of the Fox Valley Chapter in Aurora Illinois. They gathered and told me what they wished helping persons knew about pregnancy loss and the need of bereaved parents.

Chapter 8

Sexual Needs of the Dying and Grieving

Marriage Problems Are Really Grief Reactions

Many marriage problems are really grief reactions. Couples suffer unnecessarily thinking there is something wrong with the love they have for each other. If they understood these dynamics they would comfort, encourage, and be patient with their partners.

When couples experience stress and changes in their sexual relationship they frequently allude to these problems while talking to a friend. You may find that you are that friend. It is difficult for people to discuss sexual feelings therefore, the probability is low that they will seek professional help. If you are unable to respond to a friend's needs and concerns with hope for an adequate sexual adjustment, chances are there will be no help. I invite you to read this presentation from the perspective of a friend.

Sexual Adjustment of Bereaved Couples

Stress affects interpersonal relationships and may necessitate the adjustment of sexual activities as well as other aspects of a relationship. Sex is sometimes thought of as being synonymous with orgasm however, when we consider the sexual needs of a human we must consider all facets of what it means to be a sexual being. There is a need for a healthy masculine or feminine self-image, for touching, hugging, cuddling, and being close. There is also a rhythm of intercourse fulfillment among couples. Grief produces stress which has a significant impact on these interactions. Changes in sexual responses confuse not only the affected person but also the mate.

Purpose

In this chapter I will be discussing the dynamics of sexual needs as it relates to the roles of supportive friends, caregivers, and helpers. I will include examples of sexual adjustments that occur during the change process and will conclude with an exercise you can use to recommend to others as well as facilitate your own sexual communication.

Personal Death Awareness; Personal Sex Awareness

Sexual Self Awareness

It is understood that to work with the dying and grieving the support person must first come to terms with their personal death awareness. We who support others need to get comfortable with our own discomfort about dying and grief before we reach out to others. Our personal agenda needs to be familiar, comfortable, and clear, otherwise our own material will frighten us enough so that we avoid the person's grief. The same is true for personal sex awareness. Our own sex agenda needs to be familiar and comfortable to us before we can support others who are dealing with sexual adjustment. Then the therapeutic listener is clear what their agenda is and what the other person's agenda is.

Academic or Humorous about Sex

In America we can be academic or humorous about sex but, it is not acceptable to be personal. We cannot talk about our emotions as we go through life's changes. Our society considers it acceptable to use sexual humor to reduce tensions but it is not acceptable to speak honestly about sexuality.

One of the difficulties is that Americans tend to think of themselves as sexually liberated. Although we frequently talk about sex we seldom talk about our own sexual feelings and concerns. People feel more at ease if I tell an off color joke than they do when I say, "I like sex," or declare, "I would be distraught if I lost my sexual response because of the drugs I have to take or because of this illness, surgery, aging or grief that I am experiencing."

We know that being sexual is the essence of being human. That sexual adjustment takes place at every stage of life. It occurs when we are prescribed a drug for illness, go through a grief experience, body mutilation, or body changes from surgery. In all of these events we have to adjust our sexual self-image and sexual interactions. Yet that is not something we talk about with other people. We do not ask, "What is going on with me? What is going on with my partner? How do others handle similar situations?"

This denial of personal emotional adjustment to sex means there is less help available for the average person, yet the need of adjusting sexually is still there. I am not talking about pathological sexual adjustment. I am talking about normal people who have had to alter their life style and self-images because of illness, aging, and mutilation. I am discussing human concerns that we all share as human beings.

Dr. Granger Westberg said we have given up our willingness to give advice that comes from our human understanding in favor of recommending that everyone go to a specialist. This is sad because it forces the majority of people to go through these changes alone without sharing helpful information. No one listens. The vast majority of people do not go to a sex specialist. We have given up much of our birthright to provide caring interaction.

Not a Sex Therapist

I am not recommending that a caregiver be sex therapist. That is a special profession. I am talking about caring listening that can be the catalyst which makes the difference between sexual adjustment and sexual tension after someone has been mutilated, deformed, weakened, or is dying.

This is not presented as a how to fix someone's problems or to cure them. What I will be discussing are some of the normal dynamics around sexual adjustments so that when you listen you will be able to listen with hope, not with answers, that you will listen with the belief that somehow they will see this through. That you will exude a conviction that sex is a valued part of the human condition and that it is important to suggest processes and adjustments so that both parties receive pleasuring. We start with accepting the premise that sexual activity is for the pleasuring of one another and that this is at the heart of what it means to be a couple. Remember that sometimes your greatest asset is your mere presence. Bear in mind that you are needed because you are there, not because you are a specialist.

You, the Wounded Healer

Help is given by the person next to the receiver at the time of need. It comes from the neighbor, co-workers, bartender, hair dresser, and friend. This material is presented to you as someone who will be, often inadvertently, supporting others in identifying their sexual adjustments while offering them encouragement. Either you meet your friends need to talk and discuss this issue or chances are he will live and die without the opportunity of having someone listen to his concern.

If you experienced sexual adjustment in your own life you will find that you are suddenly aware that it exists in the lives of many people around you. That is natural. For those people who had a child die, they suddenly become aware of many bereaved parents. Once you have been sensitized to a need you see a world of similar struggles. That is because you now have the gift of grief and that means insights, compassion, and understanding that come as a result of your personal struggle. This is not to say that you had to go through the same struggle to be a therapeutic presence to another. You do not.

It is the nature of human beings to need other people. Support groups meet a real need in today's society. We are grateful for their existence. Many people would benefit by being a part of a support group but do not attend. These people need special outreach.

Sensitized to a Special View

My husband and I adopted children. We searched for information for over a year. We looked for information on how to, with whom, differences in adoption procedures and results. It was like talking a foreign language to most people. Eureka! Success! We had two wonderful adopted children. Now it seemed that everyone we met had an adopted child or relative who adopted. Information was suddenly everywhere. My daughter lost a finger at the age of three. Suddenly everyone I talked to experienced someone who lost a finger. From that I gained insight about care, coping skills, and hope for my daughter's ability to have a useful hand.

So it is with the call for sexual adjustment support. The world acts as though the need does not exist. Once you are sensitized through the reading of this material and other sources you will see the need everywhere. Yes, we live in a stratified society and view the world through our own experiences, our rose colored glasses. Some of us have the gifts of grief to see the colors of loss and adjustment in the world.

Granger Westberg's diagram of who is the caregiver shows 60% of the care at the time of need is given by the person next to you, 30% is provided by a first level helping person such as a minister, nurse or teacher and only 10% of help is received is by a specialist in that field. He noted that the distribution of money for education and equipment by government, churches, and insurance is proportionally the opposite with only 10% of the money provided for education to the lay public. Yet lay people are the ones providing most of the support. It behooves us to provide them with educational tools, insights, and information for the good work they are doing in sex adjustment.

Who gets help from a specialist for sexual adjustment? To whom would you go to get help if you chose to have it? When we talk about sex and dying we are combining two taboos. We are not supposed to talk about our feelings concerning either one. It is very difficult to get help in an area of taboo. Think, if you have a brother who is caring for a dying mate and he wants information on their changing sexual adjustments, who would you recommend they go to? If you cannot come up with one resource person to send someone in need to, the chances are that those struggling with sexual adjustment as part of the dying or grief experience are not going to get help from anyone.

Your Emotional Preparation

Faith and Hope are often only in the person that stands beside someone who is in need. When a catastrophic event occurs the victim's world is shattered. The spirit that emanates from someone who stands quietly by with faith and hope is different than the energy that emits from someone standing by in shock and horror. The person that stands beside emits hope that somehow the victim will have the inner resources to see this through. It is hope that is not for happiness but hope for acceptance. Hope that the victim will find a joyful approach to life even with their loss.

Sixteen year old Girl Paralyzed

I had a teenage daughter at home when I worked in the emergency department. The ambulance brought in a 16 year old girl who was lying on a cart. She was beautiful. She was brought in from a gym class. It appeared she had a spinal lesion and was likely to be paralyzed. Believe you me, that was one quiet emergency department! She was alert, saw everything that went on, could not move a finger or a toe. Everyone walked around hushed, deeply pained. It was devastating. We had to keep her with us while stabilizing her for transfer. Each of us went to her one by one and stood quietly, touching her, stroking her, fiddling with her tubes, just to pass caring energy. In memory it is still one of the saddest days of my life. We waited for her parents and when they came we met them with such sorrow.

Then I was gifted. I was assigned to sexual re-adjustment studies in a rehabilitation unit at a veteran's hospital. There were 100 men and only a few women. All were paralyzed. Some were quadriplegic and some were paraplegic. My assignment was to be their nurse for the day. The protocol for the rehabilitation department was: The nurse would greet the patient with, "Hi, I am Clarice, your nurse for this shift. What are your goals and objectives for today and how do you see me fitting into them? In what way can I help you?" This approach is different than in other areas of the hospital.

This is a wonderful philosophy for a support person. If you go with an agenda you may or may not be correct. In rehabilitation nursing we were taught, "The client is not sick; they are disabled, there is a significant difference. We do not impose goals and objectives on them. This is their life and their home. They just happen to live in our institution right now. It is still their home.

22 Years Old and Impotent Now

My first client was 22 years old and very angry. He was suffering from a recent injury. He said, "My brother never married, he never will marry, he is forty years old. I was a late in life baby and my whole purpose for being conceived was to carry on my father's name. Now I will never reproduce a child!" The young man was so frustrated and angry.

What I learned from the disabled people was that when I asked them their goals for the day I was met with such enthusiasm for the days events. "I am going into the swimming pool; I just can't wait to get into the water." "This is what I will do in the pool. The way you can be helpful is to help me at this point, and you can help me with this maneuver." One said, "Today is the day I get my paint brush. I have always wanted to do art work. I got this new gadget. Will you fit it over my arm? The brush goes into this slot. That feels firm. Let me see if I can draw a line." There was such joy on his face as he watched the picture appear on the canvas from the brush which was attached over his limp hand. I wondered why the disabled people responded with such joy because I was feeling just awful. Then I became aware that his focus was on the sturdy brush and my focus was on the limp hand. I was grieving. He had accepted.

The next client was a twenty eight year old man. When I introduced myself he responded quietly with, "Today is the anniversary of my accident. It is eight years." They always remember that day! After he worked that issue through he said, "Today is a special day! I am going to drive the van today." He was a quad and could do very little. With the slightest stimuli his body responded by going into severe spasms. In dressing him we had to wait for the spasms to pass. It took four of us to dress him because the spasms were so intense. Getting him up into the chair and all his special braces and gadgets fitted was time consuming and a lot of work.

Once in the special wheel chair, he said, "Thank you very much," and he was off like a shot. He went down the hall to the elevator, out the door to the van, used a gadget to fit his key in the door, pressed a button, the lift extended out and down, on he went up to the driver's area. There was no seat. He locked the wheel chair in, hit all the special buttons on the van, and drove like a son-of-a-gun all around downtown Chicago. I was terrified. He was a good driver. He was as powerful as anyone else on the road and most of the other drivers were unaware that this assertive sometimes aggressive driver was a quadriplegic who could not even dress himself.

I learned that there was hope. The newly paralyzed coming into the unit could not see hope. Many wished they would have died in the accident. Many wanted to die now. Some family members and friends sincerely thought it might have been better had the paralyzed person died and even prayed it might still happen. It took about a year after the accident for them to glean any hope. For those that came to acceptance, life was exciting, full of purpose and value.

What You Can Offer

Do you think I was the same when I went back to the local hospital? Do you think I reacted emotionally the same way the next time a paralyzed person was brought in from an accident? No. Now I knew there was hope and I had faith that with lots of intelligent help and love there could be a meaningful life ahead.

There is no way I would have said to those parents of the sixteen year old girl, "This is not so bad. Your daughter can still have a full life with both value and love as a complete part of her experience." I would not say that because this is not the time. They could only look at the very real tragedy that had occurred to her body and her dreams. Each loss would have to be identified and grieved, then the long process of rehabilitation and the redevelopment of a self-image that will be very different from the one that she had before the accident and very different than the one her parents had for her. Only then could she begin to fantasize a future that she could step into with great effort. However, there is a difference in the way one stands beside someone with hope and faith then when one stands beside in despair. We emit a different energy; a different light shines out from us.

That is what we can offer people when it comes to their changing sexual self-image as they adjust to the changes in their life and their partner's life. You do not need to give them much information and they do not even have to tell you a lot about their struggle. It is healing for them to sense in you, "Ah, I understand, your concern is real."

If you know some of the dynamics of sexual adjustment around grief and dying, and if you have thought out your values around them you will listen from a different perspective. You just have to value their concern, their adjustment, pass on your encouragement, and give the gentle permissions such as, "It is alright to crawl in bed with her. It is alright to cuddle and caress him."

Family Systems Approach

I will be writing about family care. Not just about the person with the difficulty because we always do a systems approach. We care for families who have a person with a disability among them.

This is especially a challenge with families who have a terminally ill person amongst them. The well partner is grieving the loss of their past self-image as well as their past sex activity. These are culturally unworthy concerns when a partner is dying; therefore they are unspoken and struggled with in silence, alone. It is important to be aware of these concerns and make a proper assessment. In the dying process the well partner is going through an assortment of adjustments. Very quickly they wonder, "What is changing about my sexual self-image? I never thought of this before." The sex patterns with the dying mate change because of immobility, drugs, apparatus, and odor. The well partner begins to fear the future. If their partner is impotent or terminal they wonder if they can live without sex, they worry about entering the singles world again.

Dying can be an instant, one hour, a day, a month, year, five years, or a ten year event. These changes occur over a long period of time. Some people even go through a pregnancy and birth before the mate dies. For those who are disabled this is a lifetime. Once you understand that this is a long time it will help to understand this material.

No Easy Way to Say

There is no easy way to say, "I am concerned about my sexual behavior and sexual capability. I wonder how it will be affected by this experience?" There is just no easy way to say, "I like being sexy. I like feeling my sexual response to someone. I like being sexually attractive to the opposite sex. This is delightful to me. I would be concerned and feel bad if this illness, surgery, emotional upset, or injury took away these feelings from me."

No One Responds Sexually to Me Anymore

We cannot freely voice the concern, "If I were to lose the sense of feeling sexy and attractive I would feel terrible." Even though the need is common to all people the cultural taboo of expressing personal feelings about sex causes contradictions which bring difficulty to people when they want sexual advice.

People worry and think, "Because of grief and stress my sexual responses are not the same as they were before." Or a woman thinks, "Men are less responsive to me sexually than they were before. This is a loss I mourn. It is very difficult for me to handle. I care about my femininity and what is going to happen to me. I care about my mate's sexuality and what is going to happen to my mate. I worry about our sexual adjustment to these changes."

There is no easy way to say, "I like being sexy." If you don't believe that, say it at the next party you attend.

Need to Feel Acceptable

One of the basic human needs is to feel acceptable to members of the opposite sex. This is a growth and development task. It still needs to be fulfilled at the age of ninety. When it comes to elderly people, handicapped persons, debilitated persons, we neuter them. We take away their male and female roles and we think of them as, "Its."

As a helping person there are some things you can do. You can seek out male and female attributes to mention. To find out what is an appropriate male or female attribute, look at their age and decide in what decade they were ten years old. People are acculturated at the age of ten. They may pick up the new mannerisms at a later age but they have to deal with the difference. They are still emotionally affected by what was appropriate when they were ten years old.

Holding the door or coat for a lady is a male role play for an older gentleman. That may not be an affirming role behavior for a younger gentleman, but something is. It is common to see a feeble old man intending to hold the coat or door for a female companion, while someone from church, a granddaughter, or a health care assistant rushes past his outstretched arm and says, "Here, I will get the door for you." The older man is frustrated because he was already reaching to open the door. She has just emasculated him. Her behavior spoke louder than words, "I have neutered you." A young man might let her do it because he was not acculturated the same way, so he receives the act graciously. Often we see family or a helping person treating a dying man like a little boy, assuming physical deterioration is accompanied by mental regression.

If you are a woman with an older, sick, feeble, dying man who wants to hold your coat or the door for you, let him. He may be slow in opening the door or helping with your coat, but what you are saying by your behavior is, "I recognize your maleness, even though you are old, even though you are feeble, even though you are dying. I respect your masculinity."

Female Beauty

In some ways it is easier to affirm the sexual role of women. We compliment women easier and have numerous words to describe a pretty dress or robe. In the hospital this is easy because women wear pretty bed clothing, fix their hair, and put on makeup. However for a man there is not much variety. After you have commented on the striped pajamas, and then the checkered pajamas, and then the plain colored ones, you are at a loss about what to say.

However, in our society we do not usually describe a female as pretty if she is over the age of twenty five, but caring people see beauty in all ages. It may be easy and good to praise the appearance of a woman's clothing and accessories, but she needs appreciation of her person as well. Choose some characteristic that is uniquely her such as, tenderness in her look, sensitivity in her touch or the loving response she gives when listening to another. Perhaps she has attractive hair or perhaps she is really a pretty woman no matter what her age. Look for these attributes in both men and women and verbalize your thoughts about them. Everyone needs to know that someone sees him or her as a person, man or woman and it does so much to reaffirm their sexuality.

We are All Sexual Beings

It is not socially acceptable for someone to say I like sexual intercourse. We live in a sexually orientated society so people think we are broad minded and can work out our sexual adjustments with each other. It is all right to be academic or humorous but it is not acceptable to be personal about this subject. That should give you some idea why it is so difficult to ask for help and to talk about normal sexual adjustment with a changing body. Yet, that is the task of everyone at various times as they go through life. That should help put this matter into perspective. Yet, we are all sexual beings. We engage in sexual intercourse or dissipate the energy needed to satisfy our needs. If that is not available we use sublimation to dissipate the energy.

Most people identify their sex role before any other. They say, "I am a man," or, "I am a woman." Or they might say, "I am a Mother," meaning female, or, "I am a Father," meaning male. Then they describe other characteristics. We use perfumes and after shave lotions to enhance our chances of being accepted by members of the opposite sex. However, it is not proper to say, "I like being sexy, I like being attractive to the opposite sex or I enjoy sexual intercourse."

Although clothing is usually chosen to please our own sex we feel more confident and comfortable in our clothes after being complimented in them by a member of the opposite sex. We delight in other people's sexual response to us. This is a healthy feeling however, it is difficult to discuss this response. People find it difficult to say, "Because of grief and stress my sexual responses are not the same." Or, "Women are less sexually responsive to me than they were before." Such changes do not occur for all mourners however, when they do occur each feels a great loss. We cannot freely voice the concern, "If I were to lose the sense of feeling sexy and attractive I would feel terrible." Or, "I would be concerned if people no longer responded to me as a female."

I invite you to scan your closet in your mind. Think of each piece of clothing. Are there some outfits you tend to choose over and over again even though you have many others? Do you sometimes have to use discipline to keep from wearing the same thing again and again? Chances are someone of the opposite sex has complimented you in that attire.

Knowing this gives you great power. If you see someone of the opposite sex in a garment that fits them well, drapes well, flatters them and the color is complimentary, say so. If you keep that thought to yourself it makes you feel good but does nothing for them. If you share it with the other person it is very powerful. They will be much more self-confident and experience a greater sense of security as a result. Instinctively we tend to wear those pieces of clothing over and over.

No One will ever Ask me

Most patients presenting themselves for trauma care, surgery or any type of long term care are concerned about the effect this will have on their sexual function and their sexual compatibility. The well partner of a disabled, ill or dying person is also concerned about their own sexual needs during and after the change takes place or the mate's death.

It is not necessary that you be an expert on the subject, but it is helpful to identify the problem and refer the person to competent help. It is likely the person only needs to know that someone recognizes their difficulty, is willing to talk about it, gives permission to be concerned and accepts them in their entirety.

People say, "No one will ever ask me for sex help. I am a lay person; nobody ever talks to me about that." If this subject is taboo, how do people ask for help? The behavioral responses indicating sexual struggle are varied. Do not be surprised if people have trouble verbalizing their concern and have difficulty talking about it. Yet the concern is there. Remember when a subject is taboo in a culture, that culture does not provide a language for its people to express concerns about it. We have not heard anyone talk like he needs to yet; the need for sexual adjustment is common to all people who are going through a change in their own or their mate's sexual self-image and sexual function.

How do People Ask about Sex?

Allude To and Skip Off

A patient or family will often allude to the problem and then quickly skid off on a tangent because of embarrassment. Many folks do not ask about sex directly. That is all right.

Tentative and Clumsy

They may say a few words watching carefully for your non-verbal reaction. Just show concern. And reflect back their thoughts. This often is a practice run for the person. Perhaps this was enough to give them courage to confide in another such as their minister, a social worker, or therapist.

Testing You, "Will You Listen?"

Sometimes a worried person makes an awkward remark but the look in his eyes tells you that he is testing to see if you are willing to discuss such a subject. Reflect back their concern to show you value it. They may not go any further with the subject on this visit. Today they are only checking to see if you will talk about it. Often they won't respond immediately but if trust is gained, they may bring up the subject again at a later visit after they have had time to put their concerns into words.

In all of these cases it is best to give third person information for the purpose of validating the concern. Say, "Many people on drugs find--, many who have your kind of surgery wonder--, some people have told me this helped them--, sometimes this is a difficult time for both patient and mate--, it is good that you are willing to talk this through." Again they may not respond to these remarks. However, by saying them in a kind parental tone it provides them permission to proceed with this painful adjustment.

Sexual Jokes

Perhaps the concern will be manifested by sexual jokes or inappropriate behavior. When this occurs respond simply with concern. Look for the concern that is expressed under the vulgar remark. Treat it seriously and with respect. Inappropriate behavior and exposure are often seen in the hospitals. It shows up as improper advances and sexual jokes. Again, this often hides a serious concern and good intentions. People do not have a language or a way of speaking about personal sexual feelings. The person talking to you may never have heard anyone voice or say in words the concern that he has. Don't notice the inappropriateness of the advance; reflect the feeling with remarks by saying, "Do you think your illness has affected your relationship with your mate? In what way? Has your illness or surgery affected your wife's sexual response?" Affirm, "That often happens. She needs to talk to someone who understands her."

You may get a variety of responses such as more vulgarity, raucous laughter, silence, changing the subject to the weather or an outpouring of pain and concern. Either way, leave graciously and quickly when that seems appropriate or listen with an empathic ear for the struggle of this person.

Overly Modest Behavior

The person may show embarrassment or blush. Some people become overly modest when they are physically dependent. They are quick to cover up all of their body. I found that more prevalent in men of good intention than in women. Perhaps they were reacting to the fact that I was a woman or perhaps because healthy men suddenly incapacitated have never exposed themselves except in sexual ways. A woman on the other hand has known since she was a little girl that she would give birth and that meant exposing her body in trust to other people for the help she and her baby would need. In an accident or sudden illness she is mentally prepared for non-sexual care and touch in private areas from helping professionals. The man may have never given that a thought. So look for the nonverbal behavior and validate the concern with simple statements.

Inappropriate Advances

It is sad to see these patients, "Zapped," put in restraints, talked about unkindly and their reputations ruined just because of their inability to express very real sexual concerns in so called proper ways.

In Full Body Restraints

I came to work one morning and was briefed about a patient that I would be giving primary care. He had been put in full body restraints because of inappropriate behavior. I was cautioned not to remove more than one limb at a time for bathing. I was advised the guard was stationed outside the door for the past 24 hours because of the man's behavior and I should call immediately if I needed help. I was assured the guard would be there instantly to help hold the man down. He was very strong.

The chart indicated the gentleman was hospitalized after a stroke eight days before. He had no visitors, was in his late 50s. He was diabetic, could not speak, use his hands, arms or walk. He flailed his limbs about with great force. He repeatedly exposed his genitals by throwing off the bed covers whenever a female aid or nurse came into the room.

With great caution and some trepidation I went to give extensive morning treatments and bed care. I started by introducing myself pointing to my name tag and explained what I would do. His eyes expressed concern as he followed every move. Beyond that I did not talk. I just explained every move I made and what I saw. When he winced I said I was sorry. When I knew the treatment would hurt I told him and asked if he had the courage to manage the pain. Then I gave him feedback on how it worked. It was quiet. For an hour and one half we did fast-moving tandem team work between patient and nurse. He said no words.

Then I informed him that I was going on break and would return to give him a complete bath and clean bed linen. He responded in a gentlemanly voice. "You go on break. You deserve it. You have worked so hard. Take a good rest." I was stunned! I said, "You talked! They told me you couldn't talk."

I gave him a bath. When I uncovered his genitals, I was shocked. I had been giving full baths since I was sixteen years old. Some days I gave as many as fourteen full baths but never had I seen someone in this condition. Clearly some inappropriately overly modest caregiver had been assigned to his care. I called his physician and together we designed a treatment with prescription care. He was diabetic which leaves skin excoriated. His skin came off with the washing. He was in excruciating pain.

I asked him why he had not asked for help. It became clear that he had no language, no words to describe to a woman what was happening to him. Then with tears he said, "I tried, I showed the condition of my bottom to every nurse who came into my room. Not one of them would help me."

For this, the man was tied to his bed and his reputation ruined. He had no clue his behavior was interpreted as lewd. People do not feel sexy in deep pain or great fright.

Facets of Sexual Needs

Skin Touch

Skin touch and hugging are part of being human. Parents of young children become so used to being touched all over they have no idea what it is like to live without touch. Yet, many people live with tactile deprivation. There are people who have lived a full life raising families and relating to people only to find they are repulsive in their dying. They benefit from someone who reaches out to hold their hand or stroke their hair.

Many Americans go through life with the hugs of only one member of the opposite sex. If they remarry this may increase to two or three members of the opposite sex in a lifetime. Previously generations of extended families fully expected to be hugged by several members of the opposite sex. When our grandparents were young, families consisted of many children as well as many aunts and uncles. As a result there was close interaction and numerous opportunities for culturally acceptable skin touch. If hugs were inappropriate in that culture other acceptable ways were found to satisfy the need for touch and stroking.

We live in a mobile society that is far removed from uncles and aunts, brothers and sisters. Families are smaller today. As a consequence the potential for strokes has decreased. If we are not hugged by those around us we remain untouched. Today we need to identify and relate to our social family when our natural family is not available. We need to support and hug social brothers and sisters, better known as tribe.

Tactile deprivation seems to be considered normal in the adult state. During a conversation, the Italians and the French touch each other about 100 times per hour while Americans touch each other about three times per hour. I have observed in my personal interactions with very dear people that I was being touched less than three times per hour. If three times an hour is the average for Americans someone is getting my share. In Asia and Africa one witnesses men in groups all touching and grinning. Notice the news films. Notice the expressions of Afghanistan and Iraq men. Americans live in a tactile-deprived society.

Quality of Touch

Everyone has skin touch and hugging needs. These needs do not change. Tactile stimulation is elevated for a baby and continues high for lovers in their twenties. If young people are open and free and life is good to them they get their tactile needs met in healthy ways.

What we fail to realize is the need for skin touch remains elevated into old age. Yet the amount of skin contact an individual receives decreases with each wrinkle and bag. Not only do numbers of touches decrease but the quality of the contact decreases as well. The older and feebler a person becomes the less touch they receive.

Painful Hugs and Handshakes

We punch and rough up young people, we usually let them hang on us; they lean right into us for all-body contact. As people approach middle age we give a quick handshake but, for the elderly we just greet them and seldom touch them at all. When we do greet with a touch it tends to be only finger tips, hardly contacting their skin. Part of the reason for withdrawal is that we are acutely aware of their pain. We know that stroking, especially squeezing, causes pain for many elderly. They put up barriers. This does not take away from their emotional need to receive touch.

There are ways to do a lot of skin contact with very little pressure. It is good to learn and practice it. Greeting is often accompanied with a bone crunching handshake or a bear hug so the elderly recoil at the advance of touch. Instead of gripping your hand, extend an open hand to them. Tense the muscles in your hand so as not to present them a limp handshake. Have your palms up and fingers extended. When they place their hand on yours, place your other hand over the top of theirs with palms down and fingers extended. Linger the hold. You cause no pain and you pass tremendous amounts of warmth and energy. When you hug, tighten your muscles and enfold them without pressing them. They will feel the tightness of your arms and enjoy what you convey while not afraid of having their backbone crushed. Many instances of crushed vertebra happen to the elderly during a bear hug.

Permission to Hold

During grief the need for skin contact is increased. Yet, there are only two situations during which Americans will permit another adult to hold them. One is for health care purposes and the other is during sexual foreplay. Many people enter affairs to satisfy a basic need for touch. If an individual could be held in a caring way for twenty minutes many affairs would never be initiated. Some individuals frequent prostitutes because of their need to be held. The sad result is that very little contact occurs with a prostitute. There is no socially acceptable way to say, "I need to be held. Will you hold me in a parental, loving, and compassionate way?"

The alternative way to receive skin contact is to seek out individuals who are licensed to touch. Hairdressers and barbers provide touch because of the nature of their work. Society dictates that an ill person may receive touch in socially acceptable ways. Many individuals continue therapy procedures such as ultra sound, massage, heat treatments, physical therapy, and water baths long after the precipitating physical ailment has vanished. They continue to receive the value of skin contact. It is often unconscious but it underlies their motivation to keep rescheduling. That is perfectly acceptable. It is a sign of maturity to identify needs and get them met in an emotionally healthy way. Touch needs are real. If a massage fulfills it for someone, fine.

In our culture there is no opportunity to receive fatherly holding or motherly cuddling that we all need. It is permissible to ask to be held during intercourse but not for brother/sister love. There is no culturally acceptable way to say, "Please hold me for twenty minutes, cuddle with me, I just need to be close." To fulfill touch needs Americans need to be ill, engage in sex or live lives of no skin contact at all.

People do hold each other when the situation is so dire that they act on their natural inclination. But some become confused about their personal reaction. Many times I have been asked by a comforter if they did something wrong because they felt a sexual response in themselves. They worried even when they carried out nurturing in a proper manner. One reason for escalation of the sexual response is that our nerve endings are familiar only with sexual holding. If that happens to you just take a second to be grateful that you are healthy, continue the platonic conduct and parental caregiving and let the feelings come and pass right through. Health professionals become comfortable with this as they become more experienced with therapeutic touch.

Waiting for the, "Want to"

When someone is feeling insecure, when their body is not trustworthy, their world is fragmented, they yearn for the warm and comforting arms of brother, sister, Mom or Dad. Older people become dependent on others and need stroking just as much as a dependent child does. Yet, touch is often not available to them.

Those who were once demonstrative and lived full lives of contact suddenly find that in their illness or old age that they are repugnant to others. Persons who smell bad because of illness or have grotesque features know this. Do you think that hurts? Do you think they know they are repulsive? Yes, they do. What happens is that visitors recoil and step back. The sick person is aware of the recoiling.

One of my nineteen year old students looked at me with wide eyes when I explained this. In a firm voice she said, "But who wants to hug a wrinkly, smelly, old person?" She said, "I work in a nursing home, elderly people are not appealing! When you see a cuddly baby or an attractive member of the opposite sex you just want to go over and hug them. Lovers want to be close, everyone wants to hug the little ones that come to visit but, nobody has a desire to go up to the elderly and caress them."

While I was trying to figure out how to react to her she continued, "I know the, *want*, isn't there so I don't wait for desire. Every day I touch every patient on my care-list with as full a body hug as I can." Then she looked wide-eyed to the group again and said, "I can get a lot of me on a lot of them. I make sure I do it twice in a shift. I start the second round a couple of hours before quitting time to make sure that I don't miss anyone in case something unexpected happens. Everybody on my team gets a full body hug twice a shift."

We were all aghast. She was amazing. I thought that was beautiful! She expressed the need to bring in the will when making a decision. She understood that we need to make a choice and not wait for desire to come from natural feelings. An act of will is often necessary in love relationships.

Touch Deprivation

People who live in busy families are used to being touched all over. It is difficult to realize what it is like to live without being touched. I grew up with nine children. There were four of us each 13 months apart. We were always tangled together; I think we were more like a litter. All my younger memories were with a lot of arms and legs. All four of us were under a bed, our favorite spot, or the four of us rolled together as a ball down the hay stack, or the four of us engaged in group wrestling. One of my most vivid memories is the four of us in the back seat of the car. The old cars did not have big back seats or seat belts. Of course on the farm there were always flies on the legs. It never mattered whose leg it was, when we saw a fly we swatted it. Then we discovered who jumped and knew whose leg it was.

Suddenly I was jettisoned into Chicago. I came from a farm community where residents always greeted. So I greeted everyone on the Chicago streets. I found out that in the big city individuals are treated the same as moving telephone poles. There is no significant difference between the pole and a person except that if they were in your direct path individuals moved to the side; the telephone pole did not move. The individuals never spoke nor looked each other in the eye. They stood and waited at the bus stop for 20 minutes but not a word passed between any of them. That doesn't mean they were not nice people. If asked a direct question they were helpful. But God! It was lonely.

After living in Chicago for several months one of the physicians at work was explaining a procedure to me. He put his hand on my shoulder. I remember later that day feeling warmth where his hand rested. It came to my attention several times during the evening. I was surprised, thinking, "My, that touch stays warm so long, I can still feel his hand." I realized that I was so accustomed to touch while in my family that I was totally unaware of what it felt like not to be touched.

The touch you give people will stay long after you have left. It will be there to warm them when the night is too long and the hours are too many. The benefit of touch stays a long time. Many elderly who lived interactive lives with large families and friends spend the last 10 to 30 years with no meaningful touch at all.

Family and Friends Confused

The family needs permission. You need to say very directly, "Go ahead and touch her, cuddle him, crawl in bed and cuddle for a while, be close." Both the patient and the family have these needs. The family needs to touch their traumatized loved one. They need to hold and be held by the injured or terminally ill member. They need modeling if you are coming to visit and notice that others are holding off, take the patients hand in your hand, do a double touch or a hug. If the person draws comfort by having their arm stroked or a foot rub, do that. Sometimes friction gives a burning sensation so be aware which result you are achieving. If in doubt, ask him. Many people get comfort from the stroking with a wet washcloth on the brow or arm. You are modeling by doing and saying such as, "Does this help?" This can make a big change in family interaction.

Machines and Tubes

Both families and patient are confused. Frequently families who were demonstrative and responsive when the person was well, withdraw when the person is sick or injured. Avoidance increases with each tube or machine that is attached to the patient. Families and friends give up normal habits of relating in a hospital environment or when something unusual has happened to a loved one.

As soon as the outside apparatus moves into the room people feel they don't have a right to move in close. Give gentle permissions, say, "Be sure to get close. He needs touch right now. Don't be afraid to get in around the machines." If you are not sure how to do this, ask a nurse to show you. Relatives and friends will not touch an arm with an IV in it for fear it is going to come out. That is too bad, medical personnel do a better job of securing it than that. If it is delicate they will tell you. Don't let machines and tubes separate you from those who need you to give and receive touch.

It is sad to see intimate family members separated by paraphernalia. They need you to give permission. They need to know where and how to touch to prevent pain to their loved one. Show by your action; provide gentle massaging on their neck, back and arms. Stroke the brow, grasp their shoulder, take hands when greeting and leaving, and suggest they do likewise. Walk with your arm around their waist. It may sound strange but families often need this kind of permission.

Teach How to Cuddle

The sick person thinks, "I am causing all of this work. I can give nothing." However, the sick person feels powerful when they can give love and physical closeness that is welcomed by their mate or child. Even though they cannot care for their own body they can give presence, comfort, soothing, encouragement, caressing, and soft whispers of love. Encourage the family member to crawl into bed and rest. Put a pillow under the caregivers head; they often doze in this position. So much comfort and rest comes from this.

Kubler Ross said that when a child is dying be sure to order a hospital bed that will fit two persons, the child and parent. She says the parent is not going to get quality rest in a separate bed when their baby is dying. They will not sleep soundly because they are tuned in to the child. When the parent or mate sleeps with the dying person they have a more restful event knowing they will hear and feel every move. They can be at peace. If the sick person is dead when they awake they know that if the dying person had struggled they would have wakened. The caregiver is comforted knowing the spirit of their loved one left while feeling the warmth of their skin as they lay beside them.

One of our patients said when her husband was dying she really needed to be close to him, but he found touch too painful. She said the nurse asked if it would please them to be close enough to cuddle. Both the husband and wife said yes but, they had no idea how to make this happen. From her story we get this protocol.

Practice In and Out of Bed

It is helpful to have the well person practice going in and out of the bed while the support person is present. It is less embarrassing for the well person if the helping person goes to the head of the bed. Say to them, "I will watch the tubes, bags, and hookups." Then step by step direct her or him to slowly crawl into bed with the patient. As they move, direct how to handle the tubes and machines. If the patient is in pain, have the well partner go slowly to within two inches of the patient's skin. At this distance ask if they can feel each others warmth and energy. This alone, is enough to bring tremendous feeling of love to each other. They can hear each others whispers, feel each others breath and take in each others warmth.

There are times when after being near for several minutes they can ease closer to the point of touch without causing pain. If the patient is touched fast the stimuli is too great but slowly as the skin gets used to the warmth it may not send pain signals. At other times the patient may not be able to tolerate touch but can enjoy a pat on their hair or the touch of their legs and feet. The couple needs to be encouraged to explore and to communicate to each other. By being aware of situations like this one can facilitate their behavior by giving simple permissions and encouraging suggestions about how to make it happen. You do not have be a magician to enable magical opportunities.

Power in an Otherwise Powerless Position

A grieving woman said, "Here I am crying all day, angry at life, depressed, and without ambition. I can do nothing to save my child who is dying but– ah yes; I can pleasure my wonderful husband." This is empowering.

The dying person needs to be touched but also remember that just as important is the reality that relatives and the friends need to receive touch blessings from the one who is dying. We sometimes forget that they need to feel Grandpa's goodbye hug or Daddy's cheek on their forehead. The emphasis is on family care not just for the person who is dying.

All Energy Going Out: Nothing Coming In

A student said, "It never dawned on me to crawl into the hospital bed with my husband. We were sexually active up to the day the hospital bed was delivered. The curtain came down that day. We were never physically close again. It never occurred to either of us, not even once in the long months of caregiving that I might crawl in that bed and cuddle with my man. Oh, just to have felt the warmth of his body, just to sleep with the smell of his skin next to me, just to have whispered sweet nothings and nibbled on his ear, how that would have fed my soul."

His illness progressed very fast and the lady said, "Suddenly I was managing the care of a dying husband, getting nurses, working with pharmacies, learning how to use hospital equipment and techniques, giving total night care, being a full time Mom for two young children and of course I had to work. He was going to die and I needed to acquire money and health benefits to take care of our children. Everything was going out from me. I was giving, nurturing, comforting, running, and managing. Nothing was coming into me; everything was going out. I was stressed with this management role, overcome with grief for my dying husband and needed something so bad. Everything and everyone that came into the home was for Jason. Every enquiry was about Jason, asking, is Jason okay? Does Jason need a massage, does Jason need to be propped up in this position, and how would Jason like his food? Does he need to sleep more? Nothing was coming toward me. No one was asking, how are you doing,

Judy, how is your sleep, do you need a massage, a facial, or a hairdresser? Everything, everyone and all concern went to the dying person."

Caregivers Get Weary

Caregivers get emotionally worn out and physically exhausted. They become worn out socially because their acquaintances begin to stay away. Friends already have completed their goodbyes, done everything they could, the mess gets messier and the individuals get angrier. The caregiver does not get a dinner out or dancing, she doesn't get laughter and silly conversation. Many caregivers die before the patient dies. This is very serious indeed.

It is astounding how many couples give up pleasuring altogether. Caregivers get so tired. We work with very tired families. There is no reprieve during long term illness which extends for years. It gets wearisome. There is no up time, no laughter in their lives. They yearn, "Just to be close, to feel his hands caress me again." Ask them. "Are you able to be intimate? Are you able to pleasure one another?"

Petting and Fondling

Husbands, wives and lovers have special needs. When a mate is hospitalized they find themselves in a situation where they are expected to be as platonic as they were in grade school. At a time of great emotional stress they are denied privacy, closeness, and fondling, the kind of intimacy that relieves tension among couples. Husbands, wives and lovers have special needs that are inherent in the relationship. The intimacy of fondling, kissing, and petting relieves tension between lovers. They need to hold each other, cry, kiss, and reassure. These activities do much to prevent misunderstandings and reduce tensions among lovers.

It is while engaging in kissing and fondling that couples find courage to talk about their heartfelt fears and loves. This is when they cry together, express love for each other, state the importance that they have for each other, ask forgiveness, and give forgiveness. It is out of that process that comes, I am sorry, and reassurances of love for each other. As long as that energy is held back it is not going to happen.

So often in a hospital situation a person will come in as a trauma victim. When the family arrives there is uptightness. They stand back in fear, holding all their feelings in. These people need to hear from a caring outsider, "Go ahead, hold each another, kiss one another, embrace each other, take the time you need, cry with one another." We don't say these things out loud except as part of foreplay so it seems unnatural to voice it out loud. We need to say, "It is important to lie close to your partner at times of stress, surgery, chemotherapy, illness, accident, and trauma." Both parties need to be stroked and fondled as well as be near to each other and cuddled.

Intercourse Desires

Helping persons as well as institutions often make believe they don't know that married people engage in physical intimacy and demand by their implied behavior that the patient and family also make believe that intimacy does not exist. Couples are denied privacy and closeness. It is important to create privacy, pull curtains, give time security and verbalize permissions such as, "Be close now, you two need this time." Or, "He needs you to be close right now. Love him."

When I worked recovery in a small hospital it was policy that the nurse accompanied her patient to his unit. There she gave the report to the unit nurse and together they got the patient comfortable in his bed with all the tubes and machines working. I was taking a young woman back to her room when her husband came toward us. He was loving and concerned. It was my nursing philosophy to engage the family in as much caregiving as they were able to handle comfortably. So I asked him to take her legs in the move from the cart to the bed.

The floor nurse took over firmly directing him, "Out in the hall! No family in here!" The husband protested which provided the nurse with a good opportunity to exert her power. She apparently needed it for her own personal growth and advancement that day. He was in the hall while we adjusted all the paraphernalia with his wife. It was my poor misfortune to be the first nurse to open the door. He leapt angrily at me shaking his finger saying, "You want me to pretend that I have never seen her legs!" It was true; we did want him to pretend.

Everyone was looking at me. I was standing in the middle of the hallway with all kinds of feelings running through me. One of them was, "My Gosh, don't make me acknowledge that I might think you have intercourse with your wife! Not here! Right here in the middle of the busy hospital hallway! Please make believe with us that you have never seen her legs." Of course, I stood there speechless. I couldn't say this out loud and I couldn't think of anything bland to say to that caring husband. It is so difficult to admit out loud that the very essence of coupling is physical intimacy and that they have a need to relate to each other intimately. We often deny partners opportunities for closeness which is what couple means.

Never be afraid to intervene assertively, yes, kindly but assertively for a relative, friend, fellow church member, or neighbor. If they need privacy to be together just simply say, "Yes, you do." Then go about helping them get their privacy need met. One of the ways is to close the door.

One of the most often spoken sorrows at Compassionate Friends around the death of a baby was from a husband or wife saying how badly they needed to cry in each others arms. They needed to roll together in grief, to hug and say over and over, "I am so sorry, I am so sorry." It is known that without this preliminary opening of hearts through intimate touch, grief becomes stilted. It becomes difficult to say and process words like, "Please forgive me. I forgive you. I love you, together with God we will see this through."

Privacy Time Security

As a concerned person you can create privacy by drawing curtains and pulling up chairs. Some people are free about showing their love and others are awkward and need verbal permission.

I often heard nurses and assistants say something like this, "The mate came to visit. I could see they needed to be alone so I stepped out to give them privacy time," intending that the couple hold, pet, fondle and be close. Later when I attended a support group, I heard the couples speak of how badly they needed privacy and that it was not given to them. When I asked about this dichotomy one Dad replied, "Nothing very intimate is going to happen if you think that someone is going to barge through that door in five minutes!" Grieving people said they sensed the nurses cared but they were inhibited with their partner because they needed better assurance of privacy.

One young father said, "I brought masking tape and put it across the door frame on the outside of the door. I did not trust the sign that says do not disturb." That caused me to remember that when I was nursing in the hospital and saw a, "Do not disturb," sign, I did not think it meant me. That man was correct; I would have gone right in. Had there been tape, I would have gone to the desk and asked, "What is that about?"

Time Security

If you are going to give privacy time you must verbalize it. If you don't put it in words it isn't going to happen. If you are in a home and wish to give time-secured-privacy simply say, "Now that you two are together I will trust that you will call me when you need me so I am going to go into the kitchen. I will not come back until you call me. I am going to bake cookies or read a book. I will answer the phone and take messages, I will answer the door and entertain your visitors but, I will not come back until you tell me you want me to come back in." That is the way you give time security. If you think you need to check in on them for one reason or another. Say, "I will return in twenty minutes, it is 2:10 pm and I will not come back until 2:30. I will come then; here is the bell or the call light." Then verbalize the permissions, "Go ahead and hold her, she needs you now, go ahead and crawl in bed, be close, it is okay." Strangely enough, people always tell us that they need permission for this. You would think that they would not, but they do because it is not their territory, it is not their turf. Even in their own home if the patient is in a hospital bed or has equipment attached to them, they do not consider that to be their turf. As soon as the outside apparatus moves into the home people feel they don't have a right to move in close.

It is sad that in the hustle and bustle of the medical regime couples forget to get close. Permission must be voiced, "Are you able to be together, are you able to cuddle, are you able to hold, pleasure, and stroke one another. Are you comfortable crawling in bed with her or him. Would you like some guidance around the tubes and machines?" You must put the permissions into words.

Factors that Complicate Adjustment

There may be no medical reason to refrain from intercourse but there may be a psychological or emotional inability to achieve orgasm. Since we rarely admit to or talk about these concerns even among couples, the inability to achieve orgasm is often perceived by the partner as rejection. This compounds the problem because one partner is unable to respond and the other partner has hurt feelings. This can have a snowball effect.

Instead of the partners comforting and caressing without an expectation of orgasm they disengage. The partner with the problem becomes even more insecure, avoids physical contact, and further decreases the ability to become aroused. A problem that may have been only temporary can result in a total avoidance of intimacy for fear of rejection. If the couple understood that this should be a time for comforting, for affirming each other's self-worth and for pleasuring by touch, both could have their needs met. If desired, one of the partners could achieve orgasm without intercourse.

Stress

Stress affects interpersonal relationships and may necessitate the adjustment of sexual activities as well as other aspects of a relationship. Sex is sometimes thought of as being synonymous with orgasm however, when we consider the sexual needs of a human we must consider all facets of what it means to be a sexual being. There is need for a positive self-image, touching, hugging, cuddling, and intercourse. Grief produces stress which has a significant impact on these interactions. Changes in sexual responses confuse not only the affected person but also the mate.

Sexual Rhythm

People are unaware of their sexual rhythm and sexual intercourse fulfillment pattern. Each person has a biological fulfillment pattern that varies between two days or two weeks. If someone regularly wants sex more than every two days there is a possibility of a motivator other than biological rhythm. If they want sex less than three weeks it is also wise to consider an issue other than biological.

Couples adjust to each others sexual rhythm. What happens is that an every two day person marries an every two week person and discovers that out of love they have intercourse about once a week. One person feels they are being put off a little and the other feels they are a bit generous. It works out. If they go on without interruption individuals are unaware that they have this need and rhythm. After years of sexual fulfillment it is taken for granted. Awareness of the need for sexual intercourse is often quite startling and difficult to accept. Many people are embarrassed and ashamed to speak of it. It comes as a shocking surprise that in the time of enforced abstinence they are suddenly aware that they have strange thoughts such as, "I am not sure I can get along without sex. I am having a difficult time adjusting to not having intercourse. I need to get help in understanding my adjustment needs."

There is a myriad of feelings including guilt for wanting pleasuring at a sad and difficult time as well as worry about being selfish. All you need to do as a sensitive listener is show acceptance and let them know that their fears and concerns are a normal part of adjusting to changing health and marriage patterns.

Pleasuring Criteria vs. Performance Criteria

When talking to people remember to use criteria that do not emphasize performance but rather criteria that emphasize satisfying their needs and the needs of their partner. The well partner should be encouraged to hold, hug, kiss and give gentle massage over the entire body of the loved one. Encourage them to let each other know which areas give the most comfort and pleasure. These areas seem to differ from person to person. Encourage them to explore alternate methods of giving pleasure.

The restricted partner can still give full sexual pleasure to their mate. Even if he or she cannot have an orgasm they can receive pleasure and encourage their partner to seek it. The well person needs to communicate to the mate that love still exists and that there is hope for their sexual future. Knowledge that there is hope will do more to insure satisfying sexual responses than any technique.

The Capital "O"

An obstacle to receiving sexual pleasure is the popular myth of the, "Capital O." There is a tendency to worship orgasm as the god of sex. This is unfortunate because sex involves more than a climax. Our society considers orgasm to be the most important sexual response. It is not true that good sex must terminate with orgasm of both parties. Often one party needs to enjoy pleasuring without orgasm. The other party may enjoy pleasuring and orgasm.

In many cultures couples come together for pleasuring and deliberately withhold orgasm. They repeat this three or four times before enjoying full orgasm. People of these cultures consider this a more complete pleasuring and enjoyment of each other.

Orgasm Not Possible

When one of the partners cannot achieve orgasm it can be devastating. It often results in the couple discontinuing all sexual activities. Caressing, cuddling, and skin touch are withheld from each other. It is even more significant during bereavement because holding and skin touch are so important at this time of self-image fragmentation.

In our culture foreplay is employed only for the purpose of excitement to achieve orgasm. We think both partners must have an orgasm and they should have their orgasms simultaneously for best sex. Wrong. The idea of simultaneous orgasm as the best of sex is erroneous. Many couples thoroughly enjoy seeing their partner's pleasure and then enjoy their own release. The nature of orgasm is a spontaneous reaction that completely consumes the person. At that time one is unaware of the other person's pleasure so if the orgasms are simultaneous they miss a pleasurable part of sexual communication which is to experience the joy of the partner's orgasm.

Loving one another is the essence of good sex. If people are coupled for a long time there are many periods of life where one of them needs to refrain from orgasm for medical, surgical, drug reactions, periods during pregnancies, child birthing, depression, fatigue, and other reasons. The pressure of orgasm prevents people from enjoying each other at these times.

No Provisions for Intercourse in Care Centers

There are seldom provisions for intercourse in hospitals or nursing homes in spite of the fact there is no reason why sexual intercourse should not occur. Some stays are for weeks or months. Besides denying the essence of what coupling means, couples are forced into long periods of abstinence which causes additional performance difficulties. Sex is integral to a couple's relationship.

Many people are hospitalized for tests or treatments and sent home for the weekend with the instruction to return to the hospital again on Monday. They are not given adequate instructions for their state of health. They are not told which activities are dangerous, which positions are unsafe, the effect their new drugs have on sexual performance, or what to do if adverse reactions occur during lovemaking. Seldom is a couple talked with about these issues. We assume, "Of course they will go home and sleep in separate beds." I always thought that sleeping separately was not too significant because smart people knew how to handle separate beds.

When we listened to couples in Make Today Count and hospice groups we heard them say that if they had regular intercourse before hospitalization they engaged in intercourse when the sick mate came home from the hospital-- but, with tremendous anxiety and fear. The persons who had a heart attack told us about their fear but, said that they made the decision to have sex anyway. The ill mates were surprised to discover that it was the well partner who was frightened out of their wits. The well mate, because of fear, is not able to maintain an erection or get lubricated enough to perform. This is very scary and troubling to the couple. They often need help to talk about this.

Grief Affects Sexual Response

Grief affects the sexual response in several ways. Some people desperately want to be held and cuddled. When a griever's previously stable world is shattered and broken apart, they lose awareness of their boundaries. They benefit from being held so they can define their perimeter. They need to know where they end and where others begin. This helps them to re-center. This can be clearly seen as one observes the bereaved attempting to do this for themselves. They keep their arms folded tightly as they attempt to hold themselves together. They sit immobilized, fearing any activity will cause them to fall apart. Mourners feel fragmented.

Loss requires a redefinition of who they are as a person. The old role designation of self as mother, brother or lover doesn't fit anymore. There is also a need to redefine who they are as a member of the community. Sex is the only acceptable way to ask to be held. For this reason many grieving persons desire more frequent intercourse.

Can the Dead See?

This philosophy is not common to all bereaved. This thought can be disconcerting to a mourner after the death of someone near to them. To think of Mother or a dead mate being in the room with them during sexual activity is not conducive to intimacy with a partner. It is imperative that people develop a more complete philosophy to cover life on earth. If this is the view of an afterlife they need to apply good mental health principles to modify their understanding.

Some grieving parents believe the dead child continues to live in another dimension and can see everything that occurs. They express an embarrassment about this thought during sex. Perhaps they can rationalize that since most parents want their child to grow up and experience a fulfilling sexual life it would follow that if their child is present in another dimension the child's spirit-self would want the parents to have a full and satisfying sex life as well.

Grief Stimulates Excessive Sexual Arousal

Because there is no obvious way of addressing these fragmentation and holding needs, grievers often seek sexual intercourse within or outside marriage in an attempt to satisfy the need to be held. This desire for increased sexual activity may confuse a mate. A mate will say, "I don't know what to do about my partner. He or she wants intercourse repeatedly but doesn't seem to get much satisfaction; she does not seem to be fulfilled by it." The unaffected mates say, "I am willing to go along with it but I don't understand." That is because it is not orgasm response that is sought, it is centering with an attempt to heal fragmentation.

One couple taught us this when their child died a withering, long term death that took three years. Each day they sat with their child and watched him fade away. The Mom said she discovered the only time she was relieved of the excruciating emotional pain was during orgasm. As the years went on she yearned for the brief reprieve. As soon as her husband arrived she begged him for intercourse. He said, "I was glad to accommodate her but I knew there was a different motivator." She feared that she was a nymphomaniac.

Grief causes Inability to Get Aroused

Grief can affect sexual response by causing a feeling of deadness. Mourners can experience both responses during the bereavement cycle. They go from desiring frequent sexual stimuli to feeling totally dead inside. Even though they are willing to satisfy their mate's desire, many are too unresponsive to achieve an erection or to lubricate enough to enjoy intercourse.

Both ways of responding are normal. The problem arises when one partner desires regular stimulation and the other cannot respond. When both partners understand that these are normal reactions to grief many misunderstandings are avoided.

Problems come when the one who cannot respond avoids being close instead of communicating with their mate. They stop dressing in the same room as their partner. They keep away from close hugs for fear it will lead to the partner's excitement. They shun the other and appear cold and unloving.

They become very concerned that the sexual response will never return. The couple needs to discuss the fact that temporarily one of them cannot become aroused. The withdrawn partner needs reassurance that the behavior is understandable and in time the sensation of deadness will pass. The worried mourner has suffered a double whammy. Not only are they suffering from bereavement but they have lost physical comforting from their mate as well. This makes two great losses.

Couples need to understand it is a grief response. It is not a physiological or a love dynamic. There are many divorces after a death because grief reactions are misinterpreted to be marriage problems. This is not a marriage problem it is just one of the adjustments after a significant loss.

This is why you do not have to be a sex therapist. Often all that is needed is your encouragement of loving expressions in ways that are effective for the couple. Know that this loving reassurance is more healing than any other thing a mate can do. The couple should verbalize their desires and need for fulfillment and together learn how to achieve this goal. When a depressed mate is approached in this loving way they often have a desire to please in a passive way. The depressed partner benefits from feeling close with the knowledge that they are able to fully pleasure their partner.

Few experiences are more difficult than to be expected to perform sexually when one just cannot. When the performance pressure is gone and the pleasuring criteria is used the couples develop a strong bond and sense of appreciation for each other. This is especially effective and healing because no expectations of performance are put on either partner, both partners achieve pleasure.

Alternate Methods

Married Couples Intimate? No

Couples must be willing to discuss intimate matters in a frank and caring way. We assume married couples are intimate but this is not always the case. When dealing with intimate needs and wants it is difficult to ask for gratification and pleasuring. People may be able to identify needs and attempt the initiation by saying, "I think I would like to be cuddled and caressed for about 20 minutes." If the partner is absorbed in a book or a project and doesn't respond the asker gives up and tends to drop the matter. If the mate seems to need convincing the asker is likely to suffer a loss of self-confidence resulting in a lack of follow through to make sure their gratification needs are fulfilled. Problems compound from this point on.

Touchless Sex

Touchless sex is common. Many people limit their physical contact to basic positions during sexual intercourse. There is little touch outside of that which is essential to complete the act. Even though we claim to be sexually liberated, couples still ignore most of their partner's bodies.

Sexually free lovers claim to know everything about the erogenous zones but ignore the greater part of the body. Even couples who are sexually active experience tactile starvation.

Dr. McGinnis from the Valley counseling center in Glendale, California and author of the *Friendship Factor* says that almost all couples coming to him were literally, "Out of touch with each other." The caressing, fondling, embracing and kissing that once were central to the bond between them had gradually diminished. The onset may begin before the grief but the grief often accelerates the isolation. Having engaged in touchless sex previous to the sorrowful event makes it even more important that a supportive person verbalize the needs of couples to hold and caress each other.

Orgasm, the Ultimate Letting Go

Terminally ill patients are frequently able to be sexually active. When a partner begins the dying process many couples talk over their sexual activity. Many terminally ill persons who engaged in sex as an important aspect of their relationship choose to continue sexual activity with the intention to live life fully right up to the dying day.

Dying persons sometimes feel they are hanging unto life by their finger tips. They are afraid that if they let go in orgasm they may inadvertently let go of life and die right then. The relaxation necessary to experience orgasm is too frightening. No one should feel required to have orgasm. Each partner needs to give and receive the pleasuring that is possible within their loving relationship.

Mini-Orgasm

One of the greatest helps is mini-orgasms. Most people are not aware of it. In a sexually active healthy person there is a build up of tension in the body. In orgasmic response there is a complete release. But when the big orgasm is not possible then the body has built in what is referred to as the mini-orgasm response. It creates a release of congestion and tension. Couples need to work with each other to find which areas are responsive to stimuli. Each person is different.

The person who chooses not be orgasmic or who cannot have an orgasm can get release and pleasure from a mini-orgasm. For paraplegics the area of sensitivity is from waist up. For quadriplegics the sensitive response is only from the neck up because there is no feeling below the break of the spinal cord. Somewhere there is a sensitive area where loving and caressing from the mate will bring about a reflex response.

Each of us has this response; each of us triggers this response. It is considered a very good practice to increase your mini-orgasmic responses. It is the feeling you have watching a spectacular sunset, the shivers you get with a certain passage of music, the freeing of mental activity when you look at a spectacular vista, it is the joy of rhythm, the laughing in the rain, the spontaneous shout and singing in the car, it is the,Yeah! with its quick release of shivers all down your body. Increase these experiences. You can do it right now by choice. The bio-energetic response is the ripple response that goes down and flows out your fingertips, genitals and feet. This technique is very satisfying for the well mate when they can pleasure the non orgasmic partner. This is a real sense of power in an otherwise powerless condition.

Lady with Vulvectomy

This need and caring for each other's sexuality was vividly impressed on me by an elderly lady who was hospitalized for her eleventh surgery. Many years ago she had a vulvectomy, complete removal of the female sex organs and vagina. At a later surgery she had a colostomy and since then other deforming surgeries. She had a great deal of work to do in order to build her image of self. She was a lovely woman whose company I greatly enjoyed as I cared for her.

After lunch she was resting quietly so I asked if she would like me to sit with her for a few moments. I asked what she thought about during the many hours that she lay in bed and if she had a philosophy of life which gave reason for all that had occurred. She welcomed the opportunity to share her thoughts with someone. She spoke lovingly about her husband and said it could not have been done without his love and devotion.

I asked about the vulvectomy stating, "That must have been a great adjustment for him." She said, "I felt hapless; that I was done with the joy of life. When they brought me back from surgery I thought that it was the end of my sexual life forever."

She spoke at length about her husband's reaction to the surgery. She described how he reassured her that she was still sexually attractive. That he was so proud of her because she had the will to live and continue with him. He assured her she could still satisfy him sexually and he wanted the opportunity to try to please her. Then she added, "It has been beautiful! Our sex life is just as active as it was before that surgery and just as satisfying." She said, "I found I have very strong pleasurable reactions that leave me very relaxed after lovemaking." I am able to bring him to climax in many satisfying ways. We have a lot of body touch, a lot of caressing and cuddling. She repeated, "Our touch life is absolutely wonderful!"

I thought, "What a marvelous man to encourage his wife that way." I couldn't wait to meet him. Her husband came in with a bouquet of roses while I was with her and their greeting was tender and sweet. To my surprise he looked like just an ordinary man. No halo, no crown.

It is through this sharing from patients that helped me understand the adjustment difficulties that so many people have to go through. It showed me hope for other couples to share in a full partnership. This story is an example of hope that stands beside, because he had hope for her; she had none. In time she was able to borrow his hope and his willing to work with the adjustments until she got hope of her own. He could not give it to her. All he could ask was, "In love for me, are you willing to work with me?"

I have always been grateful to that dignified lady for sharing something very intimate with me and permitting me to gain an insight into a special area of human need.

McGinnis says, "The sex act is often referred to as making love however, there are many types of love. There is a playful game, passionate desire, enduring friendship, warm companionship, comfort giving, receiving and providing affectionate respect. The sex act can be an expression of all of these as well as dominance, aggression or submission. The good sex act results in pleasure and release of tension. Mutually satisfying sexual activity can reaffirm the sexual identity and bolster the self confidence of the persons."

There is no substitute for love and it is a beautiful thing to witness. Supportive people who facilitate the adjustment of a couple under stress until they can achieve a wholesome enjoyment and expression of their sexuality do a great service.

Problems in Adjustment
Deformed, Mutilated, Incapacitated due to Disease, Trauma, or Surgery

Previous Problems

When discussing these matters with someone take into consideration past sex history and any problems that existed before the trauma, surgery or disease. Generally if there were previous problems they will not be minimized by the added stress. Also, make some determination about the pain level. It is difficult to become sexually aroused when in extreme pain.

Functioning Problems

Nearly all people involved in trauma care, surgery or long term care are concerned about the effect this will have on sexual functioning. There are positioning problems, drug related problems, pain levels, arousal difficulties and self-image adjustments which differ somewhat for each person. If there are questions resource professionals should be consulted.

A friend does not have to be an expert to listen to someone as they struggle to adjust. A friend can reassure them that sexual modification is part of normal adjustment with changing health. The couple needs encouragement to work at a meaningful solution for pleasuring one another.

Sexual Excitement Curve

The following are some ways that the ability for sexual excitement is affected by the results of surgery, illness, drugs or the ageing process.

Paired Pleasure Pain Association

The nature of some losses is such that the pain of grief is paired with the pleasure of lovemaking. This is often true of peri-natal deaths either with or without complicated pregnancies or an immediate subsequent pregnancy. It may also occur when the intense emotion of grief at the death of a child is paired with the memory of the intense emotion of love that was felt when, "Making the child." One Mother expressed her overwhelming feelings when she first viewed the dead body of her daughter who succeeded in suicide. She thought of the terrible tragedy of this girl who perceived herself as unloved. All this mother could think of was the joy and anticipation of her child's conception that she experience during the act of making her. For an entire year the tragedy of the child's death came to her each time she felt sexually excited. That interrupted her sexual excitement curve instantly. When this happens it is valuable to seek therapy with a kindly person. This reaction is not abnormal; it is understandable. Paired associations can be managed with intelligent help.

Guilt

Often people have guilt feelings around sex. Perhaps they feel previous sexual behavior was inappropriate or perhaps now that the partner is unable to respond sexually they feel guilty about times they were unavailable to fill their needs. Some think that once they become dependent on others for care that they are unworthy of the time it takes for pleasuring. Sometimes sick and terminally ill people think they should be sad all the time and therefore feel guilty for wanting pleasuring. Often the person just needs to talk to a kind listener about their guilt.

Time of Abstinence

The couple needs to know it is normal to experience some difficulty during the first sexual attempts after trauma or surgery. If the first attempts are failures at achieving orgasm it can be devastating and cause a snow ball effect. Sometimes the abstinence is temporary and sometimes the inability to achieve orgasm is permanent.

Avoid Each Other

When a physician recommends refraining from sex for a period of time couples tend to refrain from all physical pleasuring, caressing, cuddling, and skin touch. "No sex," is subconsciously interpreted as no pleasuring. This is because they have been led to believe that intimacy without intercourse and orgasm is of little value. They do not realize that the need to touch and be touched is even more essential to their relationship while refraining from intercourse.

Couples need to be encouraged to hold, hug, and stroke even though orgasm is not the end result for either one or both parties. It is important that when intercourse is not advised for a period of time that the couple is told to continue all other pleasuring. They need to hold, kiss, and pleasure one another.

What Activity to Omit

Find out exactly what is to be omitted. If it is intromission such as with some pregnancies or radiation treatment, then only intromission should be avoided while both parties continue to have an orgasm. If it thrusting that is dangerous as in the case of some bone cancer, perhaps positioning can make a difference. It is possible that it is not intercourse that needs to be omitted only thrusting. If there is no way to avoid the danger of shattering the pelvic bones, pleasuring of both parties including orgasm is still possible. Yet, we have tremendous numbers of couples that won't even get close to each other at a time when they need closeness so badly. This is sad.

Snowball Effect

For one reason or another, couples may abstain from intercourse for long periods of time. When they do make an attempt they may find their reactions have changed. This can cause confusion and a lack of understanding of what is happening. It often produces an ongoing reaction. If intercourse has been delayed for a period of two weeks or more the ability to maintain an erection or to lubricate is frequently decreased. This is especially true when the partners have been under stress, grief, trauma, surgery, illness, or taken drugs. Their bodies do not respond at the same rate as when they were on a regular rhythm of intercourse. Instead of the partners comforting and caressing without an expectation of orgasm they disengage. The partner with the problem becomes even more insecure, avoids physical contact which further decreases the ability to become aroused. A problem that may have been only temporary can result in total avoidance of intimacy for fear of failure. Both partners could have their needs met if the couple understood that this is the time for comforting, affirming each others worth, and pleasuring. If desired one of the partners can achieve orgasm without intercourse. The public is not well informed and very little patient teaching is done.

Responsibility Falls on the Woman

It is a blow to the ego to realize that the ability to perform sexually has decreased. Men in particular are upset when this happens. They think, "I'm all washed up. It's over for me." This is not true. Sexual response usually returns with use and can be enjoyed by healthy people into old age. The techniques may change but the pleasuring continues. Couples need to be patient and loving. They need to look for pleasuring criteria not performance criteria. If mates think they can no longer perform, a percentage of them will stop trying. Men tend to react this way more than women. As a result, the responsibility for initiating sexual activities after abstinence often falls on the woman. This is a role reversal for a wife who has been sexually passive.

After a period of abstinence a ritual of some kind helps to initiate sexual activities. A backrub can break the ice and stimulate the nervous system. Cuddling while watching TV, hugging spontaneously in a hallway, whatever works is fine just so it is mutually satisfying. There may be long periods when sex will be initiated by only one of the partners. This is accepted when there is love and understanding which ultimately result in the pleasuring needs of both partners being met.

Couples are usually not intimate enough to communicate, "I am sorry, I can't get an erection right now," or "I am unable to get physically excited." So they avoid and withdraw. The emotional response of the mate is, "I am no longer desirable. She no longer wants me." This is the beginning of a problem.

After a couple of days the unresponsive partner might think, "I feel stronger today, perhaps I can make love." They come together but this time with fear. Fear is not a help but a hindrance. Now the snowball effect begins.

The first time they come together and one of them fails there is fear and shame. The second failure is devastating. They do not talk about it. Most couples will not give themselves a third chance, they avoid each other. Some research indicates about fifteen percent of the couples experiencing this problem will never try again after a second failure.

Become Afraid of Each Other

In the majority of cases no one talks to couples in this manner.

12 Years of no Touch

A woman described how her husband underwent bladder surgery to remove a small tumor growing on the lining of his bladder. No one mentioned the possibility of impotence and she had no reason to think it might occur.

A few days after the surgery her husband realized he could not achieve an erection. He was ashamed and embarrassed and thought the ability might return at a later time. He became nervous in her presence but did not confide in her. If she was dressing when he walked into the bedroom he walked out. At night when she reached for him he withdrew. She was hurt and confused but all efforts at communication revealed nothing.

Eventually she became aware of the problem. She met with his doctor but received no help, insight or guidance, only a shrug and the statement, "Sometimes this happens." The couple's relationship became strained. In due course she moved to the spare bedroom. She cared about her husband. She had a deep empathy for his dilemma and sorrow for his suffering.

After 12 years of sleeping separately the spare bedroom became unavailable and she moved back to his bed. One night she reached for him and told him of her need to hold him, to be close and stroke him. She explained she wanted nothing more. For years he had been deaf to this plea but on this evening he melted into her arms and cried. Each evening since then they spend periods holding each other. She said the relief and pleasure is unbelievable and the effect it has on their daily life is tremendous.

He still cannot talk about his sexual feelings and she believes he has never told anyone. Although he cannot verbalize his feelings he can hold, hug, receive, and give pleasure. This is beautiful. From that day on they discovered they could pleasure one another. She could receive a full orgasm and he could receive plenty of pleasuring. They have a very good marriage.

She believes all of this suffering of twelve years could have been avoided by an encouraging, empathetic supportive person's explanation and open communication prior to and immediately after surgery. Again it shows the importance of having someone to give the gentle permissions.

Concerns of the Well Partner

Another concern of the well person is fear of catching the disease. If this fear is realistic you need to deal with it, but if not, reassure the person. This fear is much more prevalent than one would believe. You can recommend they seek special help but most people go ahead and have sex with their partner with the fear still present.

It is important to understand the dying person's self concept. Does he still see himself as desirable? Do the patient and their mate wish to enjoy a full life to the very end? The supportive person can do a great deal to reinforce this concern and desire.

The well partner has many concerns. They fear they are taking advantage of the sick person if they have their needs filled. The concern is increased if the ill partner is in pain or generally not feeling well. This thought often runs through the mind of the well mate, "What if they should die during the sex act?" It is important to ask their doctor about this fear and the advisability of resuming sex. Death does not happen very often during lovemaking, but it is in the realm of possibilities. They must come to terms with the fact that their partner is dying and either way--whither they have sex or give up sex their partner will still die. That is what terminal illness means.

Die During the Sex Act

There was a wonderful vivacious couple who were members of a support group I frequented. They were dynamic leaders in the group. They talked openly about their sexual adjustments as her cancer progressed. They presented their insight to several other groups as a way of encouraging couples. They emphasized that they chose to continue with sexual expression to her dying day.

She lived several years; they were mentors and models for many couples. As time went on she required more and more care. She became wheelchair bound. They were always fun to be with. One day during intercourse the inevitable happened; her pelvic bones shattered. They had used pillows and all the precautions but the bones were so fragile that they were going to shatter spontaneously soon, even without sex. The couple knew this. The fractures caused her to be hospitalized and she died soon after.

His grief was extreme. Since he initiated the last sexual advance he focused on guilt for causing her death. Deep grief is not the time to intellectualize. After the funeral he admitted himself to a psych unit. What a gift. He received intelligent help to go though the loss. They recalled the discussions he had with his wife and their intention of demonstrating love for each other. A secondary benefit of the hospitalization was physical rest. After a week he was able to put perspective on his grief. Caregivers are so tired.

In six weeks he returned to work; a wonderful man and a contributor to society. The point of this case study is that even with the best communication and support grief is often overwhelming. Since the beginning of time people have had to capitulate, to go inward in order to find healing for their souls.

Joy Amidst Sorrow

Some look upon sexual activity as an expression of joy; therefore, they feel they have no right to seek sexual satisfaction while in grief. Mourners feel that if they experience joy they are somehow diminishing the significance of the relationship they had with the person who is dead. After his twenty two year old daughter succeeded in suicide, one father said he grieved for the joy of her life. He said that she was so beautiful, but toward the end she was sad all the time. After her death, each time he felt sexually aroused he would think, "Heather was so sad that she took her own life. I have no right to ask for the joy of sex when my child could see no joy in her life." When that thought came he could not maintain an erection. He told us how relieved he was after attending the lecture to find that he was not betraying or being disrespectful of her suffering. He said it made all the difference in how he felt about himself and his right to communicate sexually while in sorrow.

Seduced

Some persons experience being seduced on the eve of their mate's death or funeral. The seduction comes in the form of comfort-giving. I think it is often sincerely given by members of our culture who do not know how to give therapeutic hugs or therapeutic holding. The grievers say that it is very difficult to resist because the seduction most often is by someone they know and feel friendly toward. This is often someone from whom they want desperately to receive comfort. They want to be held close. They tell us it is very difficult to say, "Go away, I need to sleep alone even though my wife is dead."

Dynamics Affecting Sexual Adjustment

The ability to become aroused by a partner often has nothing to do with love for that partner. After change due to illness, drugs, surgery, or ageing, one or both of the partners may discover an alteration in their ability to become sexually excited. This may happen to either of the parties. The well partner may find his or her ability to become aroused by the ill partner is gone. This ill partner may find he or she is unable to become sexually aroused because of their own changing self-image.

Most people of our culture are acculturated to interpret sexual arousal to mean love. The inability to become sexually aroused with a partner is therefore interpreted to mean they no longer love or are loved by their partner. For the couple who is experiencing adjustments with their ability to become sexually excited this attitude adds insult to injury. This can be a very sad situation and cause undue emotional anguish at a time when there is enough suffering for them to contend with. They need supportive intervention to assure them that sexual excitement will come in its own natural time and that you believe in their ability to pleasure and comfort each other in their present state.

The Physiology of an Orgasm

An orgasm consists of a series of 5 to 12 contractions at approximately 0.8 second intervals for both men and women. This releases muscle tension and congestion. The male contraction begins in the vas deferens of the testicles and proceeds up the seminal vesicles through the prostate and penis. The contractions in females begin at the top of uterus and continue around the base of the uterus to the cervix, vaginal walls, and vulva. There are several phases to an orgasm. They are excitement, plateau, orgasm, and resolution. Note how a hysterectomy may affect the sexual response. The effect seems to differ in some women depending on position. Women have told me that it can be different with different partners and still others have said that the pleasure was greater after a hysterectomy.

The Weakened Male

In non orgasmic sex the engorgement of the lower pelvic area of both men and women is prolonged. This creates sore testicles for the man and low backache and frustration for the female. It is important to understand that this result is not present in the weakened or aging male. Weakened men are afraid of soreness and need to be encouraged to give and receive pleasuring without orgasm if that is desired. The weakened man should be encouraged to have sex play only until he is tired, then rest and enjoy the presence of his partner. He may go to this point of pleasure two or more times without an emission. Many cultures prefer this type of lovemaking claiming it is more satisfying. They often engage in pleasuring two or three times a week with orgasm only once every three weeks.

Orgasm is Hard Work

Orgasm is hard work. This becomes significant when there is a weakened partner or a disease where the energy of orgasm may cause complications such as a stroke or death. There is a gradual increase in the physiological functions leading up to the orgasm and the increase last from one to two minutes.

Couples ask when they can safely resume sex again. The over all exertion of orgasm is about equal to walking up a flight of stairs or briskly walking two blocks. This can be used as a general guideline.

The nature of orgasm is that the pulse rises from about 60 beats per minute to 160 beats per minute. The increased heart rate only last two minutes. For some diseases or conditions there may be pain during those minutes but orgasm is not contraindicated because of the short duration. For other physical conditions, a rapid pulse for two minutes can be scary and life threatening. Blood pressure rises from an average of 120 over 80 up to 170 over 100 and it can go as high as 220 over 100. This is still a very short period of time.

If a person had a stroke and the doctor says that there is a tendency to have more and the listener responds to the ill person's worry by saying, "Its duration is only about two minutes." This is not a big comfort to the person. They might choose not to have an orgasm but they should definitely choose to receive and give pleasuring. The capitol O may be a little rough on them. It might mean the end.

Respiration goes from resting at fourteen to twenty breaths per minute to sixty breaths per minute. Depending on the stage of the disease this may cause a lot of pain. People who are normally anoxic and cannot get enough oxygen such as asthmatics, those who have emphysema, collapsed lung or chest surgeries suffer with increased respirations. People who experience a high pulse rate have a diminished output from the heart. The lack of blood circulating, plus top-lung breathing means that their bodies are not getting oxygenated properly. Orgasm is a serious activity for these people.

All of this adds stress to the affected person and to their partners. Stress affects the sexual excitement curve. As long as a couple realizes that all these medical concerns have nothing to do with the love they have for each other they can work together and receive pleasuring at a time when it is so valuable.

Situations Requiring Adjustment

There are some surgical procedures, traumas, or illnesses that cause complete impotence. Such persons need to be encouraged to seek alternative methods of achieving sexual satisfaction. Intercourse is not the only source of pleasure and it is important that the couple continue seeking pleasure and giving pleasure. Couples will find areas of each other's bodies that respond well and provide release from sexual tension. Even though the organ needed to achieve orgasm is non-functioning or missing the person still needs to express their sexuality.

Causes for Sexual Adjustment

Below is presented a partial list to raise your awareness of the causes for sexual adjustment. You may choose to research more about each of them on your own.

In researching the following material, I must say, I enjoyed discovering the use of the term, "Sedate sex." Doesn't that sound like an oxymoron?

- <u>Vulvectomy</u>, <u>Penal</u> <u>reconstruction</u>: Often the result of cancer or trauma

- <u>Bone cancer</u>: Osteoporosis, fragile bones: Positioning is very important with the use of careful thrusting movements, alternate methods and sedate sex

- <u>High blood pressure</u>: Sometimes orgasm is contraindicated, talk with the Doctor: Giving encouragement to each other, receiving skin and hugging pleasures, sedate sex.

- Many <u>medications</u>: Cause loss of libido even those not listed as such. Often a patient will be relieved to know the lack of sexual response is drug related.

- <u>Male or female mastectomy</u>: Depends on part breasts played in foreplay for either party. What part did breast play in the orgiastic response. For some women their orgasm is through breast stimulation. Many men enjoy their own nipples stimulated as a significant part of foreplay.

- <u>Sore perineum,</u> poor <u>episiotomy</u>: Causes embarrassment, poor ability to function. Plastic surgery is often a help. The individuals need encouragement.

- <u>Heart disease</u>: Rest before sex, best to engage in morning, not after a full meal. If a man has the heart condition - use female astride position, quit when tired, not necessary to ejaculate each time. Take medication just before sexual activity. Even so, some pain is often noticed around heart.

- <u>Prostatectomy</u>: Dry ejaculation into bladder, pleasure still there but if psychologically unprepared may not perceive pleasure. Some are impotent, depends on type of surgery required.

- <u>Paraplegics, Quadriplegic</u>: 70% can achieve erection, may be reflex erection without sensation but, can still give pleasure to mate. Some can receive and give pleasure.

- Loss of <u>Hands</u>: Cannot use due to disease such as arthritis or amputation. A serious adjustment. Hands are the primary sex organ for pleasure giving.

- <u>Surgery</u>: Especially knee: Restful sex, positioning

- <u>Diabetes</u>: 50% are impotent - males are affected earlier in the disease than are females.

Sexual Excitement Ability

Part Affected Area played in Self-image

There are several important dynamics to consider when a person has been mutilated or deformed because of trauma, surgery or disease. The questions are: "How the mutilation affects the person's self concept? What part does the affected area play in the person's self-image? Does this woman view herself as a nurturer? If so what part of the body does she center that concept in?" If that part of her anatomy is mutilated it will likely affect her self concept as a woman. She may not be able to respond sexually. If she views a part of her anatomy such as hands or breast to be symbolic of this role she may develop intense fears before surgery. Much of this is unconscious. Most people are unaware of their anatomy-centered-sex-role-identity.

How does the person identify the affected area with the sex role? Did he pride himself on great physical strength? Clues that help you to assess the kind of acceptance a person will need from others will be found in his choice of clothing, diet and exercise. Was his sexual self concept depended upon a perfect body? Does he think muscles are a sign of masculinity or virility? When they atrophy he may feel he is no longer a man.

Role of the Mutilated Area in Foreplay

Consideration should be given to the role the affected area played in sexual foreplay. Often deformity of a part of the body which is not usually thought of as a sex organ such as: Feet to people who have a foot fetish and ears to those who engage in ear nibbling can seriously inhibit sexual arousal. Perhaps this area has particular significance during initial stages of foreplay by either the patient or mate. It may be that mutilation may require such a great readjustment that either one or both of the partners may be repelled instead of aroused by it.

Self-image Affirmed by Quality of Partner

If a man sees his masculinity affirmed by his ability to attract a sexy female, his wife's deformity may be seen as a direct threat to his masculinity. Even though he may be sympathetic and feel guilty he may have difficulty becoming aroused. We have all known men who dated only beautiful woman. Also, it is common to see husbands and wives chiding each other mercilessly about the normal aging process. For example, some wives constantly tease their husbands about bald heads or increasing waist lines. It could be the wife feels her femininity is directly related to the attractiveness of her husband. If he is disfigured it will be hard for her to become sexually aroused by him. If in her eyes he becomes unattractive she sees herself as depreciating in value.

One often sees a mate let their appearance deteriorate after they become discouraged about their partner's appearance.

Sexual Excitement Ability Equals Love

Routines of Foreplay

What you want to give are gentle permissions. It is helpful for people going through this situation to understand that couples who have been together a long time engage in ritualized foreplay. They usually find two or three routines that are mutually pleasuring. They do it the same way each time. We say variety is the spice of life. It doesn't quite ring true. There is a pattern of fulfillment that people use and like. If they have been together for a long time and suddenly have to change their ritual the excitement curve is affected. That is very difficult. Couples do not adjust to a new method of foreplay easily. It is so important to be patient.

The method of foreplay excites their bodies and readies it for intercourse. Look at what surgery, ulcerations, and tumors in certain areas of the body can do in terms of foreplay.

Double Mastectomy

Men say, "I am a breast man, butt or leg man." We usually laugh. Enjoy the laughter; but it is true. It is the same for a woman. There is a part of the anatomy of the opposite sex that turns us on.

People are quick to reassure a woman after a mastectomy that she is still feminine, she is still sexual. I have had women say to me, "The loss of my breast makes me feel so bad because my breast is a part of me. I feel as bad that they are gone as I would if I lost any other part of me. It isn't that I feel less feminine or less sexual. I need to grieve my breast as a part of me that is no longer here." Different individuals have different areas of sexual identity and different areas of sexual excitement. It is not always the breast. There are butt women also. Many women prefer their butt stroked to having their breasts stroked as part of their sexual excitement curve. For a butt woman the removal of her breast may not interfere much with her sexual excitement curve. Here is the point. If she is married to a breast man–, is there a major sexual adjustment for this couple?

The mate of a deformed patient may have difficulty becoming sexually aroused even though the love may be strong. Let us say she is married to a man who loves her very much. He describes himself as a breast man. Her breast has been very precious to him. After the surgery he loves her as much as he did before. Perhaps his love is even enriched by admiration for her pluckiness. He comes to her with strong sexual feelings. He hugs her. She feels different. Suddenly grief overwhelms him. What happens to his sexual excitement curve? It drops sharply. Is he going to tell her this? Chances are that he will not say anything. He will handle it by saying, "I am so glad to have you home again. I am so happy that you are healing so well, can I get you a drink of water." She finds this a bit abrupt but that happens in relationships and they go on.

As he goes to the kitchen he is dealing with shock at his reaction. He thinks, "I have to get used to this. This is different. I love her very much." Later he feels warm and loving and wants to pleasure her and be pleasured by her. He holds her while talking to himself, "I am not going to let this bother me." He begins to get excited; caressing her he instinctively reaches for her breast and, "Oh, not there." Now what happens to his sexual excitement curve? Yes, it went up a ways, but-- down again. His dilemma is how to manage telling her what is happening to him. Being Mr. and Mrs. Average American, he will not talk about it. He will say, "You need your sleep honey, sleep well," as he lovingly tucks her in. Now she is confused. This is not a measure of his love for her. This is a reaction to a totally different sexual routine and pleasuring for him.

She is likely to think, "He doesn't find me attractive any more. I am damaged goods. He no longer loves me the way he used to." In the days following he goes to work and considers, "I have got to get used to the changes, I want to get used to this. I love her so deeply; I think I can do it. I want to pleasure her and get pleasure from her. I just want to get over my reaction."

He comes to her again. Is he afraid? Does fear help or hinder the sexual excitement curve? That is how this situation can snowball into years of inactivity. Often one of them will start a fight to cover up their frustration and shame. Fights help to avoid intimacy. Sad to say, this is not about their fight, this is about their grief and adjustment difficulty. Love is still there.

Repulsed By Scars

Many people are repulsed by scars. They may have to take time to desensitize themselves to the effect of the scars. They need to make friends with the scars. To thank the scars for what they do for the lover and to appreciate that the scars enhanced or saved the life of someone so precious.

Ear Fetish

Ear and foot fetishes are common. If ears are removed as they are in some traumas or for cancer surgery that will affect the sexual excitement curve. If ear nibbling and ear blowing was a significant route of their foreplay this will be a sexual loss.

Foot Fetish

Wiping her Tears

Foot fetches are common. I remember a nurse telling the story that she was working the emergency department when a blue collar worker was brought in from the job. He was dead on arrival and his wife was called. The nurse went in with the wife to view the body. The nurse said, "I went right up to the head of the bed and turned toward her and she was not there. I thought she must have fainted and I did not hear her fall. Then I saw that his wife stopped at the foot of the bed, threw the covers off and buried her face in his feet. She wept and cried telling all her love to him and the meaning of his relationship to her." She then went on to say, "I am so sorry you had to go, I am so sorry you had to die." All the while she was caressing her face and wiping her tears with his feet. She was completing all her forgiveness work, good-byes, loves, and closures with his feet caressing her face. The nurse said, "I was so shocked I said nothing." Thank God for shock!

She added, "I noticed that this man who did heavy labor had perfectly manicured feet. His nails were filed and his toenails painted." Yes, this is something we greatly respect.

Anatomy-Centered-Sexual-Self-Image

Just as there is organ-centered stress so there is a part of the anatomy where we center our sexual self-image. Mutilating surgery, trauma or tumors to this part of the anatomy will have a greater affect on the emotions of a person who centers their self-image in that part than if it were to a sexually neutral part of their anatomy. This can be very sad and cause undue emotional anguish at a time when there is enough suffering to contend with. Individuals need intervention to assure them that some ideas and myths are not necessarily true, that adjustment takes time, and that you believe and hope in their ability to pleasure and comfort each other in the state they are now in.

When losses seem equal we tend to ponder, "Why does one person adjust and have a full life while another mourns and loses confidence." This is because there is much more to the human person than meets the eye. We are holistic beings and as support person we need to honor all facets of the person.

What part of the body does a person think of when he presents himself as a sexual being? Does he take pride in his height? Does she think of her trim waistline or slim hips? If an area which is thought of as being sexually attractive is damaged it may be difficult to feel acceptable enough to become sexually aroused with a partner. People tend to center the image of self in a bodily area. As an onlooker you can often tell what that person is demonstrating and how they want to be seen by others.

Some women and men always have perfect hair. They keep a perfect cut, perfectly coffered and every hair in place. Others could care less if the wind blows their hair askew. Some people's slacks and jeans fit their thighs and butt like skin while others want their slacks baggy for comfort. For some people it is the way they carry their shoulders, the feel of their waistline or how they fit sweaters over their bra. Where is your anatomy center for your sexual role? Many of us are unaware of this dynamic in ourselves. I was surprised when emergency kidney surgery necessitated a fourteen inch scar on my waistline, the swelling of my waist completely confused my ability to feel well dressed or presentable.

If a man's concept of masculinity depended upon a perfect body? If his manly sex role was seen as being strength and now he needs someone to carry his briefcase for him it may be very difficult for him to approach a woman for sex. This is because he doesn't see himself as possessing male qualities. It may be that he is not able to become aroused if he no longer thinks of himself as a man. He may no longer feel like a man. Another man may center his manhood in his singing voice. It could be that he was similarly disabled and yet his sexual self-image would allow him to croon to a lady and his sexual excitement curve may not be affected very much. Or it could be that a man is always seen with a stunning woman on his arm; that is how he struts his manhood. Now he is disabled and walks with a cane.

It does not matter what part of the body a couple choose to enjoy for pleasuring. If that part is injured, mutilated or diseased their pleasuring is affected. They need acceptance of this adjustment period and your support and understanding as they move through it. This is communicated to them by your caring, accepting, kind, empathetic, non-verbal presence. That communication is very different from a shocked, horrified, overwhelmed, non-verbal or joking response that is usually given.

Again, it is important to be aware that what often looks like a marriage problem or a change in the love of a couple is not that; it is a change in the routine that seems out of order for either one or both of them. We need to give them encouragement and gentle permissions to take the time needed for their changing routine.

Date for Sex

What happens in stress during bereavement or while taking care of an ill or dying person is that the persons heighten awareness causes the sensitivity of the nerve endings to recede deep into the skin. There is benefit in a nerve sensitization exercise to help resuscitate the nerve endings.

Even though this subject is discussed for couples in the following material it can be effective with friends or support groups. Platonic friends can eliminate the sexual activity and wear bikinis to get a quantity of skin touch while still feeling modest.

Mourners and caregivers get fatigued and tired. It is important to be aware of coupling needs. They need to go away to a different environment at least once a month for the sole purpose of pleasuring. It is important to get into a different atmosphere that is not their home.

Time for Intimacy

It helps to make a date for intimacy time. Sex is important enough that it deserves a specific date. A time should be agreed upon, put on the calendar, and honored as a commitment. For example, a couple might reserve Friday evenings from 6:00 p.m. to 10:00 p.m. as their time to be together. They may go out to dinner and spend the rest of the time engaging in physical intimacy.

My friend had seven teenagers in the house at one time. There were constant interruptions, conversations and activities. She and Joe realized they could lose their sense of being a couple in the busyness of the home so they reserved Friday evenings to be by themselves. First they went shopping and ran couple type errands, then they went out to dinner and finally to bed. No matter how frustrated she felt throughout the week she knew that on Friday she would be able to catch up on conversation, planning, sharing, and cuddling with Joe. You can put up with a lot of harassment if there is an assurance that in a week you will have your special person's undivided attention.

Couples are reluctant to make a date for sex because it might lose spontaneity. They think planned sex is of less value than spontaneous sex. They need to ask, "Does spontaneous sex meet their needs? Does it correspond to their natural sexual rhythm?" If sex is spontaneously initiated by one partner and the other cannot respond, there is a tendency for the initiator to feel rejected. Also there is a tendency for the one who cannot respond to feel guilty. If the date is pre-scheduled each partner can prepare themselves mentally and physically. They can look forward with anticipation. A scheduled date will not detract in any way from the possibilities for spontaneous sex.

Sexual Rhythm

How does one schedule this kind of date? That depends on the partner's natural sexual rhythm. It may be two days or two weeks. They may partake of sexual activity at other times but their natural rhythm provides the greatest satisfaction. Few people realize they have a sexual satisfaction rhythm until forced abstinence makes them aware of their frustration from lack of sexual activity. Some have not identified their natural rhythm because they have adopted society's sexual myths. For example, "I'm like the Marines, always ready." The intensity of love is not related to the number of sexual encounters.

Individuals can observe for themselves at what point the anticipation of sex becomes the strongest and at what point there is frustration if the anticipated sex is not initiated. This may also be observed in one's mate. A compromise may be needed when addressing sexual needs. For example, an individual with a two-day rhythm may compromise with their mate who has a two-week rhythm and they can plan to have sex once a week.

It is good to consider the question of how important is it to honor a date with a partner? To answer this question each must examine their own conscience. If they would not break an appointment with their dentist but will break an intimate date with their mate, they must admit that the dentist holds a higher priority for time than the intimate relationship. Obviously there will be occasions when it is proper to break a date for an intimate interlude with a partner. If such is the case, reschedule the time for intimacy just as you would a dentist appointment.

Nerve Ending Educational Exercise

Masters and Johnson, sexual adjustment therapist and authors, suggest an exercise to reeducate the nerve endings. Some couples in the support groups have developed this into a happening. This exercise is helpful for any couple but is especially valuable for those who have been through emotional stress. Couples who have done this on a regular basis since the death of their child have attributed their continued communication and joy in each other to this special time they shared. A couple does not need many reasons for doing this exercise; loving each other is reason enough. All couples can gain tremendously from this exercise. If there are stress related sexual adjustment problems they will usually melt away and sex will be more enjoyable than ever.

People from Eastern countries have used these exercises for centuries. They feel that achieving orgasm during every sexual encounter is a sign of immaturity. Choose a time when you can lock the bedroom door and not be disturbed; however, do not choose such a late hour that you are both exhausted. Lie together on the bed in the nude. For a 20 minute period one is the giver and the other is the receiver. As the receiver your sole task is to lie quietly and let your partner caress you. Do not look around; do not talk, except to tell your partner what feels good as well as where and how you would like to be touched. As your partner rubs lotion on to your body become aware of the variety of sensations that your skin is receiving. This is not foreplay and for a few sessions the couple should avoid touching the breasts and genitals.

And there should be no sex afterward! Why? Because without thinking about what is coming afterward or worrying about performance you can give all of your attention to what you are feeling through this sensual experience. After 20 minutes of such pleasuring, switch roles. If you are tired, be the receiver first, you will be surprised at what happens to your fatigue. If you want to have sex with orgasm make an agreement that you will separate the exercise with a nice dinner, walk or some other kind of activity.

It is found that if a couple differs in how often they would like to have sex; the sexual needs are leveled out with this exercise. The one who complained about not getting enough sex is content with less frequent intercourse because of the glow received from intense touching. The partner who formerly was turned off much of the time becomes highly aroused by these new touching experiences and desires intercourse more frequently.

Motel It

If a couple can afford to go out for one nice dinner each month they can also afford to go to a motel once a month. The price is about the same. This is a routine that several of our couples follow. Once a month they reserve a motel room. They bring oil which has been scented with food extract such as peppermint or almond. Some like to take an oil cloth and thick towels to spread on the floor. They hire a babysitter and off they go. If they have a little extra money they may choose a motel with a swimming pool and dining room. After arriving they do the exercise with each other, then head for the swimming pool and follow this with a delightful dinner by candlelight. Then they return to the room to share each other fully with intercourse. Other couples save money by separating their activities with wine and cheese by candlelight in their room. During this time they wear clothing that is creatively appropriate to the situation.

Some couples found their children were too insecure to leave for an overnight after the death of a sibling or that the children were simply too young. In some cases the time of separation was too long for the parents, some were nursing Moms. They came up with a novel idea that works. They reserved a motel room; hire a babysitter for the evening stating that they are going out for dinner. Then they go to a motel, do the sensitizing exercises, have dinner, go back to the motel for uninterrupted love making and return home by midnight. After spending the night at home with the children they hire a babysitter the next morning and say they are going out to breakfast. They still have the motel room key until check out time. So they return to the motel with their scented oil for some more uninterrupted love making, then out to breakfast and home again.

If this activity is scheduled and carried out once a month a couple will find their intimate relationship rejuvenated, their communication exciting, their ability to enjoy each other increased and updated by new experiences. Some parents said that after engaging in this activity on a regular basis for two years their communication as a couple and joy in each other had increased far beyond where it had been before, even though they suffered the loss of a child.

In today's busy world couples must schedule their sexual activities. Grief is a special time in life. Couples owe it to themselves to strengthen their marriage and cement the bonds of intimacy. There is no substitute for love; it is a beautiful thing to witness. When patients are unable to show sexual expression to those they love because of paralysis or illness it is indeed sad, but how much more sad when perfectly healthy bodies are denied the sexual expression because of orgasmic pressures and performance myths. How helpful to think in terms of pleasuring criteria rather than performance criteria. If in the future you help a couple to achieve a wholesome enjoyment and expression of their sexuality you will have done a great service.

Appendix A

Minnie Remembers

Author Unknown

God,
My hands are old,
I've never said that out loud before,
But they are.

I was so proud of them once.
They were soft
Like the velvet smoothness of a firm, ripe peach,
Now the softness is like worn-out sheets or withered leaves,
When did these slender, graceful hands become gnarled, shrunken?

When God? They lie here in my lap:
Naked reminders of the rest of this old body that has served me well.

How long has it been since someone touched me?
Twenty years? Twenty years I've been a widow.
Respected? Smiled at. But never touched,
Never held close to another body,
Never held so close and warm that loneliness was blotted out.

I remember how my Mother used to hold me, God.
When I hurt in spirit or flesh, she would gather me close,
Stroke my silky hair and caress my back with her warm hands.
O, God, I'm so lonely!

I remember the first boy who ever kissed me,
We were both so new at that.
The taste of young lips and popcorn, the feeling
deep inside of mysteries to come,
I remember Hank and the babies.
How can I remember that but together?
Out of the fumbling, awkward attempts of new lovers came the babies,
And as they grew, so did our love.

And God, Hank didn't seem to care if my
body thickened and faded a little,
He still loved it, and touched it.
We didn't mind if we were no longer "Beautiful"
And the children hugged me a lot.
Oh, God, I'm lonely!

Why didn't we raise the kids to be silly and
affectionate, as well as dignified and proper?

You see, they do their duty,
They drive up in their fine cars.
They come to my room and pay their respects.
They chatter brightly and reminisce.
But they don't touch me.

They call me "Mom or Mother or Grandma"
Never Minnie.
My Mother called me Minnie, and my friends.
Hank called me Minnie, too.
But they're gone, and so is Minnie.
Only Grandma is here.
And God, She's lonely!

Chapter 9

Care of the Grief Support Person

Burnout Healing

You Are a Grief Support Person

Caring people are gifted persons. They are not ordinary. They manage many roles. Their secret is time management. Simply put, that means when something new comes into their life, something else goes out of their life. When something comes in the front door something else goes out the back door. Support people operate their lives on values and principles. They prioritize, they change directions quickly. They schedule crisis hours into their weekly planner. They drop other agendas quickly at the call of need. They manage crisis.

You Want to Help People

You want to help others because you have nurturing to give. Why do you have this gift to nurture? You have an overflow of love. It may come from an overflowing of gratitude for your life; or it may be that you received the gift of grief through a loss experience.

There are many gifts of grief; none of them easy to receive. None of the gifts would we have willing paid the price. That loss now provides us understanding, insight, and empathy. Life after healing grief is richer, freer, more understanding, and more sensitive.

You can recognize people who have the gift. You can hear it in the awe, as someone leans forward at the awareness of another's pain. You can see the gifts of grief in the body movement that leans in rather than pulls back from pain. This sensitivity comes to people through the gift of grief.

Gift is Freely Given to You

Bear in mind the definition of gift. Gift means freely given, not earned. The gift was given to us. We must be generous to those that do not yet have the gift. Some people simply have no foundation to go to those who are in pain, nor do they have the groundwork for empathizing. We would not criticize the athletically challenged individual for not competing in a tennis tournament; likewise we cannot criticize those who as yet have no understanding of loss.

Each of us must dig deep to find our inner value that is the driver of our caregiving. This then becomes a contributor to burnout prevention or burnout healing. I believe we are each accountable for the gifts we have received. If I received the gift of intelligence, money, space in a size limited class, and time to get an education, then, I am responsible to give back to community the results of that education. Just because I did my part by studying and self discipline does not mean I own the whole of it. The community and God provided a portion of it and deserve a return on their investment.

Why do You Want to Give?

Why do certain people want to be effective, intelligent lovers? We don't know. Many people think it is because persons have extra time and want to do something useful. However, we know that having extra time is not the answer. We know the need to nurture is in people with extremely busy lives who have very little extra time; they still have a need to nurture others. We do know the life of a giving, caring, person is a many faceted one. Support people are parents, sons, daughters, business people, neighbors, friends, club members, and church members.

People are designed to move in a tribe of about thirty people of varied ages. In America we live in nuclear families. These families are not big enough to receive all the talent that individuals have to give others. People who are healthy create an extended family to give to and also an extended family to receive from. You are one of these people.

Clarice's Definition of Burnout

Burnout is what happens at that time of your life when your ability to assess needs and your personal skills to fill those needs out-rank what can be achieved in a 24-hour day.

It happens when you are competent. You can see the need and know that you can fill the need well. You have the desire and the want to, but there are not enough clock hours to do it.

At that time there is a new growth and development task. To continue on in life with wellness you have to develop the ability to say no, even though you have the ability to fulfill the need and would love doing it. There just are not enough hours in the day, or days in the week to use all your talents.

Now you need to look at your values and prioritize your spirit-self first. When looking at holistic needs, usually the first need to be given up is spiritual. Persons give up the time to read reflective material, enjoy the river at sunset, dream with a song, listen to their spirit, time to rock in the rocker on the porch and listen to the crickets. The second most often given up need is physical; persons skip these in favor of taking on increased obligations. You need to do a holistic self care plan marking the clock hours. It needs to cover a minimum two week span.

Burnout Is Real

Yes, burnout is real. I have heard many speakers say it is not. In my experience, something happens. I have heard, "God didn't make me to burnout." and, "Be sure that burnout is not cop-out." I say, "Call it what you wish; but the burning is real."

Nine Dead Babies

One day I dealt with the grief for nine dead babies in a row. The grieving parents came to me one after another. This was at a conference where I had already related to many other losses. The mind can deny but the body will react. I noticed a paralysis in my upper lip, it began to radiate to the right side of my face and then encircled my right eye. My body was trying to block out additional pain that my emotions could no longer bear.

For a couple of years after that, the paralysis occurred as soon as someone started talking about intense grief. Then it began when I was alone thinking about lecture material on loss. I knew that I needed a long sabbatical from other people's grief. It is imperative to distinguish signs of burnout such as, objectifying, them-thinking, night dreams, avoidance behaviors, and withdrawing."

To heal from burning out one needs to realize the self responsibility of burnout healing, take mental time away, achieve something beautiful, laugh and have pure unadulterated fun. One needs to review and renew ones motives.

Validate Your Caregiver Role

Have you identified yourself as a caregiver, someone who is susceptible to burnout? Many people are the caring person in their circle at work, home, church, or neighborhood; yet, they are never identified by others or by themselves as a caregiver. Just because the role is not identified does not mean they are exempt from the strain of a caregiver. The problem rises when the giving person becomes stressed out, then intervention is necessary. However, if the caregiver is not identified, neither the antidote nor assistance is given.

We think the caregivers of society are social workers, ministers, nurses, and the like. Yet amongst each group of business folk, neighbors, church, and relatives, there likely is a major caregiver. Some of the people who carry the greatest caseload of clients are lay people who become the center, the strong person that everyone leans on.

You need to look at yourself, at your role, at your caregiving. How is it working for your life? Have you assessed your situation recently? Are you giving only from the overflow? Or are you now giving from your essence and therefore being drained.

Garfield from Berkeley Ca. felt that persons have a limited container of nurturing to give. He postulated that once you have used your container's material, it is gone for life. He noted that 10 to 15 years was about the maximum that persons could stay in the front line facing grieving people. He recommended that after 10 to 15 years the caregiver needs to choose to serve in a one step away position. By knowing this and making a conscious choice the well being of the individual and the wisdom of the caregiver is preserved.

One step away from raw pain is management, teaching, writing, consulting, and preparing behind the scenes. In this position the caregiver is able to use all their education, experience, and insights of past work. Contrast that with waiting until a blow-up of burnout occurs and the experience of the caregiver is lost to society forever.

It is important to make the choice to step away from raw grief for awhile because the tendency of people who are working with emotional and spiritual deficiencies is to try harder. This leads to a stressed out individual who continues to go, go, go until one day they are out of gas, out of resources, and they snap. Usually the snap is in a form of a professional error resulting in hurting themselves professionally, such as giving the wrong medication. Or they snap with a personal blowup resulting in damaging significant relationships.

Neither of these options is ever acceptable. Intervention must come by identifying burnout symptoms before a blowup happens. In any organization it is the responsibility of the supervisor to intervene early enough to avert loss of face to the worker. It is so sad when these beautiful intentioned and giving individuals are allowed to push themselves to the point of such personal pain.

You, the caring person are responsible to keep a close tab, close observation on your burning out component. Be personally responsible to remove yourself from the frontline of pain when the time comes. If you do not take care of yourself you may sabotage your job and your relationships. No one benefits from that, neither society nor your family. It is mature to have a contingency plan for when the burning occurs. One should know exactly what they will do to take care of themselves at that time.

Are You Receiving Love

Gifted persons are impelled to give; they tend to be very busy people. Their cup truly runs over. Self knowledge is of the ultimate importance. You need to determine how much you can do. Look at your life and know yourself better. Chances are you started out by having a balanced lifestyle, but as you continued with care-giving you have not taken time to evaluate the many add-on's to your lifestyle. You also need to become aware of what has dropped out of your life.

When you take on a new obligation, do you consciously set something on the back burner, or put it on the shelf for a year? Reality is that once your house is full, which means your 24 hours a day are full, then when you take something new in the front door, something old must go out the back door. Are you sending enough former activities out the back door, to storage, or goodwill? If not, stop taking on new activities.

Later you may choose to take some of these activities back. If you do, the most important point is: again, when something comes in the front door, even a former activity, there must also be something going out the back door. You are defined in a twenty four hour time frame. You cannot do all things. Life is a trade off.

Identify Your Role

Your sensitivity and talents brought you to this situation. People will draw from you the rest of your life. That is your lot. If you are to stay a support person your entire life you need to learn self assessment skills early in the game. Are you the strong member in your circle of relatives, friends, or church? If so, others probably come to you for help in crisis times. Most likely you are willing and glad to be of help.

As people grow in competency they add on and on to the caring tasks. In your life, what "Yes, I can do that for you," have you just insidiously added to your life?

For example, my engineer friend, Jack, knew he had skills for working on cars. Because he loved his family, he was saying yes, without realizing it, to more and more people each year. He had a car, his wife had a car, he serviced his in-laws cars, and each of three children had a car.

The joke in the neighborhood was that the best help Jack could get from all these people was that he remain on his back on the driveway all weekend. They could drive their car over the top of him thereby saving him from getting up and down. My experience is that there are certain types of skills we freely ask others to give, such as mechanical talent, help with electronic equipment, stereo, TV, computer, hand-i-man, food, baking, and babysitting. Yet we almost never ask favors of other disciplines, such as lawyers, physicians, dentists, finance counselors, business managers, and artists.

Do They Still Feed You?

My educated guess is that you are managing many more roles than you are identifying. In the next week write them down. Are there people who used to support and inspire you who are now receivers from you?

One of the factors you need to assess is: Are you receiving love? Has there been a role change in your relationship with co-workers, relatives, and friends? When I ask, do you have a sharing caring group of friends, many people say, Oh yes, I have a wonderful group of friends. We have been close and supportive to each other for years. The question is, do they still feed you? I did not ask, do they still love you. Has their role with you changed? Are they now mainly receivers of your support?

One clew is the content of your conversations. Are you still enjoying the same subjects as you did 10 years ago? Do you talk intelligently about current affairs, do you laugh spontaneously with lightheartedness and is there real humor? Or is the content relegated to physical symptoms, sorrow, regret, cynicism, and loss of hope? Many conversations of the elderly are completely composed of that type of content.

How Big is your Caseload?

Let's look at your life. How big is your caseload? Perhaps one of your friends is going through a messy divorce, another is caring for a dying Mom, one is experiencing extreme work related stress, and someone is in financial crisis. Perhaps one is having difficulty with their teenager and yet another is grieving a recent death. Are you supporting each of them? Each group has one person who rises to the occasion and looks out for the others, is that you?

If you were a social worker, you would know the number of the caseload that you are carrying. Thirty five cases a week would be a heavy load. Now count the caseload you are shouldering in your personal life, job, home, and community responsibilities. Even though not identified you are still affected by the caseload.

When role reversal occurs, when your parent becomes your responsibility, or your friend becomes your client, as often happens in life; consider it an obligation to get your filling friendship needs from another source. Role reversal or change is seldom identified because people feel guilty acknowledging consciously that a friend has become a receiver and no longer a feeder. Remember this is about role; this has nothing to do with love. This happens, surreptitiously, sneakily, covertly, without awareness.

Name the persons you check on at least daily, weekly, or monthly. As your competency increases and the years go by the chances are you have just added one person after another. The likelihood is that you completely missed naming as clients, those friends who used to feed you with humor, fun, and silliness, but are now stressed out, or filled with sorrow. It is helpful to identify the number of clients you are supporting. These roles and clients absorb time and emotions in your life even if you don't count them. This leads to weariness, stress, and burnout.

This is the personal responsibility of the helping person. To know that joy amidst sorrow is not only appropriate but also necessary in human conditions. As a caregiver you must take your own joys because now is not your time for intense personal grief. This is not your journey. Your time of grief will come but now is your time to live life freely. Take your joys. Your goal is to go freely from death bed to a birthday party. Take that happiness of life into your being so that when you go down into that well of sorrow tomorrow to help another, you will have a spirit that is overflowing.

You need to validate your grief support work by recognizing you have clients. Do not misinterpret those who draw from you to be synonymous with friends from whom you receive. This does not negate the fact that we receive from our clients; however, if you think your clients are filling your friendship needs you are likely in emotional deficit.

Circle of Life

It helps to imagine concentric circles around you. You can draw this on paper. Put a dot in the center to represent you. In the circle nearest the center put the names of the people who are closest to your heart. In the slightly larger circle outside the inner circle put names of the people who feed you. Now on the third circle put the manes of the people who you would miss if you did not see them. They are the proverbial butcher, baker, and candlestick maker. These are people in your day at work, in your town, and place of worship. These are people who we tend to take for granted. Many times we do not know how important they are to us until they are gone. In the outer circle put the manes of people you minister to.

Know when to move the name on the circle. Know when the relationship is feeding you and when it is draining you. When a friend becomes a drain on your life, put the name on your ministry list. Don't confuse the difference between those you minister to, and those who feed you. Do not confuse this as a measure of love. The love does not change with the role. Love may even increase as the person accepts more of your gifts and talents, yet you need to be fed by others. You will need to find outside support. You may need to go for therapy or counseling with a minister or therapist; not because of pathology, but because professionals are trained to listen critically and help you formulate your thinking.

It takes great maturity to identify your need, ask for help, and follow through. Yet most successful, well developed persons that I know are people who tag in and out of growth therapy or spiritual guidance. The public thinks that the use of therapist is for someone who is ill. That is not true. Therapist are very helpful for personal growth. They may be the only people who are trained to listen to what you have heard and seen. They may be the only ones who can listen to the trajectory of your thoughts and value what is happening to you beyond the needs of your client. Everyone else wants to know how the person you are supporting is doing, not how you are managing emotionally.

Give Only From the Overflow

Your first responsibility as a helping person is to make sure your own cup is full to overflowing. Your second responsibility is to give only from the overflow. Otherwise your spirit will suffer of thirst. Having additional needy people in the world is not a help to anyone.

What does that mean? That means you must stay under the overflowing cup. You must daily go to the source that fills you. What refreshes you? What is your thing?

Your Overflowing Cup

I envision it like this. There is a huge cup. To me it looks like a big beautiful goblet. Under this tall stemmed glassware are the many wine glasses of you and me. These wine glasses are so tiny in comparison to the goblet.

The goblet is overflowing, running over with the wine of life. Its overflow quickly fills our tiny wine glass and spills unto the table and over the table's edge. Around this table on a high hill are the many hungry and thirsty people of the world. They cry out for drink. The overflow runs easily from the huge goblet into ours and over the table into their outstretched hands, they sip and are refreshed.

Our temptation comes from the goodness of our hearts. We take our little wine glass and head down the hill giving this one to sip and that one to drink. Others see us coming and cry out, "Me too, I thirst." We follow the voices calling us down one hill and up the next. The sun is beating, beating, and the multitudes are stretching out their hands crying. Yes, we keep repeating our behavior. We go from one to the other, giving this one a sip, and that one to drink.

Without realizing how far we have come hearing the wounded cries, we suddenly become conscious that there is no more liquid in our tiny little goblet. Yet, we hold it above the mouths squeezing, squeezing, and somehow hoping to get another drop out of the empty glass. Alas! Too late! Our cup is dry.

Forlornly we look back to the table of the large overflowing goblet only to realize it is far, far away. We have wondered too far. We head back. Now we are thirsty, now overcome ourselves, we fall to our knees in weakness with outstretched hands crying, "I thirst!" Begging, "Someone please give me to drink."

Alas we did not stay under the source that feeds us and now have become one of the multitudes of the hungry.

You Are the Pipe, Not the Pump

You are the pipe, not the pump. The pipe just puts itself into position. The flow comes from somewhere else. The pump, however is working, working, a pump has many moving parts. Moving parts wear out. Do not attempt to be the pump! You are not the pump! The pump will still be pumping; the huge goblet will still be overflowing, after you are gone from this work and gone from this world. What is your role?

You are the Flute

You are the flute not the blower of the wind. You are simply the instrument. You merely have to present your beautiful body with right intention. The instrument is just present for flute-player. Without an instrument the flautist has no music, only wind. Be the instrument; don't try to be the music maker.

Never Give From Your Essence

You need to look at yourself, your role and the way you give care. How is it working for your life? Have you assessed your situation recently? Are you giving only from the overflow or are you now giving from your essence and therefore being drained. You need to know there will always be the hungry eyes following you into the night. We will not eradicate the poverty of the needy in the world. The bible says, "The poor will always be amongst us." You are not called to be the Messiah; you are called only to be the hands and heart of intelligent love for a chosen few. There will always be the multitudes that are beyond your reach; a difficult concept, a necessary concept to internalize. What is your role? Having additional needy people in the world is not a help to anyone. You will die and the multitude of deprived will still exist. You must be able to go from death bed to birthday party without guilt.

You are not the Savior. What does that mean? It means you must stay under the overflowing cup. You must daily go to the source that fills you. What is your thing? How do you get refreshed?

Therapeutic Distance - What is it?

Identification with the others pain is real. It is important to know whose pain it is, whose journey is this sorrow. Do not be afraid if therapeutic distance is not always there for you. It takes a long time to get used to intense grief. To be therapeutic some vulnerability is required. To achieve that combination of vulnerability and distance is important to a grief support person, you will need to develop a philosophy of loss, yes, even for untimely losses.

The goal is to have a little bit of callus. Helping persons are like harp players, they need a callus. If there is no callus, the fingers of the harpist are too sensitive to play very long. The callus must be on the tip of your finger, not on your heart, because the harp player needs to express the sentimentality of the song. I know. I gave up playing the guitar when I returned to school. Now I want to play but can only finger a few bars of music before the pain in my finger tips is too great to continue. I have lost the necessary calluses.

You need to be alert. You cannot get too callused or you do not have the sensitivity of touch to produce the feeling, the soul of the music. My brother, Harold, played since he was a boy. As a man he found that farm work caused his hands to become too callused to feel the instrument. He could no longer sense just the right touch to produce the soulful or happy sounds. How he mourned his musical instruments. Yet, he explained that he had no choice. Farm work just produced the thick calluses.

Prepare the therapeutic callus on your heart with well developed philosophies of pleasure/pain, light and dark, good and evil. Your goal is to go from sorrow and pain to enjoyment. You need to go from body function loss to joyfully feeling your own muscles while riding a bike. You need to master the ability to have joy amidst sorrow. To take your own joys and happiness while helping others who are suffering and grieving. To know at a gut level that you have your own journey. This is the other person's journey. Whose pain is it? Even though you have empathy, now is not your time to be the mourner. Know your role. Honor your calling.

Do you have an Intake Jack?

Can you receive? Many helping persons are like an electronic receiver, they have wonderful output jacks, they give beautifully to others, but they may not be able to receive. If I were to look at your receiver, would I find the receiving jack open and well used, or would I need to get an auger to rout it out before I could put something into it for you to receive? I sometimes think plugged receiving jacks are a genetic defect in persons who choose to nurture. Perhaps we need to do a little surgery, that is, make an intellectual decision around choosing to receive.

So many of us hate to be the receiver, we want only to give. I remember when the tornado devastated my home, killed, and injured my neighbors, how grateful I was when I received help from the disaster rescuers, but wow, I was emotionally confused! I knew I should be saying what they were saying and doing what they were doing. I kept repeating, "God, you have this turned around; I am not supposed to be the victim. Don't you remember? I have dedicated my life to being the rescuer. I have all these disaster rescuer certificates, why is my house down?"

Can you be vulnerable, comforted, loved? Do you have your intake jack plugged in?

Healing Measures

Not Think about Work

Change must be scheduled in order to get relief from constant grief. Dr. Kubler Ross says grief workers should not work in a grieving atmosphere for more than 4 hours a day. The other 4 hours ought to be in an area with the opposite dynamics such as a well baby clinic. A hospice volunteer, who worked among several families with dying persons, had a part time job delivering flowers and balloons for a florist. She chose to do this on purpose. She said that everyone is happy when you give them flowers. Most helping persons do not work for institutions that understand. Therefore you have to develop and schedule your own relief. See if you can do this on your job. Be creative, be innovative.

In your personal life, schedule joy time with children, family, and friends. Honor your recreation fun, such as swimming and bicycling. Then do something creative with, paint, music, dance, yoga, garden, or woodworking. Find something that is you. Be kind to yourself, be gentle with yourself. To do this, clock time must be allocated and honored. This is the point at which caregivers sabotage.

Go Home and Party

You need to leave the suffering and go home to party. Choose to be with people who do not know what you do in your nurturing role. Take time to forget about your work. That takes discipline of mind. I find most helping persons do not have the discipline of mind this requires.

Not thinking of your work means having the courage not to tell others in your recreation space the nature of your work. It means you reply to the question of what you do with something very generic or benign, such as I do office work all day or if you are an EMT, say I work in transportation. Then, show by your body language that you are not interested in pursuing that line of conversation. You fudge so well in other areas, learn to do it in the care of your spirit.

You need to do some preparatory work. That means no sabotaging behavior by taking your work with you on your recreation pursuits. This means when you take time off you have no beeper, no cell phone, no books, or papers to read or write while on your outing. Every time a remembrance of work comes to mind, discipline the mind to substitute something from the environment immediately. It works best if you use concrete thoughts such as the color of the sky, room, or clothing to focus on.

Taking work on a vacation is a way of not being present. It is a way of sabotaging your ability to be mentally away. Studies show that briefcases and computers full of work are taken on vacations. This is self-defeating behavior. Whether you use these items or never touch them, just by having work with you, you have successfully interfered with your sense of awayness.

At recreation areas I often see someone who has brought along work. Generally they do not get to the work, but they successfully sabotage their mental relaxation by being subconsciously aware and guilty about the undone work. If you take work with you, you are always aware of the paper you want to write, or figures you want to run. When you have a cell phone or beeper, you do not let yourself get to that beneficial bio energy level of relaxation because a part of you is always prepared to answer the phone. Recreation is for recreating. Leave your work at home

Find a Place to Get Away

One lawyer I know has his secretary schedule a closed conference each Tuesday afternoon. Only the Sisters at the Cenacle know the conference takes place in the gardens and reading rooms of their retreat house. He has seldom missed these Tuesday appointments for decades.

A physician friend of mine wanted so badly to achieve the ability to let go and to be truly away. After hours of discussing techniques on how to be an ordinary person he finely felt ready. He took his family on a camping trip. He succeeded to live with an ordinary person identity for 5 hours. He reported he could not tolerate the level of ignorance about medicine that was being expressed around the campfire that evening. He informed the group of his profession. He reported they were fascinated and kept him talking about his work the entire weekend. It was a nice weekend but may not have fulfilled his objective of away-ness.

Personal Rhythm

According to Meyers Briggs the majority of people need to be with others to refresh and only a small percent need to be alone. These introverts benefit by going to a retreat house, mountains, ocean or staying alone quietly in their home with the phone off.

Some people need to refresh two days every week. Others love to work straight for 3 weeks and have one week off, as is the case for airline pilots, stewards, and river barge employees. There are others who can keep going until a long vacation of two months a year. School teachers fall into this category because during the school year their minds and weekends are filled with preparation, grading, and school events.

I do well working 14 to 21 days straight. However I need two months off a year. I can write and do research during this time. I just need to be away from people's stories. It is people's stories that burn me out the fastest. Research requires a different facet of me. Contrary to popular belief, the best burnout prevention or burnout healing is likely a seminar or study course that increases skills in the field of work. This is excellent preventative mental health activity.

Validate Your Holistic Needs

Perhaps now is the time to validate your holistic needs. Perhaps now is the time in your life to validate, quiet time, fun time, conversation time. Put them on your calendar and give passive-receiving-time equal value to active-work-time.

The question you need to ask yourself is how long can I go without filling the emotional, intellectual, physical, spiritual, or social component of mine without it screaming at me? For scream it will. How long can I go without feeling out of sorts, short tempered, lonely, or yearning for an unknown?

When these feelings occur you need to ask yourself, what facet of me is starving? And then get that need met in a healthy manner. This requires time. You will find you have a fulfillment pattern. When it is filled your cup is overflowing.

You will find you can postpone that filling for a certain number of days without undo stress as long as you know you will be satisfying the yearning in the known future. Much of the benefit of a vacation is prophylactic, that is, the value is in the time coming up to it knowing that holiday time is going to happen. I need refreshing on a weekly basis; however, I can stretch to two weeks. At that point I am in emotional or physical trouble. How about you?

Make a sheet with five headings, social, physical, emotional, intellectual, and spiritual. Then list under each heading: (See John Gray's material)

- What do your need in each facet?
- How much
- How often

If you deny yourself the emotional filling time, play time, planning time, spirit filling time, then you will be harassed, have a martyr complex, experience chronic sorrow, and be a person of decreasing joy to everyone you come in contact with.

You need to ask your spirit self, "Is this what was intended when I was inspired to be a healer of persons?" Remember that if you die no one will be better off? Die? You ask. Do you kid yourself by thinking that if your body is still alive, you are alive? You need to ask, is it ethical to let your emotional self, spirit self, social self, or intellectual component die? Is that being a good steward? Remember that if you die, or your spirit, loving, or body dies, no one will be better off. Therefore, plan time to take care of your fun and refilling needs.

One Emotional Step Away

If you feel the burning of burnout coming but are required to be on the job, discipline your mind not to get emotionally evolved for a few days. You need to be creative about how to get this. Make it a point to not take work home during this phase, to deliberately not think about loss but concentrate on your personal happiness and hobbies in between patients or clients.

It is surprising that the recipients of your care often receive from you during this time even though you are keeping yourself emotionally distant. There is a great difference between distancing yourself with a purpose so that you are free to integrate past material, and the kind of distancing that is defensive which results in coldness. If you stay an involved caregiver you will need to go through this process many times as losses and ageing occur in your own life.

Finish Something

Create something; it so important that you see your finished product. Working with suffering people has no ending. It is a deep well of sorrow. Remember your place, your role is to go down into that well where they must live for now, but you are not to live in that well. If you do we now have two people in trouble. You must climb out into the sunshine, to gather fresh air of filling love to take down into that well tomorrow.

Finish your thing. It can be to wash a floor, paint a picture, play a song, knit a scarf, crochet an afghan, refinish a chair, build a ship in a bottle, or tear down a shed, with permission of the owner. What is your finished product?

To support a fellow caregiver find ways to reinforce each other's creations.

Meditation

All successful people meditate. They may not name it as such. Perhaps they call it daydreaming or fantasizing, some folks go hunting, golfing, fishing, to give their mind quieting time. Some people call it prayer and go on retreats. Many different names cause the same effect of communing with the inner self, being in the now, and opening to intuition or inspiration.

Meditation is essential to quiet the inner self, to establish your place in the universal plan, to reset your hierarchy of values, and to be a good friend to your spirit.

There is a wonderful chapter, Tips on Meditation P. 105 of John Gray's book, *"How to Get what you want and Want what you get."* I highly recommend that book. I also like Deepak Chopra's and Eckhart Tollie's methodology for meditation. Be eclectic; choose those points that speak to your spirit from many teachers.

Blue Sky Your Coming Events

They may not name it meditation. Perhaps they call it imagination, daydreaming, or fantasizing but all successful people run a detail picture in their mind of every facet of their work. Garfield gives the example of a trial lawyer sitting by the pool in the afternoon with a cool drink. To the neighbors, the lawyer looks as though he is lounging, in reality; he is running every detail of the trial over in his mind. This poolside or golfing outing is his most important preparation place.

My post surgical instructor required a detailed 24 page patient care plan. Then she put us through a grueling pre-conference oral report and quiz. She played devils advocate with the help of a co-teacher. After all of that pre-planning, the instructor stressed the most important part of a plan is that it be left on the chair outside the door of the action room, that means the operating room or court room. Then you go in and, "Fly by the seat of your pants." The way in which you play the hand while winging it, is totally different after you have done the pre-plan than when you have not prepared at all. Yes, even those times, especially those times when all hell breaks loose and you do not use even one part of the pre-plan. Your work is totally different than if you had no plan at all.

I believe this thoroughly. This is some of the best advice I have received in my life. The planning sets the goal in motion. How the goal plays out may change moment by moment but the highest goal remains the same. I spend twenty minutes before a lecture in quietude. I engage the alpha waves of my mind and then become one of the practitioners of my audience. I always say, I go into the skin of my audience and vicariously feel their experiences. If I am speaking to police officers, I visualize that

I am sitting in the squad, I observe as I receive the call, see the accident as I approach, look at the people around the wrecked vehicles, run to the injured, feel my feelings as I carry out my professional and personal duties as a Police officer.

In life how often are we reminded of the quote, "Oh, the best laid plans of mice and men?" Yet the life lived by a carefully thought out plan with meditation, reading, and daydreaming, is a totally different life then the life resulting from unplanned existence.

Worst Case Catastrophe Plan

People who handle stress well were found to be persons who knew exactly what their risks were. Garfield found that high performers worked out worst catastrophic expectation reports either in their minds or in writing before taking a risk. They set out the worst that could possibly happen and decided whether they could live with that outcome. If they were uncomfortable they did not do the activity. If they could live with the worst consequence they moved ahead confidently. Stress prone people didn't go through the worst catastrophe process, so when taking a risk they tended to be hampered by a sense of impending doom. Do not put yourself through the excruciating worry of failure. Make it a value of yours to say, I can live with that, or terminate it before you start. There is plenty else to do.

Physical Exercise

Physical exercise is absolutely necessary when working with people. You immobilize more than you realize when working with the sorrowing person. The body needs to get on an equally fatigued level as the mind and emotions. Among other benefits it allows the endorphins to rise in the brain.

We need the equivalent of two miles of brisk walking per day. This can be any type of activity such as swimming, weight lifting, yoga, bike riding, tennis, or golf. You need to move in order to circulate the blood and lymph so they collect the lactic acid and other waste products which have accumulated. You need to have flowing blood to bring fresh nutrients to your brain, muscles, and organs.

Sleep

Sleep is so important. Isn't it ironic that caring persons are amongst the most sleep deprived people? They work odd hours, are on call, and dream the events all night long.

Sleep is not necessary but lying flat and resting is. It may be hard to lie down because you feel you will not go to sleep. It is true, you may not sleep. The visions and stories may run through your mind. Some of that needs processing. Just let the images and feelings come and let them go right on through. Feel your feelings, do not stop or squelch your feelings to cause repression. This allowing to process is different than escalating.

I find having a quieting tape playing very softly helps me put my thoughts in order. If sleep does not come I get up for an hour or two. Sometimes I write, sometimes watch TV or a video, sometimes I do handiwork or something for pleasure; then I lay down flat again to rest. If for no other reason, rest is essential because the bones need to lie out and the organs need to reposition. These are some of the reasons why two short naps of twenty minutes each are so beneficial. One does not have to sleep. Sleepless periods are a good time to meditate to rest the mind as well as your body. When decompressing, I do best with a talking meditation tape, rather than silence.

Nutrition

You truly are what you eat. If you want clarity of mind make sure every bite you put into your mouth is nutritious. All diets start in the grocery store or restaurant. If it is not good for you, it does not go into the basket or on the plate. Eat food as close to the way nature made it as possible and avoid most white flour and sugar. Use the 70/30-food rule, stop when 70% full, wait 20 minutes, if you are still hungry eat more. Keep your intake of fats less than 30 grams per day.

A word about weight gain. For those of you who respond to stress with a little bit of weight gain, a gain of two pounds last year isn't much. Probably nothing to be worried about. What is two pounds? Two pounds a year between the ages of 20 to 40 is forty pounds overweight? Keep adding only two pounds a year and at age 60 you will be 80 pounds overweight.

Weight gain is a matter of decreasing volume of food each year. The metabolism slows so it takes fewer calories to maintain weight with the same amount of physical exercise. As one ages the appetite is no longer a guide of when to eat or how much to eat. The taste buds are also a fickle guide. Volume and what to eat become a matter of decision.

These are helps for some people. Keep clear canisters of acceptable nibbles such as fat free crackers and fat free pretzels for those acid tummy attacks. For crunch, add nuts to get that nutritious handful a day, have dried prunes, dates and apricots for that hypoglycemic attack, and then wait 20 minutes for the nutrients to get into your bloodstream to see if you need more snacks. Having these ready available avoids the over caloric response to these requirements.

I realize I did not mention those people who tend to lose weight under stress. I know that can be a serious dilemma. But to empathize with that dilemma is as difficult for me as it is to empathize with those who complain about having naturally curly hair. Empathize? As I pay $60.00 every three months for a permanent that no more goes the way I want it to go as does naturally curly hair. In the tornado aftermath it was a week before the disaster center weighed us. They were fearful of too much weight loss. I gained 10 pounds immediately. They say those of us who gain weight under stress are genetic survivors of repeated famines.

Nurture Those Who Support You

There is a story about a golden egg which was cherished by the princess. She was so obsessed by the golden egg which was laid each day that she completely neglected to cherish the goose who laid the golden egg. The goose died from depression and sorrowful neglect. The princess wondered why there were no more golden eggs. Moral of this story, cherish the geese that lay your golden eggs.

Watch you family manners

Don't foist upon them that which they cannot accept. This may not be their gift. They may not be able to stomach grieving and dying information.

Thank them for their support. Honest, it is true that passive support from them is enough.

Respect their time frame. It is so easy to get caught up in a grief or a dying situation that one overstays their committed time. Come home on time. Do your preparatory work. In rare cases you may choose to stay longer than promised. Prepare your family that this may occur at special times such as the dying time. When it happens, communicate with your family appropriately and with gratitude.

Don't bend their ear the minute you reach the door. This work is so emotionally overwhelming that it needs to spill out. Perhaps this is a time when you need to see your debriefer before you go home; especially if yours is a family that cannot talk about this subject. When you get home, ask what they have been doing, listen, and then share your story.

Your Family's Gift to Society

People who are too busy to help often make it possible for one member of the family to be the giver-to-society by allowing for, and tolerating: Time away, preoccupation with the case, gas money usage, child care, and odd hours.

Be Kind to Your Family

Watch your family manners. How many undiluted clock hours do you spend with them each day? We need to keep our families informed of what we do. Our families put up with it so we need to thank them and let them know how much we appreciate their support and the difference it makes to others.

Give time to activities the family chooses. Decide the time and honor it at the same value level that you would honor your doctor appointment. If you want to postpone your family appointment, ask, "Would I postpone my doctor appointment for this reason?" If you answer "yes," then go ahead and postpone your family activity. However, if you would not postpone your doctor or dental appointment for this cause, do keep your family appointment.

One movie star stated he honors two and 1/2 hours of being with his children each day. When my children were young my husband and I camped each Friday evening, Saturday, and Sunday. On Sunday we played family tennis from 9 am to 12 pm. In the winter we found one family activity per week. It was a challenge to find an activity we could all participate in. Some activities were family roller-skating lessons, swimming, and painting. When I had to be gone on an extensive speaking tour, I took my young children and husband on a Bahamian cruise immediately after so they could participate in the blessings since they had shared me as the gift.

Be clear about your helping care role, let them know you intend to do this, what the cost is to them, what the cost is to you, and what and how they will gain by the giving your services. I believe that the families of caring persons gain a lot. In order to express it to your family means you must do the homework of delineating it. You need to clarify your role and let them know what it is that you gain by the giving of yourself in a job such as this. Specify the insights care and compassion that comes back to the family. One family member's giving is truly an entire family matter. It is good to point out how the whole family gains by the community service of one of its members.

My Young Son's Bereavement Experiences

An example is my son, Craig. It began the year that schools around my area decided it would be helpful for someone to come in as a guest speaker on the subject of death and dying, grief and grieving. When my son was 9 years old, his school was off on one of my speaking days. I ask him to come along with me. He was so embarrassed for me, wanting me to cancel, saying, "Mom the kids won't listen to you on a subject like that, they will laugh at you, they will heckle you." He really suffered for me, but came along at my insistence.

To quiet his anxiety, I gave him a job to tape record the session. I can still see him clearly in my minds eye, sitting on the floor in the back of the room by the speakers. As we left the high school, he looked at me with his brown eyes and in a tone of extreme awe said, "Mom, they listened, they really listened, Mom!"

Throughout his high school years he often came with me on seminars for rescue workers and sermons I gave at churches. The lines of people waiting to speak to me after presentations were long; many people gave up and went to speak with him instead. I would glance over seeing this high school young man sincerely responding. I watched the people leave with an attitude of relief. He seemed so at ease. I never knew exactly what he said. But I knew he was familiar with the entire subject of Thanatology as it was continuously a part of his home life.

Years later he said to me. "Mom, I am the lead Officer for each death that occurs on my shift. I do my investigation and then go to the homes to inform the families of the death of their child or mate. I can do that Mom, I don't know why. The other Officers ask me about it, I just know I can do it. It just comes naturally to me."

It never occurred to him that his gift of loving service was nurtured at his Mother's knee. He thought he gained it all by himself.

Friendship Building Skills

Do You Have a Caring Sharing Brotherhood?

It is likely that you will not function freely and open in intense emotional support work for more than a year without a support group. To be effective in grief work you must allow yourself to become at least somewhat involved in the other person's grief and that means you will be emotionally drained and in need of refilling.

You need a support group for two facets of your life. One group to share your grief work material with and another group of people who appreciate you and know nothing about your work role other than your title.

Life will require that you often develop new personal friends. Losses come fast and furious about the age of 40 at which age life produces many losses. Friends take last-ditch opportunities to move up the ladder of success. Middle age depressions come to some friends who used to feed you, and others begin their chronic illnesses. Middle age is the time parents begin to age and role reversal caregiving begins.

Friendship building becomes a continuous task. It is likely that after middle age the need to build new friends will occur at regular intervals for the rest of your life. After age 60 the need arises every couple of years.

You will always need to have the kind of friends who you can call at need and say, I really need to talk to someone, and they respond with, "No problem."

Do you have a sharing caring body of friends? If not, consider it an important duty to build one, if you cannot build one, buy one. If you do not have a caring informed friend available in time of need call a professional counselor. It may be the best money you spend. It takes a type of maturity to seek help in time of need.

This concept of using a professional counselor in lieu of a personal support person is often misunderstood. There are many times when that is the most mature decision you can make, such as when all your support people are in the same boat, that is they suffer the same stress.

This happened to us in the tornado. All of us lost our homes, had family injured, and friends killed. This is a time to be talking to an outside person. Our friends needed our love and presence. We needed an objective outsider to help us sort through our own overwhelming stimuli.

Another time when people need to seek outside professional help is after moving. It takes a long time to develop the safety, trust, and shared background for a personal support group. After a move it is mature to seek a professionally trained listener to help sort out emotions and thoughts. This is just as true for the newly moved young person who is jettisoned into a new milieu as it is for adults, yes, even when his home stayed the same and only his school situation changed.

People need to know that professional counseling is available when stress and grief occur before a new personal support group is formed. So many people are in emotional deficiency after a move because they have no one in the new milieu who reaches out to emotionally support them.

Friendship Building Skills

It takes a lot of time to build a sharing, caring relationship. Many people go from family, school friends, and then directly into marriage. They simply do not grow their ability to make new friends.

There is a scarcity of mature skills of friendship building amongst adults. They are not proficient at making new friends when they become alone after a move, or when they are singled again after a marriage. The result is that we have high-rises of senior citizens who are living alone amongst other people living alone, with no ability for friendship building.

However, this is not true only of seniors; I am impressed with what a lonely society we have. We need to redefine extended family from blood relatives to tribal. Where ever there is caring sharing body of persons there is a tribe/family.

Three Strikes You Are Out

The problem is that most adults will try 3 times to make friends. If that doesn't work out they will give up. I find that three times is very generous. If you invite someone who responds with, "Sorry, rain-check," are you likely to call again? If you do and the second reply is, "Gee I'd like to but not this month." Will you call again? Probably not. The lesson for you is, if you are the one who must refuse, return the invitation or you will lose the opportunity. The other person will not have the courage to call you again for fear you will reject them one more time.

You may think the reason why someone has to say no makes a difference. In reality, it probably does not. People are just afraid to invite new people for fear of rejection. You must be assertive. The move is up to you.

You Need 5 Because:

1. The first one you call–the phone just rings and rings--. I don't know about you–but I always take it personally.

2. The second–the answering machine refers you to a number in Asia.

3. The third one would like to talk, but has diarrhea and is vomiting–both at the same time.

4. The fourth loves you but cannot come because of their work. They are the anesthesiologist and the patient wouldn't like it if he came right over.

5. The fifth one can come. It takes five calls on the average to get a positive response.

Bearing in mind the average person will only make three calls before they lose their nerve, it helps us to understand why we are such a nation of lonely people.

Children's Skills

It is good to learn from the young to try and try again for friendship. Look at young children how easily they say, "Will you walk home with me? I'll share my candy bar with you."

The next time you are in a group, look around the room, if there is someone you think you would like to know better, ask them, "Will you come home with me? I'll share my coffee cup?" When you develop a new friendship it is important to touch base within two weeks. There is a building of momentum within a two-week period, but a loss of momentum if the contact point is longer than two weeks.

Now imagine 4 working adults all with their calendars trying to find a common day free in which to meet. How long do you think it takes? Usually about 4 months. Now you see why it is such work to build a friendship base.

As soon as you build that base, it is likely they or you will move again, and you are back at square one again. There are neighborhood subdivisions around medium cities where people move on their way up the ladder of success to headquarters in other cities such as New York or Washington, DC. Ministers in those communities tell me they can use the same sermon every three years because while the church building is the same the people in the congregation are different. Is it a co-incidence that stress related illness are high in these areas?

Know the Meaning of True Love

What is the meaning of love? Rabbi Goldman asks: "Do you love me? Then, do you know what gives me pain? If you do not know what gives me pain-- then how can you say, I love you?" At the time of stress, grief, and loss, there is and excellent opportunity to say to another, "I love you."

In the time of pain, people who are suffering are often not beautiful. They are neither sweet nor pleasant company. True love goes to the suffering. Grief is interpreted as rejection, loss, and shame. It demonstrates in behavioral problems, and hostility. There may be few immediate rewards for you or for your efforts. Do you love me? Can you love me when I am not beautiful? Do you know what gives me pain?

Check List When Supporting Each Other

- Identify your caseload--perhaps you're carrying much more than you think
- Circle of supportive friends
- Remembering your spirit--know what it is that causes you to overflow
- Finished something lately
- Taking time off to be a receiver
- Taking mental time away from your work? Not thinking about your work
- Meditating
- Nurtured your family
- Exercising
- Nutritious food
- Resting enough
- Sharpened your friendship building skills–cultivated a new friend lately? What are you doing about silly friends?

Appendix A

Workshop on Burnout

Planning & Meditation

Planning and meditation time is the most important event of your day! If you must cut out something, this is the last item to cut out. The quality of all other time you spent is dependent on this hour; give your meditation-planning time the highest priority.

Meditation & Planning Together

Many persons are confused about how to make meditation and planning time work for them. The first thing to remember is that the two go together. They are rightfully part of each other. One of the greatest hindrances persons complain about in their meditations is that they are distracted, or that they are too tense because of all the things they have to do.

Yes, that is part of what it means to be an adult. You have a lot of things going on in your mind at the same time. That is as it should be. Instead of being disturbed by a planning thought, just jot it down as it comes to you. That will alleviate some worry. Stay in meditative mood.

My Personal Ritual

There is a way to work in a positive manner with many concerns going through your mind at meditation time.

First, choose the dreamiest time of your day. Are you a morning person? Can you sit with a cup of coffee and do nothing at that time? Or do you dream best in the evening? Perhaps after a nap?

I will tell you how I do my meditation and planning time, then you design yours.

Gather My Supplies

I get up an hour before I need to start getting ready.

Then I gather my supplies. In winter they stay at my couch except for coffee and calendar which is near the phone. In the summer I meditate outside and keep my things in a tote bag, they are:

- Journal--spiral note book, or computer
- Meditation book or tape–I like to sit in the dark so a tape works well at those times
- Weekly planner
- Calendars x 2

    Family and Personal work calendars.
    I usually use a laptop for this.

- Shopping lists x 2

    Groceries and General shopping

- Letter tablet
- Cell phone

Light a candle or focus on a natural beauty, flower, sky, clouds, or tree.

Let come what comes to mind for awhile

Use a relaxation tape to count down to alpha brain wave state

Read or listen to tape until a thought comes–then sail with it

Take up journal and write what comes out of the pen. Do not think about what you will write; discover what you have written when you read it. The information is in the pen or in the computer keys. You need to move these for the information to come out.

Time Structuring

Does your time plan sometimes get shot to heck? Do you plan and something seems to come up to upset it? Can it be that you are not including everything in your plan that needs to be there? Are you planning time for:

Doing Nothing

Lag Days: about 1 in every 8 days is a lag day for me.

Unplanned Time

Studies show that in an eight hour day, the average person can complete five hours of work; the rest of the time is taken up with: running errands, talking to co-workers, getting coffee and snacks, neighbors, phone calls, cleaning out drawers, rearranging things, fixing the printer, changing ink cartridges and papers, helping out your family members or work associates.

Un-validated Time

Such as how long does it really take to write a short letter? I find it takes at least a half hour including addressing and stamping. How much time does eating take? Do you include prep time, eating, and clean up when you are eating alone? Or do you only count the time you eat with others. If you don't validate these times you will always have an emotional conflict with your time schedule and say nasty things to yourself. Therefore not validating these activities can be self destructive behavior.

Crisis Time.

Are you someone who is on call? Many persons are such as: Ministers, some nurses, social workers, parish visitors, hospice workers, and emergency personnel. It is often thought that they cannot plan time for crisis. Yes, you plan crisis time. You need to chart your time spent in crisis over a period of about eight weeks and find the average number of hours you spend on crisis work each week.

Flexi Time

Now here is how you do your planning. Much of every persons work and play time is flexi time. That means it can be done with some flexibility of the hour. For instance, all professionals and para professionals including hospice and church visitors need to do professional reading to stay up on their work. The hour of this reading can change according to the schedule. Another example of flexi time work is that you may need to clean the house before company arrives two days from now, but the exact hours you clean can be flexible according to your other priority time needs.

Put in Planner

When you work on your weekly planner put the absolute time needs down such as, pick up child from school at 3:10 pm, and meeting at 7: pm. Let's say that when you were charting your time, you found you have 3 unplanned hours taken up per day, and an average of 5 hours of crisis work per week. Mark your planner with all 5 crisis hours scheduled in on Mon. Remember that studies show persons can only complete 5 hours of work in an eight hour day. The rest of the time is lag time or unplanned activities like phone conversations and people stopping by your door.

Then continue planning on Tuesday; here put in your weeks worth of unplanned activities time plus the absolute activities of this day. On Wednesday you may still need to schedule in unplanned time and perhaps now some of your flexi-time activities such as, clean the hall closet, write a long letter to your friend, go down to the river and sketch, read three hours from a book of your choice, take the dog to the vet for shots, visit that shut-in you support once a week. Finish out the rest of the week by scheduling in the activities you absolutely must do and add those you have time to choose.

When Monday arrives you have that day scheduled for crisis. Let's say your phone does not ring, you begin seriously to do your flexi work which is marked on Wednesday's schedule. You run errands, tear that closet apart, or curl up with that serious reading. On Tuesday let's say that a 1 hour of unplanned activity happened, your neighbor stopped by; other than that it is a quiet day and you are busy with the flexi time work which you have scheduled for Thursday. As you complete each task be sure to cross it out. This is a positive reinforcement stroke for you.

Wednesday goes like you planned except that you have 2 hours of flexi-time that you use to complete Friday's planned activities. See what happened? You have completed your flex-activities by Wednesday. Thursday you get a call that unexpected guests will arrive for the weekend, or your friend needs many hours of your time, or your hospice client takes a turn for the worst and you want to spend a lot of hours with the family. You still have the absolute time activities for these days but you have the flexi-time open for your pre-scheduled crisis and unplanned activities. A competent evaluator has no unplanned activities because the unplanned activities are planned for. If you evaluate honestly you know how many hours you will need and you allow for a couple extra open hours per week. It is always easy to fill those in with a walk, reading, or shopping.

Remember you need to chart the time you are active in unplanned and crisis work. Keep an accurate accounting of that time; then, when you do your weekly planning keep in mind that not all of your duties and free time needs to be on a specific time slot. Much of everyone's work and play can be on flexi-time.

Fill in Your Planner.

This is how you fill in your Calendar and Planner.

First take your calendar and mark time for the absolutes, put in information, address, directions, names, items you need to take along with you. This calendar is not thrown away at the end of the year. It is filed on the bookshelf. I have mine since 1973. It is a record and you will be surprised at how often you pull them down to retrieve information.

Now go to your weekly planner and jot the appointment down in the time-slot. Proceed to the previous Monday and write in the preparation work that is necessary to do before that event. If you need things made two weeks in advance then go to two weeks before in your weekly reminder and put down exactly what needs to be done such as shop for supplies, write an agenda, make reminder phone calls or acquire copies of handouts.

Rhythm of Life

Why does your time plan not work for you? Or, instead of easing your life it adds an additional burden? Is it that you are not validating the: do nothing times, lag days, unplanned times and crisis times? That is, you do not hold them in high value and are embarrassed to put them in written form in your planner?

Perhaps before you can properly do a good time plan you need to come to terms with some old tapes that are self destructive. Usually when you first heard these tapes they were appropriate for you to live and guide your life by because you were young and were in the process of becoming. Now you need to go to the second step of maturity. That means you must recognize you have become already, and now you must reorganize your priorities. Then, only then, go to the third step of maturity and give unto those who will receive, not to those who will throw away your gifts of energy.

You need now to review your life in the time frame of this present year. Are your old priorities still appropriate? Are the people you are devoting your efforts to still using your gifts, or are they now independent of you and you need to be looking for other recipients of your gifts? For example, do you have grown children? You have lots of talents that are free now to provide for other worthy recipients.

Are you still operating under parental injunctions such as: If it is worth doing, it is worth doing perfectly? Challenge that! Much work is worth doing not perfectly; "Strive for excellence, not perfection." Many good things are never done because of this injunction. Some people feel that, "Idol hands are a devils workshop." Their favorite refrain is, "I'm so busy." They repeat this with great pride. It really shows an inability to manage time. Calm time is important for meditation, imagination, creativity, and prayer. Perhaps now is the time to validate your holistic needs. Perhaps now is the time in your life to validate quiet time, fun time, conversation, listening to music, and thinking. Put them on your calendar and give them equal value to your other work.

What is your Rythem

You need to understand your holistic self in order to succeed at this. What is your rhythm of life? How much time does each facet of your self need in order to grow, flourish and bloom? Some persons have a rhythm of life that cycles every 24 hours, others every 2 days, and some once a week. The question you need to ask yourself is, how long can I go without filling this emotional, intellectual, physical, spiritual, and social need without it screaming at me? Without my feeling out of sorts, short on temper, lonely, and yearning for an unknown. When these feelings occur you need to ask yourself, "What facet of me is starving?" And then get that need met in a healthy manner.

You will find you have a fulfillment pattern; when it is filled your cup is overflowing. You will find you can postpone that filling for a certain number of days without undo stress as long as you know that you will be filling it in the known future. By charting my rhythm of life sheet I learned that I need filling on a weekly basis, can stretch to two weeks and then I am in emotional or physical trouble. How about you?

Make up the *Rhythm of Life* sheet and fill it in. Make 5 columns and label each. One is Physical, Emotional, Social, Spiritual, and Intellectual. Keep that sheet available for two weeks and every time you are aware of a need put it in the appropriate column with the amount of time required to get that need filled.

What do you need in each facet?
How much?
How often? See John Gray's material

Some people have a 24 hr. rhythm. They need to do the event every day, others have a seven day rhythm but perhaps any 3 days is all they need. Such as a rhythm of 1 hour of hard exercise 3 times a week will fulfill them. Perhaps two of those days are Saturday and Sunday. Our family used to play tennis all weekend. I need 3 hours of deep intellectual reading each week or I am unfulfilled. I can complete them all in one sitting at the college library. A very few people have a 14 day rhythm. They can hold off for 2 weeks, and then get really out of sorts.

Note:

Every day equals 4 x week in the life of a busy adult because three days of the week are, "Out of plan." You need to honor that so that your self talk compliments you on the four day success rather than focusing negatively on the three days that went awry.

Too Few Clock Hours

I suspect you will discover that there are too few clock hours in a week for your desires. That is why I say that:

Clarice's Definition of Burnout

Burnout is what happens at that time of your life when your ability to assess needs and your personal skills to fill those needs out-rank what can be achieved in a 24-hour day.

It happens when you are competent. You can see the need and know that you can fill the need well. You have the desire and the want to, but there are not enough clock hours to do it.

At that time there is a new growth and development task. To continue on in life with wellness you have to develop the ability to say no, even though you have the ability to fulfill the need and would love doing it. There just are not enough hours in the day, or days in the week, to use all your talents.

Now you need to look at your values and prioritize your spirit-self first. When looking at holistic needs, the first need to be given up is spiritual. Persons give up the time to read reflective material, enjoy the river at sunset, dream with a song, listen to their spirit, time to rock in the rocker on the porch and listen to the crickets. The second most often given up need is physical; persons skip these in favor of taking on increased obligations. You need to do a holistic self care plan marking the clock hours. It needs to cover a minimum two week span.

Afterward

Summary of the Course

You have just read a course on coping with loss. Most people never have the opportunity to spend time on the subject of loss; to think about it over a period of time and come back to the material. You have the opportunity to live with these concepts, insights, and skills, to try them out in your personal life and check back again. This is a wonderful way to learn new coping patterns. I am glad it was available to you.

Let's Review the Course

Holistic Model

In the health model of teaching, we use the holistic model which consist of physical, spiritual, emotional, social, and intellectual components. Each time we work with a person we automatically assess all of these components. After reading these volumes I think you are quite keen about whole person concerns as affected by loss and change.

Intelligent Loving

At the beginning of this course we talked about the need for loving when working in a field of high loss. We used the words intelligent loving. We talked about how a parent may deeply love their child but it may be dysfunctional loving. In that case it is necessary for those parents to attend a class on parenting in order to develop proper attitudes with healthy information. Contrary to the popular platitudes, loving is never enough; it must be intelligent. You can be an intelligent lover of mourners.

Three Areas of Teaching

There are three areas of teaching, cognitive, skill, and affective teaching. When a course is designed, the designer chooses the focus. It is most often either a cognitive or skill course.

Sometimes the designer may choose to design a course to teach the emotions, the feelings of the student. Then the goal is affective learning. The objective of affective learning is to have the students actually become the emitters of their new understanding. The effort is to provide the student with cognitive information, skill information, and a safe environment in which to grow and mature their emotional/feeling self. As the student grows, they change. The student changes because of what they have assimilated. You are aware that someone can have intellectual knowledge but not change as a person. They can get an A in the test but never use any of it in their thinking or behavior. However, if you have assimilated affected learning you are a changed person.

This course is designed to educate affective learning. Yes, there was a lot of theory taught, and many skills, but it is the self image that the material was directed toward.

Skill learning is the easiest to teach and the easiest to test. Cognitive learning is the 2nd easiest to teach and a little more difficult to test. Affective learning is the most difficult to teach, and almost impossible to test. We cannot tell if the life of the student has changed as a result of the knowledge assimilated from the lectures. This is between you and your God. We honor that.

You have Grown

Now Lets look at some experiences for growth that you have gone thorough.

1. You have developed both verbal and non-verbal skills on a taboo subject.

2. You have likely listened to another's debt of pain, sorrow, love, and caring without interrupting the expression of pain. This does not happen often in the outer society.

3. Looking back you realize that you were scared when others shared from their intimacy level. Now you are no longer frightened. If someone opens up and cries, you are comfortable with your discomfort. You have come a long way. That skill will go with you into the future. That is one of the gifts from this material to you.

4. You let your body show as it betrays your emotions. It is when the body reacts that most persons interrupt another's story, or they avoid the sick or grieving person. In the future when your involuntary body reactions start to happen on you, they will be familiar to you. This is another gift from this material to you.

5. You are aware of trembling and seeing others tremble as you and they put into words feelings from the inner level of self. It is not scary to you.

6. You wait kindly as others block in their verbal expressing. You find no need to interrupt nor are you frightened by the seemingly long silences.

7. You verbalize the comfort words across a room, you accept whatever your body needs to be doing at the time.

8. You send your comfort caring across space without words. Your energy goes to the one who is working their grief. It is full and rich, almost visible, tangible, and measurable. You can sense it.

9. You let your tears come and discover that you do not lose dignity, intelligence, or capability with tears in your eyes. The presence of your tears does not unduly frighten you.

10. You reach out and touch, sometimes to hug, at the inner level of giving and receiving. You discovered at this level that there are no strangers, only fellow humans in pain, or fellow humans in love.

11. You read on this subject of human pain of loss and came back to test the authors ideas coupled with your own insights. Through open sharing you learn from what others read and think.

12. When you practice on this level and add to that the hours of thinking and reading, you change! You cannot help but grow. You have grown because you have come to this study. It will be there for the rest of your life.

Blessing

May you be open and free flowing in the experience of your pain; and therefore you will be open and free in your acceptance of love.

Many you take in love at this deep level; knowing the goal of opening this deeply to the pain in your heart is so that love can go all the way into the depth of the grief wound. The energy that holds in the pain also holds out love. When the energy no longer holds in sad, the love just rushes in because the gates, the walls, the barriers are down. It is the hanging unto the sad that keeps the doors to ones heart blocked.

May your life be eased by this experience and may the lives of those you touch be eased.

Growth Through Loss & Change

Volume I & II

Goals and Objectives

Course: Learning to Live with Loss
After the study of this information the student will be able to:

Volume I
How to: Be With the Dying without Fear

Chapter 1: Emotional Preparation of the Helping Person

Goal: To enable the students to come to terms with their personal death awareness

- Understand the value of getting comfortable with own emotions
- Know one's own feelings and emotions concerning death and dying, grief and grieving
- Identify one's own personal loss awareness

Chapter 2: Americans: The Lonely Grievers

Goal: To improve the student's ability to assess and meet the sociocultural needs of the bereaved

- Be aware of individuals need for group support
- Identify the tasks of community
- Distinguish the variety of America's cultural backgrounds

Chapter 3: The Dying Person

Goal: To provide students with practical and useful techniques for interacting with a dying person

- Describe the needs of the dying person
- Identify the use of your personal loss experiences in therapeutic listening
- Describe the elements of a therapeutic visit

Chapter 4: Family of the Dying *"Stages"*

Goal: Explain the value of this experience for the family
Recognize the value of this dying situation to the family

- Identify tasks of the family at the dying/grief time
- Understand family interventions for each stage of grief

Chapter 5: Sudden Death Crisis

Goal: To familiarize the students with helpful practices to use for families and friends in the presence of the body

- Discuss the reactions at sudden death
- Effectively show the body
- Know self-care needs

Chapter 6: Dying Event *"Being There When"*

Goal: To expand the student's knowledge to recognize, assess, manage, and suggest interventions during the dying event

- Describe the physiological changes at the dying time
- Identify and implement comfort measures for the dying person
- Explain comforting measures to the family

Chapter 7: Pregnancy Loss

Goal: To familiarize the student with the dynamics of newborn loss

- Assess needs of families surrounding perinatal loss
- Recognize that many primary grievers have no primary death experience, no coping patterns

- Develop bereavement interventions for perinatal loss

Chapter 8: Sexual Needs of the Dying and Grieving

Goal: To provide the students with practical and useful techniques for educating individuals and families who are dying or bereaved

- Describe the cultural taboo around sexual adjustment
- Identify sexual interventions to meet the touch needs of the dying and their mate
- Understand the use of pleasuring criteria vs. performance criteria

Chapter 9: Burnout Healing *"Care of the Grief Support Person"*

Goal: To help students identify the signs and symptoms of burnout and when to intervene for caregivers and for themselves

- Distinguish signs of burnout
- Realize the self-responsibility of burnout healing
- Catalog your support structures

Volume II
How to: Grieve without Undue Fear

Chapter 10: The Scope of Grief *"Consciousness Raising"*

Goal: To enable the student to identity areas of loss that bring forth a grief response

- Delineate the scope of grief
- Describe culturally acceptable grief
- Identify culturally unacceptable losses

Chapter 11: Normal Dynamics of Grief

Goal: To enable the student to identify normal dynamics of the grieving process

- Recognize normal dynamics of grief
- Understand the phases of grief
- Describe the tasks needed to attain healing grief

Living Grief: *"Must Process Again and Again"*

Goal: To enhance the student's ability to identify living griefs that promise never to leave but challenge the mourner to learn to live well and productively with the loss

- Identify the many faces of grief
- Understand why the length of the bereavement period may differ
- Explain the role of the helping persons in hope for the future, and faith for a meaningful life

Physiology of Grief *"Your Body Grieves"*

Goal: To provide the students with practical and useful techniques to inform patients about how the body grieves

- Understand the fight or flight syndrome in the grief process
- Describe the role of medication in the grief process
- Develop a holistic patient care plan for the bereaved

Chapter 12: Grieving Children Need Adult Help

Goal: To improve the student's ability to assist grief processing according to the child's stage of growth and development

- Understand how children grieve
- Identify the needs of the child griever
- Understand that a grieving child needs adult help

Chapter 13: Just For Teens

Goal: To enable the student to be comfortable in reaching out to others in grief, pain, or fright

- Be motivated to help others and self to healing grief
- Understand grief as an involuntary process
- Appreciate the gifts of grief
- Understand the grief process results from loss of person, place, ideal, or thing

Chapter 14: Gender Differences in Grief Response

Goal: To familiarize the student's understanding of the gender needs of bereaved men

- Understand two etiologies of gender differences: *"what"* from physiology; *"how"* from culture
- Explain that male action oriented grief work may be genetic
- Identify helpful interventions for the bereaved man

Chapter 15: The Pastoral Visitor in the Hospital

Goal: To present Nurse's view of the role of the visiting minister in the medical setting

- Understand minister/patient interactions which the nurses assess to be not helpful
- Implement minister/patient interaction which nurses have seen to be helpful to the patient
- Identify ways to help oneself when feeling repulsed

Chapter 16: Spiritual Handling of the Holidays

Goal: To provide a sacred time to name and ponder a specific gift a loss has brought to the student's spirit

- Understand *"Grief bursts"* and know the coping patterns to deal with them as they come
- Describe, *"Escape the holidays,"* and define the positives and negatives of going away
- Identify the spiritual gift they have because of bonding and losing a special person or persons

References

Following is a list of authors and lecturers whose works influenced my writings. I chose not to list specific works from an author because I usually perused all of their writings for insights and was therefore influenced by their body of work. This is by no means a complete record of all the works and sources I have consulted; such as multitudes of professional journals of all helping disciplines, and attendance at countless hours of professional seminar presentations. It indicates the substance and range of reading upon which I have formed my ideas. As a speaker on the national lecture circuit, I made it a practice to attend the entire conference for which I presented.

If, because of limited time, I were to pick only three foundation authors, my choices for a background on the influence of loss on growth and development is: John Bowlby and for an understanding of practical applications of the principles of dying and loss, the works of Glen Davidson, and Alan Wolfelt are excellent. For readers who wish to increase their overview of dying and bereavement dynamics as well as enlarge and update their understanding, I recommend a literature search in several of the helping professions publications to get a broad view. There is a plethora of material readily available through library searches and on the internet.

American Medical Association

Becker, Ernest B,
Borg, Susan
Bowlby, John
Chopra, Deepak
Compassionate Friends, The, Inc.
Conley, Bruce H.
Cooper, Anderson
Corr, Charles A.
Covey, Stephen R.
Curic, Katie
Davidson, Glen
De Angelis, Barbara
Dyer, Wayne
Fleltcher, John
Garfield, Charles
Gordon, Audrey

Gray, John
Grollman, Earl
Hendrix, Harville
Hewett, John
Iron, Paul,
Johnson, Robert A.
Kalish, R., and Reynolds, D.
Kastenbaum, Robert J.
Kavanaugh, Robert
Kelly, Orville E.
Kohn, Jane
Krementz, Jill
Krieger, Dolores
Krieger, Dorothy
Kubler-Ross, Elisabeth
Kushner, Harold
LaTour, Kathy
LeShan, Eda
Lewis, C.S.
Lindemann, Eric
Linn, Mary Jane
Machavelli, Niccolo
Mandelbaum, David G.
Manning, Doug
McGinnis, Alan Loy
McGraw, Phillip C.

Mead, Margaret
Meyers Briggs
Moody, Raymond
Nouwen, Henri J.M.
Parks, Colin Murray
Peace, Barbara
Pincus, Lily
Rosenthal, Joel Thomas
Schiff, Harriet
Schoenberg, Bernhardt Mark
Schultz, Clarice A.
Schulz, Richard
Sheehy, Gail
Sheehy, Patrick
Shneidman, Edwin S.
Taylor, S. E.,
Tolle, Eckhart
Tournier, Paul
Updegraff, J. A.
Westberg, Granger, E.
Winfry, Ophra
Wolfelt, Alan
Wordon, J. William
Yancy, Phillip
Zukav, Gary

About The Author

Clarice Schultz has worked as a nurse-thanatologist for 30 years and presents from that perspective. A Bachelor in Science of Nursing plus a BS in Psychology, an AD in Anthropology and a minor in Theological studies augment her nursing insights. Thus she brings a well-rounded holistic approach to her subject matter.

Clarice has taught numerous semester courses in Thanatology in Illinois, Texas, and presented on the Regional and National Lecture Circuit. Students of all the helping disciplines have received graduate credit as well as continuing education credit from her work.

Ms. Schultz has published her work in Nursing Journals and in a Medical Textbook. She has shared the platform at conferences with Elizabeth Kubler Ross, Bernie S. Siegel MD, the Author of Love, Medicine, and Miracles, and Dana Reeves, wife of Christopher Reeves.

Subjects on Coping with Loss in its many arenas have been presented by Clarice at seminars with high acclaim. There have been continuous requests for an easy to read reference book to have available on the resource shelf for a time of need.